Unfreedom and Waged Work

Unfreedom and Waged Work

Labour in India's Manufacturing Industry

Sunanda Sen
Byasdeb Dasgupta

SAGE   www.sagepublications.com
Los Angeles • London • New Delhi • Singapore • Washington DC

First published in 2009 by

 SAGE Publications India Pvt Ltd
B1/I-1 Mohan Cooperative Industrial Area
Mathura Road, New Delhi 110 044, India
www.sagepub.in

SAGE Publications Inc
2455 Teller Road
Thousand Oaks, California 91320, USA

SAGE Publications Ltd
1 Oliver's Yard, 55 City Road
London EC1Y 1SP, United Kingdom

SAGE Publications Asia-Pacific Pte Ltd
33 Pekin Street
#02-01 Far East Square
Singapore 048763

Published by Vivek Mehra for SAGE Publications India Pvt Ltd, typeset in 10/12pt Minion by Star Compugraphics Private Limited, Delhi and printed at Chaman Enterprises, New Delhi.

Library of Congress Cataloging-in-Publication Data Available

ISBN: 978-81-7829-940-2 (HB)

The SAGE Team: Rekha Natarajan, Gargi Bhattacharya, Rajib Chatterjee and Trinankur Banerjee

Contents

List of Tables

List of Figures

Acknowledgements

This book dwells on our research project on 'The Political Economy of Labour in a Globalized Economy', which was conducted during 2003–06. We remain grateful for the help we received from different institutions in making it possible to initiate and to successfully complete the study. A major role was played in this venture of ours by the ICSSR–IDPAD Secretariat which provided a generous research grant to cover the three-year-long research in the project. It was possible to locate and implement the project with the generous help from the two host institutions, the Academy of Third World Studies, Jamia Milia Islamia, New Delhi and the Department of Economics, University of Kalyani, West Bengal.

The study entailed the utilization of a lot of manpower, time and strenuous efforts, both in processing the secondary data and in conducting the field study. We would like to put on record the contributions of Prasenjit Bose and Hamida Khan in Delhi; and of Amit Kumar Bhandari and Abhik Basu in Kalyani, in collecting and shaping the data in its final form. Atulan Guha helped us in a big way in doing the survey at Surat in Gujarat. In this regard, we especially acknowledge the help that we have received from Uma Rani of the Gujarat Institute of Development Research in carrying out the survey in Surat. We also thank Shahid Ahmed for his help in computation. Anjan Chakrabarti drafted a major part of Chapter 6 and we thank him for his contribution.

Comments from other scholars who were available in the two international conferences that we organized in Kolkata and Delhi were useful in formulating the ideas. Gary Dymski offered some innovative ideas to organize the data in Chapter 3 which helped us. We also mention Amiya Bagchi, Debdas Bandopadhyay, Ajit Singh, Sukti Dasgupta, Rachel Kurian, Prabhat Patnaik, Guy Standing, Indira Hirway, Pravin K. Jha, Anjan Chakrabarti and Aditya Bhattacharea, all of whom offered useful comments on our study. Help was received from Pronob Sen in gaining access to crucial data on price indices. We thank all the above for their generous help in our research in the project.

The institutes which, through their faculty and other members, helped us include the Planning Commission, Research and Information System (RIS) for non-aligned and other developing countries, Institute of Studies in Industrial Development (ISID), Institute of Human Development (IHD), Jawaharlal Nehru University (JNU), Centre for World Trade Organization (WTO), the Indian Institute of Foreign Trade (IIFT) and International Labour Organization (ILO) in Delhi, National Labour Institute (NLI) in New Okhla Industrial Development Authority (NOIDA, UP). In Kolkata the Annual Survey of Industries (ASI) Directorate, Census Office, and National Sample Survey Organization (NSSO) helped us in accessing data sources. Also the Inspector of factories in Kolkata, Delhi and Mumbai, and the Bengal National Chamber of Commerce and Industries helped us in collecting secondary data from their databases, and provided lists of factories and units in different places. We thank all these institutions for their help. We are also thankful to the Development Commissioners at Santa Cruz, NOIDA and Falta SEZs for allowing us to conduct the survey inside these three SEZs and also helping with their staff to aid in our survey effort. We received help from local trade union offices at Falta, Aurangabad, NOIDA and Kolkata. Samik Lahiri, MP, helped us in carrying out the field survey at the Falta SEZ. We thank Prasenjit Bose in providing us some of these contacts. We also remain thankful to Saikat Sarkar of DGCI&S, Kolkata, IIMC library, the Principal, faculty and students of D.N. College, Murshidabad, and local CITU leaders and workers at Falta, Kalyani, Hooghly and Kolkata. Tarun Bhowmik, owner-proprietor of Club International Soft Luggage Company, gave us of valuable time to discuss issues pertaining to industries and labour in India in the current phase of economic reform and globalization.

We would like to thank Professor Mushirul Hasan, Vice Chancellor of Jamia Milia Islamia, and the successive Directors at the Academy of Third World Studies for their generous support to the project. In Kalyani, the successive Vice Chancellors and the administration have been similarly helpful in accommodating the project in their institution. For logistic support we must mention Sanchita Datta at the ICSSR–IDPAD Secretariat; J.M. Khan and Md Azam Siddiqui at ATWS; Abhijit, Ayan and Pralay at Kalyani and all staff members in these two institutions for their continuous support to the project.

We hope that this study of labour in the organized manufacturing industry of India will be worth the value of all the help we received from various institutions and individuals over the last few years.

Sunanda Sen
Byasdeb Dasgupta

Introduction

This is a study on the unfreedom and stress experienced by workers in India's manufacturing industry. It deals with labour employed in units which are registered in terms of the prevailing Factory Act of the country. Since the set of workers relates to the 'formal' as distinct from the 'informal' or unorganized sector in the economy, one expects, in principle, some minimum safeguards for these workers in terms of jobs, their permanence, as well as some minimal labour security. However, very little, if any, of those benefits seem to exist in reality, as is borne out by the detailed analysis of secondary official statistics and data from a primary survey we have undertaken for this study.

The Indian nation-state has passed through at least three major transformations since independence in 1947. Of these, the first phase, covering the first two and a half decades of independent India, can be described as one close to a social democratic regime or a developmental state. Workers, who had jobs in the formal (organized) industries and services, also had the right to claim job tenures as well as job-related benefits from employers (paid leave, medical benefits, accident insurance and superannuation benefits). A part of these compensations (for example, pensions and provident funds) were provided by the state, which also kept a vigil on labour-related issues by ensuring the existence of trade unions and other labour rights, with the framing of appropriate labour legislations. As for the much larger section of workers, who remained outside the ambit of the regularized workforce, even these were in a position to avail of some of these basic social benefits, which the state was in a position to provide. Facilities as above started waning during the second phase of transformation which, beginning in the late 1970s, took a definite turn by the mid-1980s. Marked by a drive for liberalization in different pockets of the economy, these moves initiated a regime with the label of a so-called liberal state where labour was commoditized as with other goods and services. In terms of the liberal position, labour supply was to be seen as a voluntary response to the incentives provided in the labour market. The economy witnessed far-reaching changes during the third phase as full-scale economic reforms were launched by the newly elected government in 1991. Reforms relating to the labour market gradually absolved the employers of the responsibility of providing benefits which usually came with tenured jobs. The shift in the official position was officially endorsed in the recommendations of the National Commission on Labour (2002) which recommended use of contract labour in view of the uncertain demand from global markets. However, the suggestion for an adequate social safety net was still recognized as one that remains to be fulfilled by the state. Other concessions to capital, which worked against labour during these years, can be found in the changes incorporated in the labour laws permitting 'hire and fire' of workers, especially in foreign direct investment (FDI) controlled units and in the Export Processing Zones (EPZs). Large-scale privatization, in turn, provided a further push to labour flexibility. Thus started a phase, which continues today, of a total commodification of labour, wherein it is viewed as an input rather than a human being. Departing from the social relations that sustain people, the process places the market, which is disembedded from society, at centre stage. It is thus logical for flexible labour market norms to disregard and altogether neglect dispossession (say with unemployment), displacement (with hire and fire policies and casualization) as well as human degradation (with low quality of life for workers) as surfaces (see for conceptual basis, Polyani 1944; see also Polyani Levitt 2005).

Liberalization and the steady opening up of various markets, which came up with globalization, have also changed the structure of these economies. Dominated by big corporates—domestic and foreign—one witnesses the emergence in India of the *third phase*, with *neo-corporatist capitalism*. The state today has very little to do with the residual labour rights, if any. In this new regime it is the employer and probably the family which is ultimately expected to provide the means of survival for the worker. The ability of workers to organize and to bargain with employers is markedly less than what it used to be before, especially in terms of the prevailing mode of production that relies on the outsourcing of jobs and the flexibilization of labour. In absence of full employment policies, workers are compulsively drawn to these jobs, however inadequate these are to fulfil their needs and to compensate them for their contribution to output. Policies which define the space of the individual worker as a utility-maximizing rational being conform to positivist principles in neo-classical economics; one where the market is the final arbiter of remunerating the worker in terms of the latter's choice between work and leisure. It is even claimed in theories that in the process, labour cannot only be more productive but can also get back the much needed freedom (option) over his/her own 'time', and to choose between work and leisure. The approach originates from methodological individualism advocating complete laissez-faire.

One thus witnesses, in India and in similar other nations, the gradual erosion of a developmental state which goes with the disappearance of welfare measures. However, the identity of welfare or developmental states, as pointed out, cannot be specified by the sheer magnitude of welfare related social expenditure on the part of the state. There remain three 'multifaceted dimensions' or attributes of welfare states. These include the extent of 'de-commodification' which, as Polyani (1944) held it, extends social rights beyond or independent of the market. These also include 'stratification', which, say by insuring workers on an occupational basis, reinforces status differences and intra-class cleavages; and finally it relates to the 'form and locus of social protection' in terms of the 'state-market-family mix' which determines the ultimate source of protection (Esping-Anderson 1990: 21–23).

Our study relates to a section of workers in India who are employed in the manufacturing units registered under factory laws. Thus the study is necessarily a snapshot of the overall picture relating to the conditions of the Indian working class, comprising not more than 2 per cent of the aggregate working population in India.[1] These workers, however, are relatively privileged in having access to the legal and social safeguards to labour that are still available in the organized sector which provides a test case for judging the impact of the neo-liberal norm of labour market flexibility. This is due to the existence of large-scale and old type of industries where labour is better organized and labour legislation is relatively adhered to. Moreover, this is the sector which is better integrated with the rest of world in terms of exportability as well as the destination of FDI, both of which affect the status of labour vis-à-vis capital.

We have provided, in Chapter 1, the conceptual basis of the current wave of labour market reforms which include the plea for labour market flexibility. The conceptual basis as well as the policy prescriptions which follow, as pointed out, do not stand scrutiny, either in terms of their logical soundness or empirical validity. Rejecting the conventional interpretations, sermonized by official circles in India in support of the on going policies of labour flexibilization, we try to offer an alternative framework. In our analysis, we contest the official explanations of unemployment and labour distress in India which runs in terms of labour market rigidity and protective labour legislations. We also critique explanations which dwell on movements in product wages relative to real wage rates, as the primary factor behind the shortfall in employment.

Validity of the aforementioned critiques is borne out in our analysis of secondary statistics relating to workers and industrial units in organized manufacturing industry. Chapter 2 deals with the central observations of the present study, which concern the pattern of 'jobless growth' in the Indian economy over the last few decades. Relying on the alternative framework provided by us, we have empirically tested the relevance of different variables as explanations behind the low growth rates of employment as well as of the poor quality of jobs (in terms of casualization and lack of non-wage benefits) as are observed for workers. In our analysis we have used the secondary data set as available from official sources to test the hypotheses we have set up to explain joblessness, especially in high growth industries. Labour-displacing technology seems to be a major factor behind the phenomenon, not only in stagnant industries like man-made fibre, tobacco manufacture, publishing, etc. (which are relatively labour intensive) but also in high growth and relatively capital intensive industries. (The latter include manufacture of aircraft and spacecraft, motor vehicles, electronic valves and tubes, electric motors, generators and transformers and jewellery, etc., having individual growth rates which were well above 20 per cent.) Employment in all these industries has grown at a slow pace (or remained stationary) which contrasts the high output growth therein.

With employment growth thus low or stationary, the quality of jobs has also been poor for labour. The manifestations include long working hours (with growth in officially reported man-days far exceeding similar growth rates in number employed) and stationary or declining real wages, despite a rise in labour productivity, the latter largely as a consequence of the rising capital–labour ratios, with labour displacement which follows. Casualization, in most industries, is common, especially in the export processing zones where employers have more freedom to use labour in a manner which achieves cost competitiveness. Using firm-level data, we also observe that trade (especially net exports) or foreign equity participation had very little role in the expansion of the major Indian firms in terms of sales performance. This chapter provides detailed statistics on the basis of National Industrial Classification (NIC) of manufacturing industries at 3-digit level as are provided in the Annual Survey of Industries. It may be mentioned here that we have utilized these data, for the first time in industry studies, at a 3-digit level.

As it has been pointed out by scholars writing on the condition of the working class under capitalism, '...one needs to glance over the factory walls to the larger world the worker came from, the selection process in which the jobbers played a prominent part and the occasional strikes in which the local environment and loose associations played a role' (Bagchi 2002: 238, citing the work of Buchanan 1934). It is also important to look beyond the statements by workers on conditions of their work and life. This is because of '...the tensions that mark the relations between workers and managers, the property-less and the propertied, the ruled and the rulers' (Bagchi 2002: 213). In our analysis of secondary data and in particular, from what we observed in our field study, we came to subscribe to the view that workers in India, even in the organized sector, are rendered *unfree*, first by the authority of capitalists, which extends not only to the workplace (Braverman 1974) but also beyond; and second, by being forced to sell labour power to survive in a manner which leaves them very little option to decide as to how they would have liked to live (Bagchi 2002: 267).

Aspects as above provide the rationale behind our move to gather supplementary information, through a field survey of a set of industrial workers in different areas. The survey was conducted in 15 different sites, and spread over five Indian states during 2004–06. In soliciting information through questionnaires, we have sought to gather information, both quantitative and qualitative, relating to conditions and terms of work, the living condition and the background of the 615 workers we have directly interviewed. These help us to arrive at an assessment of their status in terms of what in the literature is described as 'labour security'. We have sought, in Chapter 3, to relate labour status in terms of the impact, if any, of attributes like trade orientation and technology of industries, skill, education, permanence of jobs, migrant status, age, union membership and social background of workers, etc. Data on the basis of the field survey, processed and analyzed in these chapters, complement the observations arrived at in terms of secondary data in Chapter 2, confirming what we observe as the unfreedom and stress of these workers in Indian industry.

Profiles of the different areas under survey come in Chapter 4. It links up the statistical profile provided in Chapter 3 to the background of the respective sites we visited. The narratives help to understand the reality which often lies hidden in quantitative statistics.

An innovative exercise, of calculating what we describe as the 'security index' of the workers, is attempted in Chapter 5. Adopting the method available in other studies we have modified the criteria to suit Indian conditions. The result is a construction of the composite and individual security indices, for the 615 labourers we have interviewed. Attributes used to construct the individual indices include the security levels defined by income, jobs, age, education, migration and union membership which is also used in the previous chapter. The findings help to substantiate the arguments on the poor status of labourers as are offered in the earlier chapters.

Chapter 6 critiques the attempt to change labour market policies in India during the post-liberalization period and its conceptual leanings. It draws attention to the official position as encapsulated in the report of the National Commission of Labour and as reflected in the advocacy of labour flexibility as the panacea for achieving efficient growth. This chapter aims to put in place the context of industrial policies towards labour which has the explicit sanction of the Indian state. The fact that labour in industry is increasingly being casualized is thus what we could expect. Thus both the capitalists managing industry and the ruling state share a common interest in aspiring the so-called efficient path of growth under competitive capitalism, by following a trajectory of labour flexibility. What happens in the process to labour is not of concern to either, as is told by the growing distress the latter is subjected to. While the state is aware of the limits to such policies, the remedial actions remain half-hearted, especially with the priority to make the economy a user-friendly terrain for the foreign (as also the domestic) investors. In effect, the state seems to be moving fast in the direction of policies recommended in conservative mainstream doctrines which view protective legislation of labour as a hurdle for investment and growth.

The aforesaid arguments are reiterated in Chapter 7, which provides the conclusion. It reflects on an issue which is highly topical and contextual in the current phase of globalization. We hope that our analysis will help in formulating policies and open up fresh debates regarding labour market policies in the current phase of globalization in India.

Note

1. Manufacturing industries provide 12 per cent of total employment in India, and the organized sector provides only 14 per cent of total employment in manufacturing industry as a whole. Thus the organized manufacturing industry provides only 1.6 per cent of total employment in the country.

Alternate Approaches to Labour Economics: Theory and Practice

1

Introduction: The Case for Labour Market Flexibility–The Mainstream Arguments

Policies relating to labour in the current era of globalization, especially with the drive for flexible labour markets, have in general the stamp of what is recognized as neo-classical economics. Analysis in neo-classical mainstream models is often carried out in terms of the forces of demand and supply which interact to clear different markets including those relating to labour. Markets in these general equilibrium models are assumed to clear at equilibrium simultaneously, thus never dwelling on the sequences through which the variables are determined at equilibrium. In these theories labour is viewed just as one more factor of production like land and capital.

In mainstream analysis, discussions relating to labour pertain mainly to microeconomic issues. There remain three agents which are considered important in the context of labour market. These include *(a)* workers, *(b)* firms (or employers) who hire labour and *(c)* the state which, in principle, has regulatory powers over the labour market. Missing in this literature is the uniqueness of the labour market, which in reality is a social institution, dealing with human beings rather than simply as one of the markets. However, given the paramount significance of the mainstream approach on labour policies in both advanced countries and (especially) in the developing countries, one needs to be familiar with the assumptions and implications underlying these versions of labour economics.

As for the three agents mentioned above relating to the labour market in neo-classical economics, initiatives of labourers, considered as voluntary, centres around the allocation of their time between work and leisure. There is an implicit assumption that workers are free to choose their options between hours of work and leisure, in a manner which maximizes their utility. However, the individual workers' choice between work and leisure is influenced by social reality, an aspect which remains totally ignored in neo-classical analysis. Workers in these models are thus assumed to have the ability to decide on how many hours to work, what skills to acquire, when to quit a job, how to choose occupations, and whether to join labour unions, etc. Each of these decisions is motivated by the desire to maximize their well-being. Decisions as above on the part of workers in neo-classical theory generate the aggregate labour supply, not only in terms of the number of persons who enter the labour market, but also in terms of the quantity and quality of skills available to employers. The labour supply curve is often upward sloping with the choice exercised by workers to work more at higher wages.

As for other agents in the labour market, there remain the firms which hire workers and are assumed to take decisions with the goal of profit maximization. These decisions include the number of persons hired, the terms of those offers, decisions to hire and fire, capital to employ, etc. If one adds up the individual decisions to recruit (net of hiring and firing), it generates a downward sloping aggregate labour demand in the economy. It pays the firms to maximize profits by offering lower wages and also by having the discretion to hire and fire.

As for the government, the third agent in the labour market, it is assumed to influence the decision of workers and firms by imposing taxes and granting subsidies, and by regulating the 'rules of the game' in the labour market. In reality much of the role of the government in the labour market remains undermined as economic reforms cater to a minimalist state.

Workers and firms, therefore, enter the labour market with conflicting interests; which balances at equilibrium where labour supply matches with labour demand at a given wage rate. However, even in neo-classical doctrines, the above does not necessarily imply that unemployment should be reduced to zero at equilibrium. The theory admits the existence of unemployment, and also identifies a *natural rate of unemployment* (NRU) (Haltwanger 1987: 610–12), even when the labour market clears itself. The pattern of such unemployment, however, is considered to be short-term and frictional in nature. As an explanation it is pointed out that the labour market is in a constant flux and workers are prone to quit their jobs or be laid off, with employers reshuffling the workforce they employ. Many of these workers, who lose jobs in the process, are assumed to re-enter the job market after acquiring more skill or after remaining idle for a while. At a point of time, therefore, some of them can be *between* jobs, thus defining a state of NRU. Both workers and firms try to locate each other in such situations, and in terms of the information as are available on the possibility of a job match.

There can also be *frictional unemployment* which, in terms of main-stream theory, does not pose any fundamental structural problem in the economy. It arises out of voluntary decisions of 'individual' workers to quit their jobs and/or a refusal to accept 'unfavourable' job offers. Hence frictional unemployment is not viewed with alarm by policy makers. It is supposed to lead to short-term spells of unemployment which even turn out as 'productive' because it generates search activities of workers and firms which improves the allocation of resources. Policy solutions to combat frictional unemployment consist of providing information to workers about job openings and to firms about unemployed workers.

Neo-classical theory also recognizes the possibility of *seasonal unemployment* which, by nature, is usually predictable. Accordingly it does not pose a problem and requires remedial actions, since most of the unemployed workers are expected to usually return to the job held earlier once the lean season is over.

However, unemployment is considered a problem even in neo-classical theory when one considers *structural unemployment*. The following factors, among others, can explain this type of unemployment: *(a)* a mismatch in numbers between the respective job seekers and jobs available at a point of time and *(b)* a mismatch in skill when persons looking for jobs fail to 'fit' in to those which are available. Thus, skill-mismatch can prevail even when there is no imbalance between jobs available in the labour market and those sought after by workers. Policy prescriptions to remedy the structural unemployment of the skill-mismatch type advocate skill formation, as a solution from the supply side. Formation of 'adequate' skill is thus treated as the standard panacea for structural unemployment as above. As for structural unemployment, which relies on an excess supply syndrome in terms of job seekers in the labour market, it is sometimes related to excess policy intervention and/or union activism on part of workers. Both, in terms of neo-classical theory, obstruct wage flexibility in the market, especially in the downward direction and even interfere with job contracts as are consistent with flexible labour policies. The panacea thus lies in labour market flexibility, the keyword for labour market reform in this age of globalization.

Various *micro-theoretic models* are offered in different versions of neo-classical theory to explain frictional unemployment (Stigler 1961, 1962). These include, among others, the search-theoretic wage offer distribution model, the inter-temporal shift hypothesis, the sectoral shifts hypothesis, efficiency wage models and implicit contract theory. In essence, all of these justify frictional unemployment, by treating it as voluntary in competitive labour markets. We offer in the following sub-sections a brief sketch and a critical appraisal of these models.

Wage offer distribution and search models (Mortensen 1986)

The basic premise of this theory is that the search for a better job may continue even when the workers accept a particular job offer. It is postulated that there exists a frequency distribution of wage offers available to a particular unemployed worker in the labour market.

Had search activities been absolutely free, the worker would keep on knocking from one door to another until he/she hits the one that offers what he/she considers as the desirable wage. Search activities, however, involve certain costs and there exists, therefore, a trade-off between the time spent and the cost involved to search jobs at higher wages while the desired wage proportionately goes up.

There also exists, in these models, an 'asking wage' which sets the threshold wage at which the unemployed worker is ready to accept incoming job offers. At this wage the marginal revenue for the worker from an additional search just matches the marginal cost of the search. Workers with low asking wages will find acceptable jobs very quickly and their unemployment spells will be shorter than the workers with high asking wages. Factors which are considered to affect the worker's asking wage rates include (a) the current orientation of the worker and (b) unemployment insurance. If a worker is oriented to the current situation, then there is considered to be a tendency to discount all gains from future searches which thus decreases the 'asking wage'. As opposed to above, the worker is prone to raise the 'asking wage' when there is unemployment insurance. It thus follows logically that at the level of policy it helps not to have unemployment insurance in order that workers remain content and employed at a lower wage!

Inter-temporal substitution

Unemployment can also be explained by inter-temporal substitution (Lucas and Rapping 1969) which determines the way workers allocate their time over the business cycle. With pro-cyclical fluctuations in real wages, labour supply is assumed to drop during recessions when real wages are low since the opportunity cost of enjoying leisure also goes down. In terms of the above argument workers can then afford to become unemployed and collect unemployment insurance benefits. From this angle unemployment, as is observed during recessions, is voluntary because workers can take advantage of the decline in the real wage to opt for leisure with unemployment benefits. The entire construction of the sequence, on a second look, does not sound realistic in a world where the workers can neither choose to remain unemployed nor can they necessarily avail of unemployment benefits.

Sectoral shifts and skill-mismatch

Neo-classical theory tries to explain skill-mismatch among workers and structural unemployment. With sectoral shifts (Lilien 1982) in industry there would be, in terms of this formulation, a pool of workers who remain unemployed for long spells because of a structural imbalance between skills of unemployed workers and those the employers are looking for. As mentioned earlier, policy proposals to combat this type of structural mismatch of skills and related unemployment entail a process of enhancement of the level of skill of the labour force. The solution ignores the possibility of deficiency in demand relative to supply in the labour market, a major factor behind structural unemployment.

Efficiency wages

In neo-classical literature it is sometimes argued that unemployment can be explained by the practice of firms to 'buy' worker cooperation with offers of 'efficiency wages' (Shapiro and Stiglitz 1984). This is because monitoring the performance of the workers turns out to be easier with such offers. The efficiency wage, however, remains as the profit-maximizing wage. In the process the firm pays wages which are above the market wage rate. The above, in efficiency wage models, generates involuntary unemployment at the ruling wage rate. Here, one can interpret the unemployment caused by the efficiency wage as the 'stick' that keeps the lucky workers, who have highly paid jobs, in line. Efficiency wage is also the wage which induces workers not to shirk their responsibilities. When unemployment rate is high, it is then costly to shirk responsibilities, because once a worker gets caught shirking his duties and gets fired, he faces a long-term unemployment spell. The firm thus will want to offer a wage-employment package that encourages its workers not to shirk their responsibilities at all. But if the unemployment rate is low, workers who are caught shirking their duties and get fired face only a short-term unemployment spell. The key message provided by the efficiency wage model thus runs as follows: *some unemployment is necessary to keep employed workers in line.*

Recent empirical work on efficiency wages documents the existence of a downward-sloping curve that depicts the relationship between wage levels and unemployment in terms of a wage curve (Blanchflower and Oswald 1994; Card 1995), which states that wages tend to be high in regions where the unemployment rate is high, whereas the wage tends to be low in regions where the unemployment rate is low. Does it also prescribe wage cuts as solution for unemployment?

Implicit contracts

The long-term nature of labour contracts (perhaps resulting from specific vocational training), as held by neo-classical theory, introduces opportunities for workers and firms to bargain. These contracts may exist even if the workers are not represented by a formal institution like a union, when these labour market contracts are treated as implicit contracts (Rosen 1985) which are often unwritten and unspoken. However, workers within a particular firm are expected to have a good understanding of the logistics of these contracts.

There can be different types of feasible implicit contracts between workers and firms. Let us consider, in particular, two extreme types: The first is a 'fixed-employment' contract, where the person works the same number of hours per year, regardless of the economic conditions facing the firm. The second is a 'fixed-wage' contract, where the worker receives the same hourly wage, again regardless of the economic conditions facing the firm. As the firm faces different market conditions over a business cycle, the firm will respond to these changes in market conditions in case of a fixed-employment contract, by varying the worker's wage, with the workers getting high wage during an economic expansion and low wage during a recession, which leads to fluctuations in the worker's income over the business cycle.

To contrast the case of a fixed-wage contract, the firm here responds to a recession in the product market by reducing the hours of work, which also lowers the annual income of the worker. However, in neo-classical theory, this loss might be offset by *(a)* the additional leisure hours the worker would voluntarily have at his/her disposal during the recession and *(b)* the unemployment compensation replacing some of the lost earnings. As a result, the worker's 'real' income may remain relatively constant over the business cycle in a fixed-wage contract. Moreover, since the workers are assumed to be risk-averse, they may actually prefer fixed-wage contracts, thus willingly accepting layoffs as part of the long-term employment relationship.[1] The typical implicit contract in the labour market would then be a fixed-wage contract—implying that the wage is sticky over the business cycle and the unemployment increases during recession, which is voluntary in nature. It does not require much insight, however, to contest the utility maximizing behaviour of workers which is a major assumption behind the above arguments.

A Critical Evaluation of the Mainstream Neo-classical Labour Theories

What then remains as the policy prescription of neo-classical theory to combat unemployment? While it is admitted that there can be unemployment, both in the short run and over the long run (the latter due to structural changes in the economy), the solutions offered rest on achieving labour flexibility by removing all distortions in the labour market and equipping labour with better skills. Both rely on what can be labelled as supply-side economics, with an emphasis on adjustments in labour supply as the sole remedial measure for unemployment.

We offered earlier some critical remarks on the mainstream theories relating to the labour market which may, for convenience, be recapitulated as follows:

1. Labour treated in these theories is a utility-maximizing rational agent who can freely allocate labour time between work and leisure. This is far from the social reality in any capitalist economy. Given the social relations of production, an individual labourer remains at the receiving end, and in most instances, can offer labour time at the prevailing market conditions which is beyond his/her control.

2. In each of the neo-classical models relating to the labour market, it is assumed that the worker is paid by marginal productivity. This 'rightful return' is also 'efficient' since there is no wastage of scarce resources, and each of these resources is used to the best of

its ability for which they get in turn their contribution. If each is getting the rightful return against their contribution there is no question of exploitation. Such theories foreclose the very existence of exploitation and indeed of surplus labour as such.

3. In these theories, the labour market is perceived as a market similar to those for any other commodity. Since production has an in-built lag before it is processed and finalized, the employers effectively enter into a forward contract while fixing wages for labour. The latter is done with the expectation of selling the final good in the future. Demand for labour, therefore, depends upon the entrepreneurs' future expectation of sale of goods. But wages are also determined through a bargaining process—collective or singular; and wages are also set by conventions, customs and social norms. Attempts to reform the labour market and the underlying institutions fail to perceive the above aspects behind wage determination.

4. In terms of efficiency wages, it is presumed that an individual worker can shirk his responsibility (Alchain and Demsetz 1972) which, however, is hard to find in real life. The above undermines the entire structure of efficiency wage theories.

5. In neo-classical theory, there is no room for involuntary unemployment in the Keynesian sense. Unemployment is either voluntary or frictional due to workers' in-between job searches. Also people become unemployed in these models when their skill gets obsolete, which can be resolved by retraining unemployed workers. Arguments as above amount to a supply-side view, which ignores effective demand as the key source of the real life unemployment problems, as pointed out by Keynes many years ago. In neo-classical theory, the phenomenon is identified as the natural rate of unemployment at a point of time.

6. Labour, in neo-classical theory, is homogeneous and is treated as an aggregate. But in reality labour remains fragmented in terms of the specificity of skills, nature of job contracts, and involvement in formal or informal segment of the economy, or even the mode of payment. Perhaps, there is hardly any space in these models to accommodate the diverse mode of labour appropriation (say family labour, casual labour, child labour, self-employed labour, sex worker, etc.) as it is averse to accommodating the notion of exploitation—which contrasts the surplus approach to accumulation as in Marx.

Globalization, Jobless Growth and Labour Flexibility

There has been a spate of jobless growth, both in the advanced countries and in the developing ones, in recent years. This puts to disbelief that unemployment can be taken care of by the rate of growth or the level of output in an economy. Joblessness is thus a common phenomenon, not only in the poor countries of the developing region but also in advanced economies with high levels of gross domestic product (GDP).

According to the *Global Employment Trends Report* (2006), published by the ILO, the number of unemployed worldwide climbed to new heights in 2005. With output growth failing to provide jobs to the rising number of people entering the job market, the phenomenon was described as one of a 'jobless growth'. Thus, as pointed out by the Director-General of ILO, Mr Somavia, 'Economic growth alone isn't adequately addressing global employment needs.'

One observes, in the literature, divergent views on the relation between the growth process in the developing economies and its impact on employment. The different positions, as can be expected, generate policy proposals which tend to be very different from each other. The differences can be traced back to the respective theoretical foundations in these positions which range from different versions of neo-classical doctrines to constructions as are consistent with Keynesianism and its variants.

Looking at the literature, 'jobless growth' is a phrase, used by economists since the early 1990s, to describe the recovery from a recession or even a spate of output growth which fails to have similar positive effects on employment. As for its explanations and remedies, one can identify divergent positions, both in mainstream literature as well as in the views held by the opponents. We document, in the following pages, some of these positions on the phenomenon of 'jobless growth', which include the neo-classical positions and are followed by their critiques as follow from an alternate viewpoint:

1. The first of these relates to the standard neo-classical position of a downward-sloping demand curve in the labour market reflecting a trade-off between (product) wages and employment, with institutional rigidities (protective labour legislation, trade union rights, etc.) preventing a market clearance at lower wages (Ahluwalia 1992; Fallon and Lucas 1993; Ghosh 2001; Lucas 1986).

It is argued that employers are prone to adjust the level of employment according to whether (product) wages are high or low as compared to the marginal productivity of labour, both measured in units of the same output. A low employment elasticity of output, by this token, can be caused by a tendency of (product) wages to be high as compared to labour productivity at the margin. The relatively higher level of wages is attributed, in this literature, to institutional factors like trade union militancy on one hand and protective labour legislation by the state on the other, both reflecting rigidities in the labour market (for a critical review of these positions, see Nagraj 2006: 253–62; Mazumdar and Sarkar 2004). A hike in wages, along with the difficulties of pushing down wages or retrenching workers may, as held by this school, deter employers from hiring more people, which also explains the low employment elasticity of output, as can be currently observed in India. Thus the problem lies entirely with the policy-induced and institutional rigidities in the labour market, which interrupts changes in wage and employment as can happen with labour market flexibility. The above remains as the dominant view in official circles which justifies their faith in labour market, reforms as the only solution for the long lasting unemployment problems in regions of economic growth.

2. As a critique of the above, it can be pointed out that the basic premise in the formulation in terms of labour market rigidity is no longer tenable for India and other developing countries, especially with the implementation of wide-ranging formal and informal labour reforms. The latter started since the early 1990s, if not earlier. Ironically, the arguments in support of labour market reforms have continued to rely on what still is labelled as labour market rigidity as well as the prevalence of rising product wages, while none of the two seem to prevail much in today's environment of flexible labour policies. With protective labour legislations on their way out, trade union militancy as well as wage hikes are somewhat *passé* today, especially with rising unemployment and the weakened bargaining strength of workers.

3. Arguments to explain 'jobless growth' in terms of the slow growth of employment and the low employment elasticity of output also sometimes dwell on *relative prices* between manufactures and consumer goods. The position, while postulating the neo-classical position on a trade-off between product wages and employment,

tries to provide further explanations for rising unemployment in India in terms of an observed tendency for product wages to move up. As argued in this literature, with real wages (deflated by consumer prices) constant, a rise in consumer prices relative to manufacturing prices, which is the domestic real exchange rate (DRER), will cause product wage rate (deflated by price of manufacturing) to rise. This is because the product wages can be viewed as the multiple of real wage and DRER. In other words, a rise in DRER, with given real wages, is responsible for an upward movement in product wages in the labour market. The consequence, according to these economists, has been a drop in labour demand, as is visible in the case of India (for details of the argument, see Ghosh 2001, 2003a). The policy conclusion is clearly a cut in money wages as a remedial process.

4. Critiquing the above position, while the logical validity of the above as an argument cannot be disputed, the inherent assumption of product wages as the sole determining factor of labour demand is questionable. Indeed, the labour demand function may be subject to downward swings with shortfalls in aggregate demand in the economy. The argument thus remains confined to the neo-classical paradigm of price adjustment theories. Again, at an empirical level, the assumption that real wages cannot be pushed down by employers also is subject to scrutiny, especially as one witnesses the declining trend rates of real wages even when a large number of industries experience high growth rates. Data on the above aspects of the Indian economy has been provided in the empirical chapter which follows.

5. In terms of another view, which reflects an advanced country perspective, unemployment in these capital exporting home countries are attributed to tendencies for outsourcing by multinational corporations (MNCs) in order to avail of the much cheaper labour cost in developing countries. Paradoxically, both free trade and capital flows (especially the FDI) are held responsible for job losses in general as well as for the skill-mismatches that results in these countries. The above encourages the protectionist lobby in these countries to introduce newer forms of non-tariff restrictions which remain permissible in terms of the WTO regime. Little, however, is realized that a deficient global demand, both with the monetarist practices in advanced countries and stagnant markets in developing countries, which result in low wages and incomes, have a role in these job losses.

6. In an argument, which is parallel to the earlier one, low employment elasticity of output in India has been interpreted in terms of a rise in product wages (as in the earlier argument) and in addition, by the share of value added as remains to meet the wage bill. The latter, as a determining factor has even been interpreted as a Keynesian construct (or post-Keynesian construct), having its origin in the Kaleckian framework (for details, see Mazumdar and Sarkar 2004). It has been argued that a rising share of the wage bill in value added (which is assumed invariant in the short/medium term) along with a rise in product wages (due to a rise in DRER, as pointed out in the previous paragraph) explain the cut backs in the hiring of labour by employers. To confirm the argument, statistics as are available for the relevant variables have been used for a decomposition analysis of changes in employment as a function of *(a)* share of wages in value added, *(b)* product wages, *(c)* DRER and *(d)* real wages. One should be aware that despite its Keynes–Kaleckian leanings, the implicit policy conclusion comes with a strong advocacy of labour market flexibility, on the ground that the rising product wages during the 1980s explain the declines in employment.

7. As pointed out in a recent work (Nagraj 2006: 256–62), figures used in the above exercise for worker remunerations are in reality the total earnings which include wages as well as other earnings. These cover payments to workers on overtime as well as the supervisory remunerations. Thus a part of these earnings are related to the additional labour hours contributed by the same workforce, as can be detected by the rising number of man-days during these years. Hence in reality wages paid per hour have been much less if one calculates these by netting out the payments against additional man-days. Also these earnings include payments to non-workers, thus reducing further the amount paid as wages. These observations contest the high wage-low employment story advanced for the 1980s in studies similar to those mentioned earlier (for example, see Mazumdar and Sarkar 2004; Ghosh 2003b).

8. There also remain other versions of the mainstream view on the low employment elasticity of output. These recognize the fact that a 'trade-off' between wages and employment is not always feasible on a day-to-day basis, unless workers are recruited on a casual contract. Two more interpretations of the low employment elasticity follow from the above position. The first uses the 'efficiency wage' argument mentioned earlier, with employers

having the option to elicit more work from labourers who are already employed at better terms. A related argument relies on the logic of the 'internal labour market' models which dwell both on the bargaining power of workers who are with jobs and on employers seeking to retain the existing workers, in their self-interest. The situation creates an insider–outsider divide in terms of workers with or without jobs. For obvious reasons output expansion ceases to create jobs between the two groups in the same proportion in these situations. The argument can also be used to rationalize the wage-gap between the skilled and the unskilled in the labour market!

9. A related issue on employment, endorsed by the mainstream factor endowment trade theory of the Heckscher–Ohlin variant (and its corollaries in terms of the Stolper–Samuelson theorem), speaks of the impact of international trade on the labour market in terms of changes in relative factor prices. It makes the point that in advanced countries (where skilled labour is considered to be relatively abundant as compared to the unskilled), trade would result in a decline in the relative wages of unskilled labourers, the scarce factor (in advanced countries), as predicted by this branch of theory. This is based on the fact that the developed countries usually export goods which are skill-intensive while the developing countries export goods primarily using unskilled labour. The argument has been used to decry the practice of outsourcing by MNCs, by setting up subsidiaries in cheap labour countries, to produce goods which compete with products originating in advanced countries. There arises, in terms of the above view, a 'skill-mismatch' (Wood 1994) in the advanced countries. This again leads to a policy conclusion which has a strong plea for protection as a remedial measure against the widely observed unemployment and the widening wage gap against the unskilled.

10. Arguments, as above, do not stand scrutiny if one recognizes the fact that unemployment and poverty (with low wages) is high among the unskilled in developing countries as well. One thus witnesses rising wage-gaps between the skilled and unskilled workers in these areas. Trade between the advanced and the developing countries has thus neither reduced the wage and employment gap between the skilled and unskilled workers in countries which trade with each other, nor has it caused any further worsening of the relatively poor status of the unskilled

(the relatively scarce factor) in advanced/developing countries (see also Ghosh 2003b). The trade theoretic arguments relating to the labour market do *not* seem to provide a clue to the observed tendencies in employment and wages in the trading nations. Instead, the rising skill-mismatch seems to be common in both advanced and the developing country trade partners, irrespective of their so-called initial factor endowments, which are far from fully utilized in either country.

11. In reality the unemployment as well as the rising wage-gap between the skilled and the unskilled in advanced countries can rather be related to the contractionary macroeconomic policies in the world economy with the related deficiency of demand over the last few decades. Much of these policies are part of the underlying paradigm of mainstream economic doctrines which dominate policy making in the developing countries as well. It can be observed that conservative fiscal and monetary policies, which constituted the basic tenets of the Thatcher–Reganite policies in industrialized countries, have contributed to limit demand and to stall employment prospects; especially for the unskilled and the disadvantaged. Jobs for these workers have also been hit by the use of new technology which is skill- and capital-intensive. In most cases the push to these cost-cutting technologies is driven by competitive capitalism with the need to cut costs in the face of growing competition under liberalization and the opening up of these economies. Use of labour-saving technology has been a common practice in manufacturing, as we observe later in this study, for both high- as well as low-growth industries in India.

12. Endorsing the above position, one can also point at the visible increases in factor productivity, and in particular of labour productivity in industries using capital intensive technology, and adopting large doses of automation. This, as is held, has led to high economic growth in many parts of the world without commensurate growth in employment.

On Notions of Labour Flexibility

We now provide some remarks to the alternate theories dealing with unemployment, especially, from the neo-liberal perspectives on labour reform which regards labour flexibility as a panacea to cure unemployment, both in the developed and developing world. We contest the position that the major cause of unemployment, as diagnosed in the mainstream arguments and also in the related formulations (in terms of DRER and skill-mismatch, etc.), rest upon the belief that product wage has remained above the market clearing level and that labour reforms are needed to address this issue by incorporating free labour markets and wage flexibility.

With labour security regulations fading out in the current phase of competitive capitalism, flexible labour policies at the firm level have already been common. The main thrust there is cost cutting to retain the competitive edge, both in the global as well as local markets. Labour flexibility can be devised in different forms influencing wage payments as well as other norms and conditions relating to employment.

We provide below four different, but interrelated, notions of labour flexibility as can be traced in the literature (see Regini 2000):

1. *Numerical flexibility:* With adjustments in the number of workers to meet the varying levels of demand as well as technological innovation (EIRR 1985 as cited in Regini 2000). This type of flexibility requires that *(a)* firms can shed those workers whose skills have become obsolete and *(b)* can hire new workers on contractual or temporary basis so that they can be easily laid off when situations demand. This is the most popular notion of flexibility, as has been practised in many countries since the last decade. It also remains one of the driving forces behind labour market reforms.

2. *Functional flexibility:* This simply refers to the individual firm's ability to reorganize its workforce to varying levels of tasks as are due to technological changes. This is also conditioned by the ability and skill of workers to adapt to the changing tasks. However, job-rotation, multi-skilling, retraining and internal mobility, which remain the essence of this kind of flexibility (see Callenberg 1990, as cited in Regini 2000), once established, leave few incentives for firms to hire new workers. Large corporate firms, and especially transnational corporations (TNCs), are increasingly adhering to these forms of functional flexibility which, in a way, reduces labour costs while multi-level processes can be carried out safely with the existing set of workers.

3. *Wage flexibility:* It refers to the firm's ability to adjust wages in a manner which suits the changing conditions of cost competitiveness and product demand in the market. Among others, labour

regulation, and particularly the minimum wage legislation, is viewed as the principal hindrance for this type of flexibility at the firm level. The above can be abolished by permitting a free hand to the workers in setting wages, and also by limiting the power and functions of the labour unions and organizations which come in the way of downward revisions in wages. As argued in this approach to labour flexibility, such flexibility is a help to attain the adjustments needed to attain market clearance in the labour market (Soskice 1990, as cited in Regini 2000).

4. *Temporal flexibility:* This refers to adjustments in the utilization of labour hours according to the temporal and/or seasonal variations in product demand (Adam and Caniziani 1998, cited in Regini 2000). This type of labour flexibility allows firms to adapt to the practices of overtime work, flexible (part-time) work, shift-work and weekly or annual arrangements of work, none of which require a change in the number of persons employed. Practices as above are gaining prominence with casualization and contractualization of jobs replacing the standard Fordist work contracts and practices all over the world, including India which is no exception.

Of the several forms of labour flexibility, the one to be chosen by firms depends on their specific strategy for competing in the product market. In the literature (the term is borrowed by Regini [1997, 2000] from Streeck [1991]) three types of product market strategy are mentioned which include diversified quality production (DQP), flexible mass production (FMP) and flexible specialization (FS). In DQP strategy, firms compete in the product market on the basis of quality of the product, and not on the basis of diversification and price. Accordingly they target the high market segment as opposed to those for the low-wage products. This calls for high levels of functional flexibility on part of the workers which is characterized by multi-skilling, retraining and a high level of co-ordination among the workers. Other types of labour flexibility (numerical, wage and temporal) are pursued with respect to the low wage peripheral workers, and not with the core sector workers with high skill and higher wages.[2]

In FMP strategy (the term is borrowed by Regini 2000 from Boyer 1987, as cited in Regini 2000), mass production of various goods is practised by the firms in accordance with the varying demand conditions while holding prices down. Even with this strategy functional flexibility is required among the core group of workers while numerical and temporal flexibility (in the form of casualization, part-time work, etc.) are applied in dealing with workers in the periphery.

Small firms in the economy adhere to FS strategy of flexible specialization which lend versatility in production process and rapid adjustments to changes in demand with diffused production systems. Here the
entrepreneur and his small group of assistants need to be able to carry out
a wide range of functions. Employees in this type of small firm are subject
to numerical as well as wage flexibility. At the same time these workers need
to adapt to different machines which adjusts their workload to changing
demand, and thus demands functional flexibility.

The above discussion makes it clear that labour market flexibility at the
firm level demands one or more of the following: (a) the ability of the firm
to control and adjust the number of persons employed and/or its ability
to vary the number of hours worked and (b) the ability of workers who
are employed to adjust and cope with multi-level skills in the production
process, necessitating high degrees of co-ordination between workers on
the one hand and with employers on the other. Forms of labour market
flexibility as envisaged above can hardly reduce aggregate unemployment, and may even increase it, especially with technological innovations
and automation which deters hiring of new workers. Multi-skilling and
retraining of existing workers further deter the fresh hiring process. From
this point of view, skill-formation as such cannot be considered a solution
to the skill-mismatch problem by generating additional employment
opportunities, unless it is targeted to those among the unskilled who are
unemployed and not to those already in jobs.

In developing countries like India, labour-related policies have been
influenced by de-regulatory measures with the dismantling of state legislations to protect labour. The above, along with the rising casualization
of workers have been responsible for marked reductions in the bargaining
power of labour, especially in the face of having little option in terms of
alternative job offers. The employers, in turn, can easily declare a lock-
out in a bid to avoid labour trouble, and sometimes to avoid potential
losses (Papola 1992). The process sometimes siphons off capital from
productive units where labour is deployed to speculative ventures in the
financial sector (Dutt 2003).

On Jobless Growth in India and Its Explanations

In interpreting the Indian scene, we reject in the present study the mainstream neo-classical explanation for the widely observed job losses,
especially among the unskilled. The critique we have offered in this chapter

on theoretical foundations of the mainstream approach to labour market is complemented, in the rest of this study, by analytical and empirical observations which substantiate these critiques. As for the impact of these growth-oriented policies we find the consequences as socially antithetic; especially in view of the uneven distribution of the enhanced growth dividends, if any, on the status of labour. Impact of these growth-oriented policies not only reduces the number of jobs as are offered but also downgrades their quality. Aspects as above are reflected in the low security status of workers, as we have indicated it in our study. The process, in our judgement, may also adversely affect output growth; both with a drop in average labour productivity (with wages dipping below subsistence), and with shortfalls in aggregate demand as are due to cuts in the wage bill in the economy. No amount of supply-side incentives as are driven by rising labour productivity with labour-saving technology, skilling of the labour force and wage adjustments can, in such circumstances, lead the economy along a higher growth path.

We make an attempt in the present study to test empirically the validity of the alternative hypotheses in the literature relating to the effects of labour flexibility on growth and employment in the Indian economy. These theories include the standard neo-classical frame of analysis as described earlier and the related prescriptions, as opposed to the Keynesian position on related issues. We have tried to arrive at an assessment of the alternative positions, with simple quantitative estimates as well as econometric analysis of the relevant variables.

Jobless growth in India and in other developing countries opens up a debate on the possible effects of economic reforms and the liberalization process which are currently underway in developing countries like India, an aspect which is well documented in official statistics (Government of India 2006). It may be mentioned at this place that estimates from official sources indicate that the growth rate of employment in the organized sector has actually been declining, not only in the public sector but also in private corporate sector. Thus the total number of male and female workers employed at end of March 2003 at 27 million started falling steadily from March 1997 when the figure was at 28.25 million. The drop in employment had been more prominent with male workers and in the public sector. Incidentally, the public sector still provides the major chunk of employment in the country, as can be seen from the employment figures for the public sector at 18.58 million out of an aggregate employment figure at 27.0 million by the end of March 2003. As for the sectoral shares of employment, of those employed in the organized private sector, more than 50 per cent (at 4.74 million) were absorbed in manufacturing at the end of March 2003 (Government of India 2006: S-50). Employment in the organized sector declined by 0.8 per cent in 2003 due to a drop in public sector employment by 1 per cent during the year (Government of India 2006: 230).

Looking now at the sectoral share of GDP at factor cost in India for 2003–04, agriculture (and related activities) along with manufacturing, construction, power and water provided a little less than 50 per cent. The rest were provided by services which include those in the defence-related public sector (Government of India 2006). Growth in the manufacturing sector, which of late has picked up, is still one of the less performing sectors in the economy, especially as compared to the booming services sector.

In this study we have chosen to deal with the status of labour in the organized manufacturing sector of the Indian economy. The reasons behind this selection include:

First, that the working population in the organized segment can be expected to have a symbolic presence in the economy in terms of collective labour power vis-à-vis capital and the state.

Second, with the regulatory norms and labour legislations still having some hold and relevance in the functioning of the organized labour market, the sector, in our judgement provides a test case for judging the impact of labour market flexibility which has been initiated in India since the early 1990s. Thus the significance of the organized labour market as the lead sector of the economy and as a base of protective labour legislation still holds in this country.

Third, as a further justification of confining our study to the organized labour force in the manufacturing industry we point at the existence of large-scale and old type of industries in this sector. With labour better organized and with labour legislation, as mentioned earlier, in principle adhered to, organized labour in manufacturing is worth analyzing.

Finally, it remains the case that despite the rise of services as a leading sector in terms of growth, the manufacturing sector is still the one which is integrated more with the rest of the world, both in terms of the exportability of their products as well as in providing the target destination of FDIs. Factors as above, as it can be expected, affect the status of labour vis-à-vis capital in this sector of the economy.

A study of labour in the organized manufacturing sector can thus be of help in throwing light on the status of labour in the market-led flexibilization regime in the new economy of India. Aspects as above have led us to select this segment for further analysis, notwithstanding the fact that labour in the organized sector covers as little as 1.6 per cent of the total labour force in the economy.[3]

As we have already pointed out, mainstream arguments relating to the labour market has considerably influenced official policies in developing countries. Most prevalent of these relate to the plea for labour market flexibility. It seeks to do away with the so-called rigidities in the labour markets which are identified in the rights demanded by the unionized workers with permanent jobs and in social protection enjoyed by workers in terms of pro-labour legislations by the state. In terms of above even labour legislation is considered a factor which can be instrumental for labour market rigidity.

Positions as above speak for wide ranging deregulation of the labour market, and for the dismantling of labour legislations in general, with an advocacy of hire and fire policies and offers of employment on a casual basis. It is expected that by reviving the market forces the demand for labour will settle at wages which also clear the labour market. The process is also expected to generate more jobs, with product wages *lowered* to a level as is consistent with the marginal contribution of labour in terms of production. Policy prescriptions as above include, in India, the recommendations of the National Commission on Labour in 2002, with its strong advocacy of labour flexibility in the interest of growth with efficiency.[4]

In our empirical study on labour in manufacturing industries, which follows in the next four chapters, we observe tendencies for product wages to remain stagnant or even decline over the last decade and half. This is evident in the official statistics relating to the real wage bill at constant prices and in the number employed in the organized manufacturing sector. Such observations disprove the current view, often shared by official policy makers, that wages are rigid at levels which are far too high for creating more employment. It also contests the view put forth by others (see Lilien 1982; Shapiro and Stiglitz 1984), who see a rise in product wages and/or in the DRER as factors behind the shortfalls in employment.

There also remains the argument that jobs fail to rise because a smaller share of value added is now available for meeting the wage bill (Shapiro and Stiglitz 1984). But one has to recognize that the plethora of funds, which seem to be forthcoming to India in recent years, have come as a result of foreign direct investments, joint ventures and even foreign institutional investor (FII) inflows. Thus, liquidity may no longer be the constraining factor for additional employment. Instead it is the stagnant demand for real output, the choice of capital-intensive technology, the relative profitability of investments in pure speculative investments in financial assets as compared to those in the physical sector which make for the final demand for labour. We will spell out some of these aspects in the next chapter where we analyze the employment aspects in India's manufacturing on the basis of secondary data.

In the four chapters which follow, we intend to look into the following aspects:

1. Employment growth in relation to manufacturing output growth rates during the post-reform years starting from 1991.
2. Patterns of labour deployment in high growth and low growth industries which respectively include those with annual average growth rates above 20 per cent and below 5 per cent.
3. Aspects as above also include an analysis of the following:

    (*i*) Growth rates of employment vis-à-vis output (the employment elasticity of output).
    (*ii*) The related technological changes which consist of the ratio of fixed capital vis-à-vis output (capital elasticity of output) as well as the ratio of labour to fixed capital, both for high growth and low growth industries.
    (*iii*) Casualization of workers, to the extent data is available.
    (*iv*) Changes in wage share and profit share in these industries.

4. We also provide, from data collected on the basis of field surveys, an analysis of labour security (as defined later in Chapter 5) for 615 workers we have interviewed in our field survey from various locations.
5. Data from the field trip is also used to provide a profile of the individual areas where the survey was conducted. The above helps in the analysis which follows.
6. Data from the field survey is used to relate labour status to the nature of industries in which they are employed. Industries here are classified according to trade orientation (export/import intensity), factor intensity (labour/capital intensity) and similar other binary attributes.

Notes

1. The utility function of risk-averse worker exhibits diminishing marginal utility of income. Because of this, the increase in utility resulting from the higher incomes paid during an expansion is not enough to offset the loss in utility resulting from the lower incomes paid during a recession. Firms that offer fixed-wage contracts, in effect, offer 'insurance' against wage declines during recessions, and hence can attract risk-averse workers at lower average wages.
2. There exists in the labour market a polarization of workers between the high-skilled ones who belong to the core group and those who are un-skilled, or having skills which are obsolete, and thus in the periphery.
3. Manufacturing industries provide 12 per cent of total employment in India. Of the total employment in the manufacturing industry the organized sector provides as little as 14 per cent. Thus the organized manufacturing industry provides only 1.6 per cent of the total employment in the country (Government of India, Annual Survey of Industries).
4. See Chapter 5 of this book for details.

The Indian Manufacturing Sector and Labour: An Aggregative Picture

2

Introduction

Manufacturing industry in India had been subject to marked shortfalls in output growth since the year 1990–91 which also marked the beginning of economic reforms in the country and has continued since then. Thus the index of manufacturing output, with base in 1980–81, at 207.8 in 1990–91 fell considerably during the next few years with the respective figures for three years (1999–2000) at 159.4, 167.9 and 196.6. There has been a recent turnaround in the industrial growth with the indices moving up to 214.6 in 2004–05 and 263.5 in 2006–07. Much of this improvement was confined to a handful of industries. Thus, out of the 18 industry groups classified according to the NIC 2-digit level, indices relating to only three in the year 2006–07 recorded an impressive growth with levels above 300. In contrast, four major industry groups which included 'jute products' (90.7), 'wood products and furniture' (91.0), 'cotton textiles' (157.3) and 'metal products' (183.2) recorded low growth, as indicated by the respective indices provided within brackets. While the picture of manufacturing sector as reflected in terms of its overall trend in growth rates is quite robust, the overall picture, especially relating to labour is not so, as will be pointed out in the rest of this chapter.

Employment provided by the manufacturing sector has generally been stagnant or even declining over the last few years. Thus there has been little response, if any, of these spurts in output growth to employment in manufacturing. The number of workers employed in the organized sector which stood at 6.33 million at the end of March 1991 started falling steadily with the respective figures at the end of the financial years 1996, 2001 and 2005 at 6.04 million, 5.88 million and 5.61 million. There has been decline in both public as well as private sector employment since the inception of economic liberalization in 1991 with little turnarounds in between (Government of India 2007: S–50, Table 3.3). As pointed out in the Eleventh Plan document, employment in the organized sectors as a whole fell from an annual percentage growth of 1.53 per cent during 1983–94 to –0.70 per cent during 1994–2005. Employment in organized private sector recorded similar trends, with annual average percentage rates hovering between 0.44 per cent in the earlier period to 0.5 per cent in the later period (Government of India 2007: S–50, Table 3.3). Considering the spurts in the growth of the services sector in recent years, the low employment growth in private organized sector is revealing. While decline was observed in organized sector male employment, both in public and private sectors during 1990–2005, the corresponding female employment actually increased during the same period (Government of India 2007: S–50, Table 3.3). So, if we exclude the rate of growth in female employment during 1990–2005 from the total employment growth rate, then we will find that the male employment has declined at a faster rate than the overall decline in the growth rate of employment in the organized sector.

The aforementioned figures confirm the joblessness aspect of India's manufacturing sector. We probe further into the related issues of jobless growth in industry in this chapter, using data for organized manufacturing industry at 3-digit level from the Annual Survey of Industries (ASI), as provided by Government of India's Central Statistical Organization (CSO). The related information on labour includes, among others, figures for employment, wages, nature of labour contracts, factor use, and so on. These are used in our analysis to arrive at conclusive arguments relating to the status of organized labour in India's manufacturing industry, as offered in the rest of this chapter.

The Data Set and the Methodology

The empirical analysis in this chapter is based on data set relating to the organized manufacturing sector which is available from the official sources mentioned earlier. The ASI data set consists of two series corresponding to *(a)* the census sector and *(b)* the factory sector. The census sector consists of only those units, which employ, on an average, 50 or more workers with the aid of power and 100 persons or more without the aid of power. The factory sector is more comprehensive in that it covers establishments which are registered under the Factory Act and thus employ 10 or more workers with power and 20 or more workers without power. The survey, carried out annually since 1959, covers all manufacturing establishments. In our study, we have chosen the data for the factory sector since it is more comprehensive.

ASI data provides industrial classification at different levels of digits which allows detailed specification of industries. Depending on data availability we have used 50 3-digit level industry groups[1] covering the period from 1980 to 1981 through 2002–03. The industrial classification in ASI was changed to NIC in 1973–74 and hence the data prior to that period are not strictly comparable with the data set relating to the later years. We have, however, confined our analysis to the period which starts from 1980–81. The data set covers almost the entire organized manufacturing sectors in India.

Industries are re-classified in our study by using the concordance procedure in terms of the latest available (National Industrial Classification, 1998) industry classification. The ASI data reports monetary values of the data at current period prices. We have used the wholesale price index (WPI) series for different industries to deflate these into real values at 1993–94 prices. Nominal values of the respective variables are used at 3-digit levels of classification of industry groups and then deflated by the WPI as above. Annual values of the respective WPI, in turn, are derived from the monthly indices of wholesale prices. For deflating the value of capital stock we have constructed a separate deflator by using the WPI for machinery, transport equipment and construction (see Hasan et al. 2003 for a similar study). These values have been used in the present study to arrive at different ratios as well as to test a set of hypothesis in terms of a model set up with regression equations. We may mention here that so far industry data at the 3-digit level has not earlier been worked out in other studies relating to labour and industry in India and this study will probably be a pioneering one to venture it.

The variables we have worked with in the rest of this chapter include the number of workers, value of output, wages, profits, capital stock, etc. In dealing with the variables we realized that while net value added (NVA) is considered a better measure of output, it entails the problem of double indexing if one has to obtain NVA figures at constant prices. We have accordingly used the gross value added (GVA) figures which, as pointed out elsewhere in the literature, avoids the related problems of double indexing (Balakrishnan 2004). The employment series is calculated as annual averages with workers defined as persons employed (both permanent and causal), directly or through an agency (including a contractor) on payment of wages/salaries, and engaged in any type of manufacturing or its ancillary activities. Wage per worker in each industry refers to the product wage which is derived as the total wage bill deflated by the WPI and divided by the number of workers of that industry. It excludes the imputed values of other benefits, employers' contribution to old-age benefits and other social security expenses on workers, which are reported separately. Volume of output is measured as the total value of output at constant prices produced by each industry over a year. The value added is measured as total value of output minus total value of raw material as well as intermediate inputs. To measure capital stock we have derived a series which include capital stock at a constant cost in terms of their replacement value. Capital stocks for successive years are obtained by using perpetual inventory method which is obtained as a sum of new investment and the depreciation of adjusted capital stock at the beginning of the period.

The time period considered in our study is divided into the pre-reform (1980–91) and post-reform years (1991–2003). The practice is consistent with India's liberalization and economic globalization efforts which have been intensified through policy reforms since 1991.

The Analysis

The starting point of our analysis is the phenomenon of 'jobless growth' as can be observed in the Indian economy over the last two decades. We notice the lagging employment scenario, even in high growth industries, a paradox which has generated wide-ranging debates on the success of economic reforms in general, and of liberalization as well as trade opening in particular, in improving employment and the related level of living in the economy. We can observe, at the 3-digit level of data for industry groups at constant prices, *that employment growth had been either low or near stagnant, even in industries which are high-tech and/or with high trade intensity*. We have mentioned earlier in Chapter 1 some of the explanations offered in the literature on factors which affect employment in Indian industry. We reiterate here briefly the points mentioned in Chapter 1.

One of the arguments mentioned earlier in Chapter 1 points at the rising gap between the product wage and real wage, when the two are respectively deflated by the WPI (product prices) and the consumer price indices. The gap, as has been erroneously argued, explain the declining labour demand over the last few decades. This apparently happens because of the increase in the WPI relative to the consumer price index (Mazumdar and Sarkar 2004). Attention has been drawn, in other studies, to possible reductions in the reported employment figures due to the stretching of labour hours through overtime (and probably also non-payment of overtime labour) in industries. Closure of big industries, especially with lockouts in the textile industry has also been cited as a major explanation of the dwindling employment situation in the 1980s and 1990s (Dutt 2003; Mazumdar and Sarkar 2004; Papola 1992). In addition, the reductions in employment due to a shift in the size class of industrial units have been cited as an explanation of low employment growth (Uchikawa 2002). Attention also has been drawn to the declining bargaining strength of workers and especially of the labour unions, both at industry level and for the economy as a whole (Papola 1992; Roy 2002; Shyam Sundar 2005). Tendencies as above have been considerably aggravated during the recent years with labour flexibility in operation.

While dealing with employment in the organized manufacturing industries, it may be relevant to point out that the current share of small and medium enterprises (SMEs) is around 44 per cent of the aggregate industrial production in the country which provides more than 35 per cent of the country's exports. In terms of their socio-economic importance, the total number of SME units at 11.39 million today is nearly 95 per cent of all industrial units of the country, providing jobs to nearly 27.13 million people, which is nearly 86 per cent of the total employment in the country (Government of India 2007: 147–54). However, employment generated by these small units is mostly outside the organized sector.

Issues have also been raised in the literature on trade opening and its impact on employment, particularly in the context of what is observed as the skill-mismatch in advanced areas (Wood 1994). Declines in job opportunities for the unskilled and the widening wage gaps between the skilled and the unskilled, as observed in advanced countries, are attributed to the spate of rising imports of labour-intensive manufactures from a set of developing countries, in particular from Asia. Tendencies for TNCs to outsource or even relocate production in these cheap labour destinations are identified as major factors behind these tendencies. However, the new pattern of trade and its impact on employment, as pointed out in a study, cannot be explained by standard trade-theoretic models (of the Stolper–Samuelson variety) as are implicit in the above argument (Ghosh 2003b, 2005a, 2005b). Thus, trade has failed to bring about a levelling of factor prices including wages, across countries. While the prevailing gap in wages between the skilled and unskilled has been rising in advanced countries, a similar trend is also visible in developing countries in terms of the rising wage gaps between the skilled and unskilled. Explanations may include global recession, use of labour-displacing technology and even low trade intensity, which are common for both areas.

There is a need to analyze, at an aggregate level, the employment-elasticity aspect of industries in the context of trade liberalization and opening up of the economy. An exercise as above, attempted elsewhere for an earlier period (Mazumdar and Sarkar 2004) could not be replicated by a follow-up exercise for later years due to data limitations. The earlier exercise was based on the input-output analysis constructed by the Planning Commission available for 1991. The results arrived at in that study are clearly not suitable to arrive at a conclusion on subsequent years because no update of such input-output table has been constructed by Planning Commission or by other agencies after 1991.

We have based our analysis on the data set as is available for the post-reform years up to 2003. We try to provide a 'reality check' with an industry-wise break-up of the relevant variables as concern labour. We notice the performance of a group of manufacturing industries (at 3-digit level) with high rates of output growth at around 20 per cent or above over the post-reform years. The related issues concerning employment include the following five aspects:

1. Did high output growth rate in these industry groups contribute to employment growth in the same proportion? If not, was there a tendency for displacement of labour by using labour saving techniques in these industry groups?
2. Was there also a tendency for the deepening of capital by using higher levels of capital per unit of output?
3. Does one also observe higher levels of labour productivity in these industries? Do these confirm labour saving practices, if any, in these industries?
4. Do the changes in product wages and profits as share of output in these industries reflect the weaker bargaining power of labour in terms of the sharing of the national dividend? And are these changes also related to casualization of labour in terms of the labour flexibility norms?
5. For the top ranking manufacturing firms, detailed statistics on which is available for selected variables, we ask whether liberalization and opening up of the economy contributed to (a) higher growth rates

of output or *(b)* sales in these units, as is expected in terms of the neo-liberal doctrines. In particular, is there a positive correlation between sales/value added on one hand and foreign equity holdings and export earnings on the other? Also, has foreign equity holdings in these units been functional in generating exports as is expected in terms of the mainstream doctrines?

High and Low Growth Industry Groups—Output and Employment Growth

Let us first identify the high growth (from now on HG) industry groups. The top five of these, experiencing an annual average growth rate (AAGR) at 23 per cent or above over the five years ending in 2003 include, in a descending order in terms of growth, manufacture of aircraft and spacecraft (111.0 per cent), motor vehicles (30.2 per cent), electronic valves and tubes (26.2 per cent), electric motors, generators and transformers (25.5 per cent) and jewellery and related articles (23.4 per cent), with percentage growth rates given in the respective brackets. If we look at a broader set of industry groups experiencing AAGRs at 10 per cent or above over the same period we arrive at a larger set, which also includes textiles (17.8 per cent), telephone, television and radio apparatus (17.2 per cent), plastic products (11.7 per cent) and refined petroleum (10.8 per cent).

As for employment, it is revealing that the corresponding rates of growth in employment in these HG industry groups has been consistently lower than their respective output growth, a pattern which speaks of the prevailing employment elasticities of output at low levels. (See Table 2.1A for output and employment growth and Table 2.2 for capital and employment elasticity of output in top 10 industries over the five years ending in 2003. Also, see Table 2.1B for output and employment growth in industry groups having an annual average growth rate above 10 per cent. See Figure 2.1A for share of output and employment of each industry group ranked according their AAGR in 2003.) It is even more revealing that the gaps between the respective AAGRs of output and employment have been the highest for manufacture of aircraft and spacecraft (353), the industry group with highest growth rate. Similar large gaps also prevail between growth rates of output and employment for other high AAGR industry groups during the post-reform period.

Table 2.1A AAGR of output and employment for industry groups (AAGR of output above 10 per cent) (Post-reform years: 1999–2003)

Industry group name	NIC code	AAGR of output	AAGR of employment
Aircraft and spacecraft	353	111.10	65.00
Motor vehicles	341	30.27	4.90
Electronic valves and tubes and other electronic components	321	26.25	14.72
Electric motors, generators and transformers	311	25.56	10.85
Jewellery and related articles	369	23.45	7.69
Watches and clocks	333	23.31	–6.36
Other textiles	172	17.84	12.22
Television and radio transmitters	331	17.23	2.81
Knitted and crocheted fabrics and articles	173	15.05	10.25
Furniture	361	13.25	4.71
Wearing apparel, except fur apparel	181	12.93	5.25
Repair of ships and boats	351	11.92	5.66
Refined petroleum products	232	11.76	5.54
Plastic products	252	10.88	3.59
Basic-precious and non-ferrous metals	272	10.79	0.79

Source: Annual Survey of Industries, Central Statistical Organization, Government of India (various issues), as downloaded from www.indiastat.com (last accessed on 15 April 2004).

Table 2.1B AAGR of output and employment for industry groups (AAGR of output above 10 per cent) (Pre-reform years: 1980–90)

Industry group name	NIC code	AAGR of output	AAGR of employment
Other fabricated metal products; metal working service activities	289	46.91	1.12
Electronic valves and tubes and other electronic components	321	27.63	9.61
Products of wood, cork, straw and plaiting materials	202	26.70	0.27
Optical instruments and photographic equipment	332	24.66	7.47
Footwear	192	21.80	6.48
Man-made fibres	243	20.89	5.92

(Table 2.1B continued)

(Table 2.1B continued)

Industry group name	NIC code	AAGR of output	AAGR of employment
Refined petroleum products	232	18.34	4.29
Transport equipment n.i.e.	359	17.50	7.73
Plastic products	252	16.76	6.03
Wearing apparel, except fur apparel	181	15.93	8.89
Office, accounting and computing machinery	300	15.40	1.28
Television and radio transmitters and apparatus for line telephony and line telegraphy	322	15.32	1.46
Non-metallic mineral products n.i.e.	269	13.93	13.24
Aircraft and spacecraft	353	13.86	1.68
Knitted and crocheted fabrics and articles	173	13.63	11.58
Watches and clocks	333	12.42	3.17
Jewellery and related articles	369	12.25	5.34
Basic chemicals	241	11.14	0.96
Television and radio transmitters and apparatus for line telephony and line telegraphy	331	11.00	1.48
Other chemical products	242	10.64	3.01
Motor vehicles	341	10.31	1.52
Rubber products	251	10.05	2.39
Beverages	155	10.04	3.97

Source: Annual Survey of Industries, Central Statistical Organization, Government of India (various issues) as downloaded from www.indiastat.com (last accessed on 15 April 2004).

Table 2.2 Labour and capital elasticity of industry groups (AAGR of output above 10 per cent) (Post-reform years: 1991–2003)

Industry group name	Capital elasticity of output	Employment elasticity of output
Aircraft and spacecraft	0.943	0.585
Motor vehicles	1.062	0.162
Electronic valves and tubes and other electronic components	2.173	0.561
Electric motors, generators and transformers	1.387	0.424
Jewellery and related articles	1.323	0.328

(Table 2.2 continued)

(Table 2.2 continued)

Industry group name	Capital elasticity of output	Employment elasticity of output
Watches and clocks	–0.300	–0.273
Other textiles	0.943	0.685
Television and radio transmitters	0.627	0.163
Knitted and crocheted fabrics and articles	1.257	0.681
Furniture	2.058	0.355
Wearing apparel, except fur apparel	1.082	0.406
Repair of ships and boats	2.201	0.475
Refined petroleum products	3.671	0.471
Plastic products	–0.058	0.330
Basic-precious and non-ferrous metals	2.442	0.073

Source: Annual Survey of Industries, Central Statistical Organizations, Government of India (various issues), as downloaded from www.indiastat.com (last accessed on 15 April 2004).

A similar pattern as above has also prevailed for low output growth industry groups (LG) which have experienced average annual growth rates even at less than 5 per cent. All these low growth industry groups like man-made fibres, tobacco, publishing, etc. (with the exception of those with zero or negative growth rates of output), experienced growth rates in employment which were lower than those for output. It was thus natural that employment elasticities of output in these industry groups had also been low.

On the whole employment growth seems to have fallen much behind growth rates of output in most of these industry groups in the organized sector over the five years which ended in 2003. This is reflected in the relative elasticities of labour and capital vis-à-vis output (Table 2.2). Probing a little backwards in terms of time, a similar pattern seems to have prevailed over the pre-reform years before 1991 (Table 2.1B).

Cumulative Shares of Individual Industries in Aggregate Manufacturing Output

The pattern, as described earlier, is all the more evident when industries are grouped according to their cumulative share in total output of the

Figure 2.1A Employment and output shares of industry groups (As percentage of aggregate manufacturing employment and output) (2003)

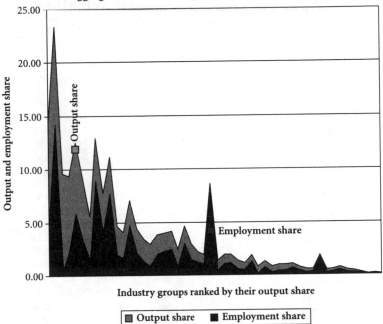

Industry groups ranked by their output share

☐ Output share ■ Employment share

Source: Authors' own calculations based on data contained in *Annual Survey of Industries,* Central Statistical Organization, Government of India (various issues), as downloaded from www.indiastat.com (last accessed on 15 April 2004).

50 industry groups at 3-digit level considered here. As indicated in Table 2.3, industries[2] with individual shares between 5.8 per cent and 9.9 per cent of output in the organized sector of Indian manufacturing industries collectively contributed 47.66 per cent of aggregate manufacturing output while their cumulative contribution in terms of aggregate employment in these industries had only been 30.73 per cent. Paradoxically, for the low growth industries (with individual contributions between 0.04 per cent and 0.95 per cent of industrial output and cumulative contribution of output at 13.21 per cent) their aggregate employment as is contributed stands at 22 per cent. The pattern indicates, once again, the rather poor contribution of the high growth industries in terms of employment which contrasts the relatively substantial contribution by the low growth industries (see Table 2.3 and Figure 2.1B). *It is revealing to note this inverse relation between output share and employment share for individual industries.*

Table 2.3 Cumulative shares of all industry groups at 3-digit level classification (Shares of output and employment as percentage of aggregate manufacturing output and employment respectively) (2003)

Industry group code at 3-digit level	Share of output (%)	Share of employment (%)
271	9.94	4.40
171	9.11	14.27
232	9.05	0.56
241	7.08	2.30
242	6.61	5.90
341	5.88	3.30
Subtotal	47.67	30.73
151	4.09	1.46
154	4.01	8.93
153	3.62	4.12
269	3.38	7.76
252	2.70	1.93
359	2.45	1.62
181	2.33	4.75
291	2.29	2.13
311	2.12	1.30
272	2.02	0.87
Subtotal	29.01	34.87
292	1.90	1.92
210	1.75	2.26
289	1.73	2.42
251	1.63	0.83
152	1.63	3.03
369	1.47	1.43
Subtotal	10.11	11.89
173	0.95	1.22
155	0.92	1.05
160	0.91	7.72
313	0.90	0.44
281	0.89	1.08
172	0.80	1.18
321	0.79	0.56
331	0.69	0.45
192	0.63	1.28
300	0.62	0.16
191	0.57	0.71
322	0.55	0.26
243	0.53	0.41
293	0.52	0.42
261	0.44	0.64
221	0.36	0.39

(Table 2.3 continued)

(Table 2.3 continued)

Industry group code at 3-digit level	Share of output (%)	Share of employment (%)
314	0.35	0.26
231	0.28	0.30
222	0.27	1.60
351	0.25	0.27
315	0.24	0.30
202	0.21	0.51
361	0.18	0.28
352	0.13	0.26
333	0.11	0.17
332	0.05	0.07
201	0.04	0.12
353	0.04	0.03
Subtotal	13.21	22.14

Source: Authors' own calculations based on data contained in *Annual Survey of Industries*, Central Statistical Organization, Government of India (various issues), as downloaded from www.indiastat.com (last accessed on 15 April 2004).

Figure 2.1B **Employment and output shares of industry groups (As percentage of aggregate employment and output) (2003)**

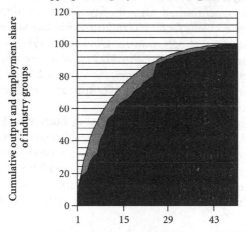

Industry groups aggregated in terms of individual
output shares arranged in descending order

☐ Cumulative output share   ■ Cumulative employment share

Source: Authors' own calculations based on data contained in *Annual Survey of Industries*, Central Statistical Organization, Government of India (various issues), as downloaded from www.indiastat.com (last accessed on 15 April 2004).

Does it indicate the wider application of labour-saving technology in high growth industries which generate the major part of industrial output in the organized sector?

Volatility of Output and Employment

As for the fluctuations in the pattern of output and employment, we observe that three among the top 10 HG industries also in terms of AAGR went through the maximum variations in output over the post-reform years. The three include manufactures of aircraft (353), watches and clocks (333) and electric motors and generators (311). Variations in output growth, synchronous with similar variations of employment growth, were relatively higher (than those for employment) for as many as eight of these 10 HG industries. As for the LG industries (experiencing less than 5 per cent output growth over the same period), fluctuations in employment in at least two of these exceeded those in output. On the whole, *volatility of employment was thus common for most industries, including industries in a state of stagnation*; with low or negative growth rates of output. *The synchronized pattern of variations in output and employment, observed especially for the HG industries indicate the impact of uncertain output market on job opportunities. Obviously, workers absorbed at the time of high output growth were shredded off at a time when there was a reverse turn from the upward trajectory.* (See Tables 2.4 and 2.5 and Figures 2.2 and 2.3 for standard deviations of output and employment in the HG and LG industries over 1999–2003.)

Labour thus seems to be having a raw deal, with fluctuating job prospects even in some LG industries where output growth tends to be zero or negligible. As it has been pointed out, in absence of compensatory measures by the state and/or the certainty of getting an alternate jobs in a full employment economy (where unemployment can only be voluntary), *labour becomes a risk-bearing factor of production in a capitalist economy* (Johnsson 1978).

Structural Changes in Industry between the Pre- and Post-reform Years

Structural changes, as seem to have taken place in the Indian manufacturing industry between the pre- and post-reform years, had a lot of significance

Table 2.4   Standard deviation of output and employment for industries (AAGR of output above 10 per cent) (Post-reform period: 1999–2003)

Industry group	NIC code	Standard deviation of output	Standard deviation of employment
Aircraft and spacecraft	353	297.19	196.42
Motor vehicles	341	73.91	23.21
Electronic valves and tubes and other electronic components	321	31.72	28.05
Electric motors, generators and transformers	311	91.94	71.36
Jewellery and related articles	369	43.45	12.83
Watches and clocks	333	106.05	17.37
Other textiles	172	21.18	13.04
Television and radio transmitters	331	27.78	8.71
Knitted and crocheted fabrics and articles	173	33.46	24.20
Furniture	361	29.97	19.53
Wearing apparel, except fur apparel	181	15.54	6.92
Repair of ships and boats	351	60.65	58.44
Refined petroleum products	232	20.50	11.35
Plastic products	252	17.14	7.41
Basic-precious and non-ferrous metals	272	24.45	16.70

Source: Authors' own calculations based on data contained in *Annual Survey of Industries,* Central Statistical Organization, Government of India (various issues), as downloaded from www.indiastat.com (last accessed on 15 April 2004).

Table 2.5   Standard deviation of output and employment for industries (AAGR of output less than 5 per cent) (Post-reform period: 1999–2003)

Industry group	NIC code	Standard deviation of output	Standard deviation of employment
Manufacture of special purpose machinery	292	12.815	9.664
Manufacture of man-made fibres	243	31.636	24.186
Manufacture of television and radio transmitters and apparatus for line telephony and line telegraphy	322	18.885	14.199

(Table 2.5 continued)

(Table 2.5 continued)

Industry group	NIC code	Standard deviation of output	Standard deviation of employment
Printing and service activities related to printing	222	20.552	39.494
Manufacture of paper and paper product	210	10.191	4.863
Manufacture of tobacco products	160	17.342	9.256
Manufacture of other food products	154	7.243	4.629
Manufacture of products of wood, cork, straw and plaiting materials	202	29.908	14.152
Manufacture of coke oven products	231	15.327	10.601
Saw milling and planing of wood	201	28.213	10.182
Publishing	221	14.326	16.657
Manufacture of railway and tramway locomotives and rolling stock	352	22.240	24.286

Source: Authors' own calculations based on data contained in *Annual Survey of Industries*, Central Statistical Organization, Government of India (various issues), as downloaded from www.indiastat.com (last accessed on 15 April 2004).

Figure 2.2 Standard deviation of output and employment in high growth industries (Post-reform years: 1999–2003)

Source: Authors' own calculations based on data contained in *Annual Survey of Industries*, Central Statistical Organization, Government of India (various issues), as downloaded from www.indiastat.com (last accessed on 15 April 2004).

Figure 2.3 Standard deviation of output growth and employment growth in low growth industries (Post-reform years: 1999–2003)

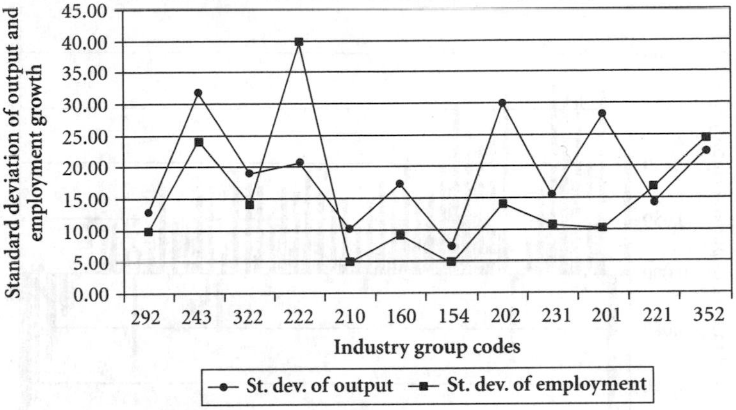

Source: Authors' own calculations based on data contained in *Annual Survey of Industries*, Central Statistical Organization, Government of India (various issues), as downloaded from www.indiastat.com (last accessed on 15 April 2004).

from the point of view of labour. High growth industries (with average output growth at 20 per cent or above) during the pre-reform years of 1981–90 included, in a descending order of growth, optical instruments, footwear, man-made fibre, refined petroleum and transport equipment. It is interesting to note that none of these feature later amongst the top high growth industries during the post-reform years. A definite structural shift in production pattern did thus take place between the pre- and post-reform years; with office equipment, aircraft and spacecraft, ships and boats, jewellery, electronics, furniture and motor vehicles emerging as sunrise industries of the current decade, experiencing growth rates at 20 per cent and above (see for the contrast Tables 2.1A and 2.1B).

As already mentioned, there has been a noticeable gap between the growth of output and employment, as can be seen from the trend rates of output which had been much higher than those of employment over the period 1991–2003 (see Figure 2.4). *The changing composition of the top HG performers over the recent years might have reduced the potentials for labour absorption, along with the use of labour-displacing technology* (see Tables 2.1A and 2.1B). However, as for the divergent rates of growth between output and employment for most industries, the gap seems not only to prevail but actually wider than that during the pre-reform years. This is also reflected in the widely divergent capital and labour elasticities of output over the period, as can be witnessed from Table 2.2. *A tendency for shredding labour in industries has thus been an established practice.*

**Figure 2.4   Trend growth rates of output and employment
(Post-reform period: 1991–2003)**

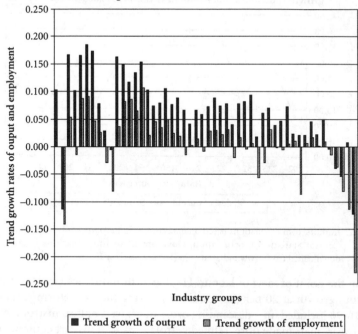

Source: Authors' own calculations based on data contained in *Annual Survey of Industries*,
Central Statistical Organization, Government of India (various issues), as
downloaded from www.Indiastat.com (last accessed on 15 April 2004).

Technological Shifts in Industry

Observations offered earlier in this chapter relating to lags in employment
growth as compared to those of output are captured better as one looks at
the changes in the choice of technology which seem to have taken place
in these industries. As already mentioned, this is reflected in the values of
employment and capital elasticities vis-à-vis output during the post-reform
years (Table 2.2). *Labour elasticities fell short of the capital elasticites not only
for the HG industries but also for the LG industries.* This is also indicated
in the technological shifts as are reflected in the trend growth rates of
capital–labour ratios which have been positive during the post-reform
years for most of these industries (Figure 2.5). Deviations as are found
among the LG set do not make sense given that some of these industries
have been subject to negative growth rates of output.

Figure 2.5 Trend growth rates of capital–labour ratio of high growth industries (Post-reform period: 1991–2003)

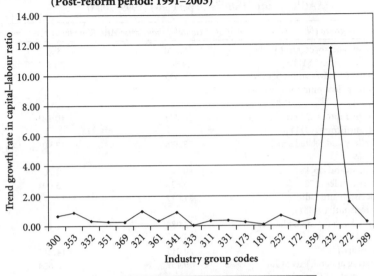

Source: Authors' own calculations based on data contained in *Annual Survey of Industries*, Central Statistical Organization, Government of India (various issues), as downloaded from www.indiastat.com (last accessed on 15 April 2004).

Capital Intensity, Labour Productivity and Wage–Profit Ratios

We observe a strong impact of the rising capital intensities on labour productivity. As it is evident from Table 2.6 and Figure 2.6 the two moved together for most industries. The rise in labour productivity also explains much of output growth rates, as indicated in Figure 2.7. We will deal with these aspects of rising capital intensity later in this chapter with econometric testing.

We also observe in Table 2.6 and Figure 2.7 the responses of labour productivity to capital–labour ratios in different industries. In most cases higher capital–labour ratios have pulled up both labour productivity and output growth rates (Figure 2.7). As we point it out later, little, however, has reached out to labour as wages, as can be witnessed from the growth rates in wage rates which, if at all, had been negligible. *Thus technology had hardly been favourable to labour employed in organized industry.*

Table 2.6 Average capital–labour ratio, labour productivity for industries (AAGR of output above 10 per cent) (1999–2003)

Industry group (NIC code)	AAGR of capital–labour ratio	AAGR of labour productivity
Aircraft and spacecraft (353)	5.700	39.072
Motor vehicles (341)	19.869	20.245
Electronic valves and tubes and other electronic components (321)	29.032	13.733
Electric motors, generators and transformers (311)	16.772	10.781
Jewellery and related articles (369)	25.376	17.905
Watches and clocks (333)	–0.123	24.200
Other textiles (172)	5.638	5.091
Television and radio transmitters (331)	11.017	16.571
Knitted and crocheted fabrics and articles (173)	13.084	8.189
Furniture (361)	28.017	14.215
Wearing apparel, except fur apparel (181)	9.452	7.664
Repair of ships and boats (351)	134.683	20.462
Refined petroleum products (232)	42.108	18.740
Plastic products (252)	–2.232	7.460
Basic-precious and non-ferrous metals (272)	33.970	12.821

Source: Authors' own calculations based on data contained in *Annual Survey of Industries*, Central Statistical Organization, Government of India (various issues), as downloaded from www.indiastat.com (last accessed on 15 April 2004).

As for the links between the four variables which include output growth (O), capital–labour ratio (K/L), labour productivity (LP) and wages (W) we notice, from the estimates of Pearson correlation coefficients provided in Table 2.7, a strong association of K/L on LP which in turn is associated with O. While the causal sequence can only be established by a regression analysis (which will be provided at the end of this chapter) we can observe the noticeable impact of the rise in capital–output ratios in the HG group of industries on labour productivity.

Improvements in labour productivity as are related to the technological upgrading, pointed out earlier, open up the question as to whether the benefits are being passed on to labour in the form of higher wages. We notice from our calculation of the correlation coefficients that there exists very little association between wages and labour productivity.

Figure 2.6 Trend growth rates in capital–labour ratio and labour productivity (Post-reform years: 1991–2003)

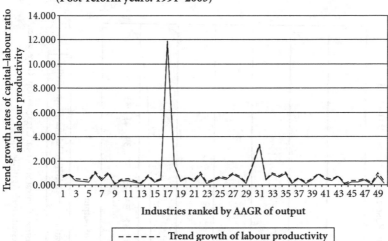

Source: Authors' own calculations based on data contained in *Annual Survey of Industries*, Central Statistical Organization, Government of India (various issues), as downloaded from www.indiastat.com (last accessed on 15 April 2004).

We notice that for the group of 17 HG industries, annual growth rates of wages as share of output during 1999–2003 have been lower than the corresponding profit shares for as many as 12 (see Table 2.8). The exceptions are due to relatively higher labour intensity, as indicated by detailed statistics.

As can be expected, reverse movements in wage and profit shares are observed in most of these industries (Figure 2.8). In most cases wage shares dipped as profit shares rose further. Trend growth rates in wage shares, both for the high and low growth industries, hovered around zero during the post-reform years (Figure 2.9). For low growth industries one witnesses a low level steady growth path for wage share which results in negative trend rates for these shares in most industries (Figures 2.8 and 2.9).

On the whole, the pattern of wage and profit shares in the organized industries thus tells a story which is familiar, of stagnating wage shares and steady improvements in profitability across industries. The sequence was a consequence of the ongoing technological upgrading with rising capital intensity in most industries. Labour, however, had little to gain from the latter, even with improved labour productivity as resulted with these changes.

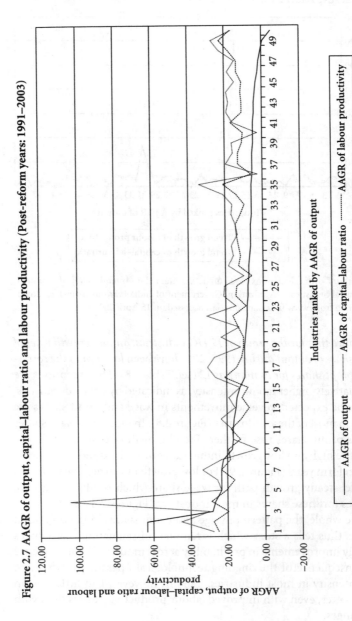

Figure 2.7 AAGR of output, capital–labour ratio and labour productivity (Post-reform years: 1991–2003)

Industries ranked by AAGR of output

——— AAGR of output ——— AAGR of capital–labour ratio ········· AAGR of labour productivity

Source: Authors' own calculations based on data contained in *Annual Survey of Industries*, Central Statistical Organization, Government of India (various issues), as downloaded from www.indiastat.com (last accessed on 15 April 2004).

Table 2.7   Pearson's correlation coefficients (1980–2003)

	AAGR of output	AAGR of capital–labour ratio	AAGR of labour productivity	AAGR of wage
AAGR of output	1.000			
AAGR of capital–labour ratio	–0.007	1.000		
AAGR of labour productivity	0.513**	0.317*	1.000	
AAGR of wage	0.018	0.599**	0.103	1.000

Source: Authors' own calculations based on data contained in *Annual Survey of Industries*, Central Statistical Organization, Government of India (various issues), as downloaded from www.indiastat.com (last accessed on 15 April 2004).
Notes: * Correlation is significant at the 5% level.
** Correlation is significant at the 1% level.

Table 2.8   Share of wages and profit in output for industries (AAGR above 10 per cent) (1999–2003)

Industry Group (NIC Code)	Average wage share	Average profit share
Aircraft and spacecraft (353)	0.109	0.044
Motor vehicles (341)	0.044	0.040
Electronic valves and tubes and other electronic components (321)	0.036	0.051
Electric motors, generators and transformers (311)	0.046	0.064
Jewellery and related articles (369)	0.028	0.082
Watches and clocks (333)	0.103	–0.063
Other textiles (172)	0.041	0.047
Television and radio transmitters (331)	0.042	0.081
Knitted and crocheted fabrics and articles (173)	0.031	0.045
Furniture (361)	0.065	0.036
Wearing apparel, except fur apparel (181)	0.049	0.086
Repair of ships and boats (351)	0.066	0.012
Refined petroleum products (232)	0.007	0.045
Plastic products (252)	0.022	0.029
Basic-precious and non-ferrous metals (272)	0.027	0.081

Source: Authors' own calculations based on data contained in *Annual Survey of Industries*, Central Statistical Organization, Government of India (various issues) as downloaded from www.indiastat.com

Figure 2.8 Average wage and profit shares (Post-reform years: 1991–2003)

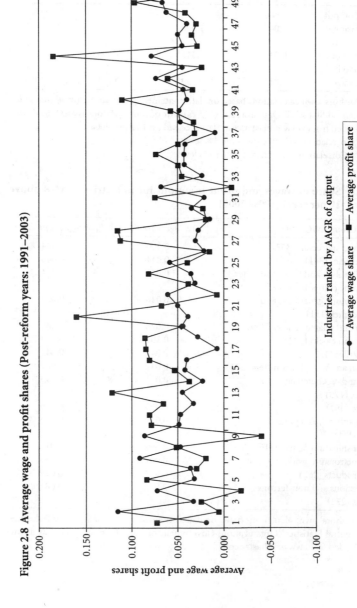

Source: Authors' own calculations based on data contained in *Annual Survey of Industries*, Central Statistical Organization, Government of India (various issues) as downloaded from www.indiastat.com (last accessed on 15 April 2004).

Figure 2.9 Trend growth rates—wage share of output in high growth industries (Post-reform years: 1991–2003)

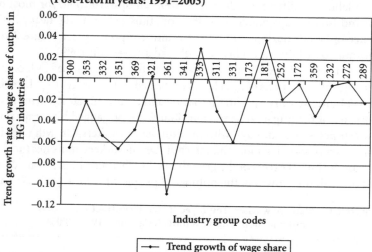

Industry group codes

—•— Trend growth of wage share

Source: Authors' own calculations based on data contained in *Annual Survey of Industries,* Central Statistical Organization, Government of India (various issues) as downloaded from www.indiastat.com (last accessed on 15 April 2004).

On Labour Flexibility in Indian Industries

Status of labour in the new economy remains incomplete unless we look into the quality of jobs offered in the new regime. This has to do with labour flexibility, a notion and a policy tool which is much in use in the Indian economy today. The *jobless growth* scenario of the Indian industry can also be linked to the current spate of labour market flexibilization in the country which permits wide-ranging casualization of the labour force along with hire and fire policies.

A rough estimate of the above may be found from the growth rates for workers in the manufacturing sector who are directly employed, as against those recruited through contractors. We treat the latter as solely casualized while keeping in mind that even those directly employed include a fair number of casualized workers. The weakened status of labour in organized manufacturing is very clearly reflected in the large numbers employed through contractors. These are the workers with casual status with purely flexible job contracts. As mentioned earlier, the remaining ones (who are employed directly by employers) also often have a casual status. We find that shares of workers employed through contractors in total labour in different industries exhibit an upward trend for most of the industry groups under consideration, thus reflecting the heavy incidence of labour flexibility in their recruitment policies (see Figure 2.10; for more on labour flexibility, see Felstead and Jewson 1999).

The impact of flexibilization on labour status can be assessed by looking into the various aspects of what has been termed as 'labour security'. Later in this volume, we will deal with this notion and try to estimate it. An indirect measure of the impact of labour flexibility can be gauged by comparing the estimates of 'man-days' with the number of workers. Growth rates in man-days reported, if more than the number of workers, indicates the use of labour time in excess of the growth rate in scheduled hours as are consistent with the growth in the number of people who are at jobs. We can

Figure 2.10   Share of workers employed through contractors in total employment in different industry groups (1992–2003)

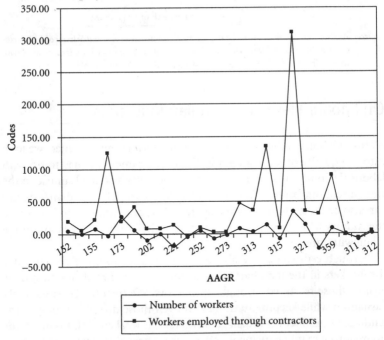

Source: Authors' own calculations based on data contained in *Annual Survey of Industries*, Central Statistical Organization, Government of India (various issues) as downloaded from www.indiastat.com (last accessed on 15 April 2004).

have an idea of the extent of labour expropriation by having a look at Figure 2.11 which shows a consistently higher growth rate in man-days as compared to those who were employed. If one puts together the unimpressive growth rates in wage shares, it becomes evident that workers in organized manufacturing have of late been bearing the brunt of labour reforms, both with low share of wages in output they produce and also by working longer hours which seem unpaid.

Figure 2.11 AAGR of employment and man-days worked (1999–2003)

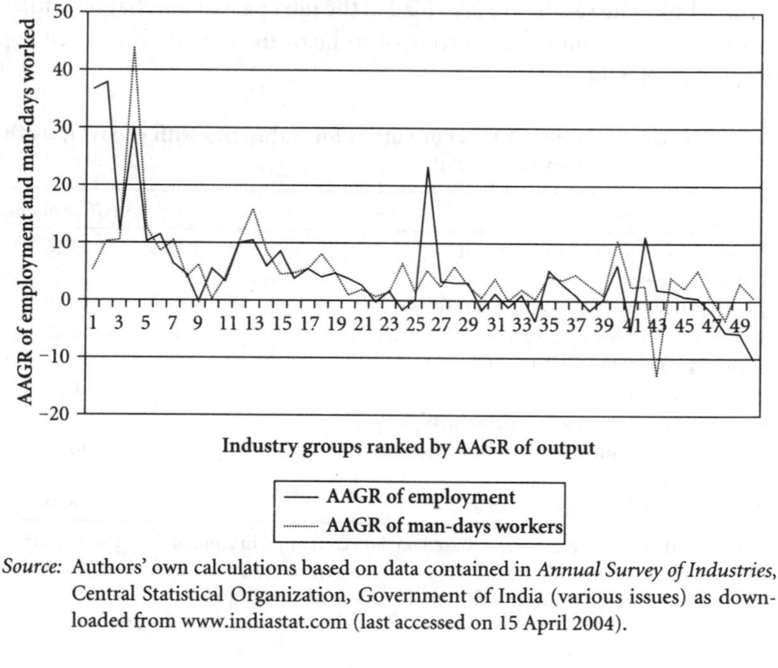

Industry groups ranked by AAGR of output

——— AAGR of employment
·········· AAGR of man-days workers

Source: Authors' own calculations based on data contained in *Annual Survey of Industries,* Central Statistical Organization, Government of India (various issues) as downloaded from www.indiastat.com (last accessed on 15 April 2004).

Trade Opening and Efficiency

With economic reforms geared to gaining competitiveness by achieving competitive efficiency, one expects that these also make for better exportability. While improvements in labour productivity, as has come with increases in capital–labour ratio, indicate an upturn in efficiency of labour use, we failed, however, to find any link between output growth and growth in exports at the 3-digit level of NIC of industry groups. Instead there seems to be an arbitrary combination of high/low output and export growth rates. Table 2.9 vindicates this observation, as industries with export shares of more than 10 per cent of their output did not necessarily translate into high annual average growth rates during the post-reform period under consideration. Industries with higher output growth rates are not necessarily the ones which also have either high export growth rates or high export shares of output (Figures 2.12 and 2.13). We also try to look at the above relation, if any, by means of a regression analysis on the data which confirm an absence of a high output growth–high export growth link. The results are provided in the next part of the chapter which deals with the econometric testing of some of the hypotheses by relying on firm level data.

Table 2.9 Growth rates (AAGR) of output for industries with export growth greater than 10 per cent

Industry group (code)	AAGR of output
Manufacture of jewellery and related articles (369)	23.26
Spinning, weaving and finishing of textiles	6.20
Production, processing and preservation of meat, fish, fruit vegetables, oil and fats	5.47
Manufacture of basic chemicals	6.27
Manufacture of other chemical products	7.20
Manufacture of knitted and crocheted fabrics and articles	16.41
Manufacture of basic iron and steel	6.35

Source: Authors' own calculations based on data contained in *Annual Survey of Industries,* Central Statistical Organization, Government of India (various issues) as downloaded from www.indiastat.com (last accessed on 15 April 2004).

Financial Status of Industries

Attention may be drawn here to the financial status of these industries (debt liabilities in particular) in relation to their investments. Did these industries invest more when their debt also moved up? Statistics as are available, however, indicate that there is no relation between the two. It may mean that industries in general do not rely on borrowings to finance their fixed investments. Rather these units may be relying on other sources of finance, which include re-invested earnings, for which we do not have adequate statistics.

Figure 2.12   AAGR of output and exports (Post-reform years: 1991–2003)

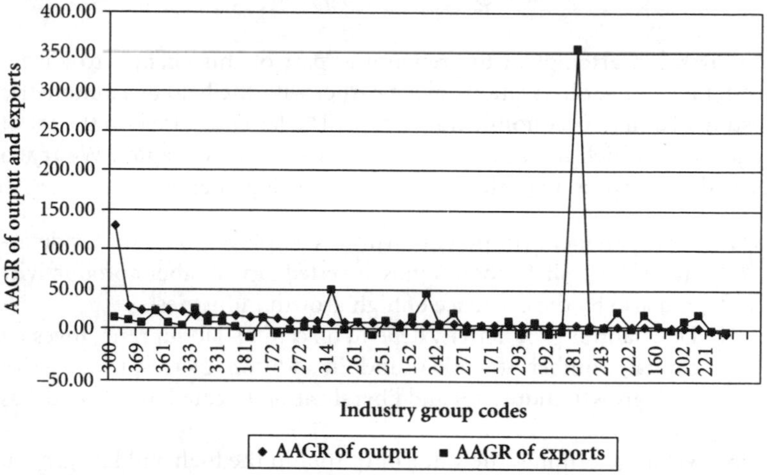

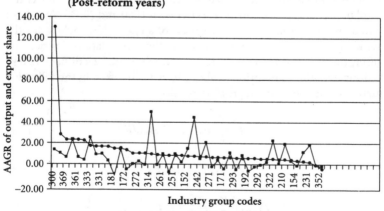

Source: Authors' own calculations based on data contained in *Annual Survey of Industries*, Central Statistical Organization, Government of India (various issues), as downloaded from www.indiastat.com (last accessed on 15 April 2004); and website of Ministry of Commerce, Government of India (http://commerce.nic.in, last accessed on 20 April 2004).

Figure 2.13   AAGR of output growth and export shares of high growth industries (Post-reform years)

Source: Authors' own calculations based on data contained in *Annual Survey of Industries*, Central Statistical Organization, Government of India (various issues), as downloaded from www.indiastat.com (last accessed on 15 April 2004); and website of Ministry of Commerce, Government of India (http://commerce.nic.in, last accessed on 20 April 2004).

Econometric Testing of the Hypotheses

We make an attempt in the remaining part of this chapter to have a fresh look at the observations made earlier with the help of econometric testing of a macroeconomic framework. The latter is based on the set of hypotheses which has already been advanced in this chapter. We try to provide an answer, in particular, to the following queries:

1. Is employment (number of workers employed) in industry determined by capital–labour ratios, invested capital, labour productivity and also by the existence of high growth industries?
2. Does labour productivity depend on capital–labour ratio, invested capital, number of workers and, in addition, by the prevalence of high growth industries and liberalization (treated in the model as a dummy)?
3. What determines the value of output in the high and low growth industries? Do these include capital–labour ratio, invested capital, labour productivity and liberalization (as a dummy)?
4. What determines labour productivity in high/low growth industries? The same set of factors mentioned in (2)?

We provide the results of a regression analysis which is based on the data set we have generated for 50 industries at 3-digit levels, for the entire period of pre- and post-reform years between 1980 and 2003. We did not try to arrive at a conclusion on the basis of a regression analysis for the post-liberalization years, 1991–2003, for the same data series because limiting the time period to post-reform years would make it difficult to test. The four hypotheses mentioned above have been tested in the following equations to arrive at the regression results:

$$L = f\left(\frac{K}{L}, IC, LP, HGI, LIB\right) \qquad (2.1)$$

$$LP = f\left(\frac{K}{L}, IC, L, HGI, LIB\right) \qquad (2.2)$$

$$O = f\left(\frac{K}{L}, IC, LP, LIB\right)$$

$$(2.3)$$

where

L = Number of workers
O = Value of output

K/L = Capital–labour ratio
IC = Invested capital
LP = Labour productivity
HGI = High growth industry
LIB = Liberalization

Results arrived at on basis of these regressions run on the relevant variables, and reported in Tables 2.10–2.21. These confirm the observations which have been presented earlier in this chapter. The results indicate the following:

1. Employment growth (L) is negatively impacted by rising capital–labour (K/L) ratios as well as average labour productivity (L/P) ratios (Table 2.10).
2. Labour productivity moves up with increases in capital–labour ratios and rise in fixed investments (I) but goes down when employment (number of workers) rises (Table 2.11).
3. Value of output is impacted favourably by raising labour productivity (LP) and fixed investment but negatively impacted by capital–labour intensity (Table 2.12).

From the preceding discussions it appears that neither employment nor output growth in the organized manufacturing industries seems to have a favourable impact from technological changes with higher capital intensity. These represent results which are rather unexpected if one follows the mainstream doctrine. Moreover, with rising employment growth, labour productivity seems to be on the decline, an outcome difficult to explain by any kind of economic theory (Table 2.12).

If high growth (industry) is taken as an additional explanatory variable the result is similar but for the fact that both employment as well as labour productivity is negatively impacted by growth in HG industries, a result once again is difficult to interpret. However, inclusion of both HG as well as liberalization (LIB), the latter as a dummy variable has to be looked at with caution, given that we are considering the whole time series from 1980 onwards. Neither the high growth segment of industries as defined elsewhere in the chapter nor liberalization seem to feature till the 1990s. In any case the liberalization dummy variable does not, as is expected, turn out to be significant as an explanatory variable. Finally inclusion of output growth as an explanatory variable entails the question of endogeneity and causation.

We also have run regressions using only the high growth industry data (Tables 2.13, 2.14 and 2.15). The results are similar to those for the industries as a whole.

**Table 2.10 Dependent variable: Number of workers
(Time period: 1980–2003)**

Variables	Model 1	Model 2	Model 3	Model 4
Constant	2.074**	2.014**	2.153**	2.381**
	(9.359)	(9.900)	(12.743)	(12.823)
Capital–labour ratio	−0.487*	−0.468*	−0.440*	−0.440*
	(−24.271)	(−24.281)	(−23.280)	(−23.240)
Invested capital	0.795*	0.836*	0.790*	0.802*
	(51.623)	(51.613)	(54.792)	(55.793)
Labour productivity	−0.206*	−0.218*	−0.304*	−0.302*
	(−8.284)	(−8.224)	(−15.194)	(−15.024)
High growth industry	−0.712*			−0.735*
	(−11.794)			(−14.227)
F values	934.582	949.458*	1075.21*	1066.22*
Adjusted R^2	0.978	0.975	0.979	0.988

Source: Computed by the authors.
Notes: Significance less than 1% (*), 2–10% (**); Figures inside parentheses denote
t values; Models 1 and 2 use deflated values; Models 3 and 4 use undeflated
values.

**Table 2.11 Dependent variable: Labour productivity
(Time period: 1980–2003)**

Variables	Model 1	Model 2	Model 3	Model 4
Constant	2.3001**	2.554**	2.528**	2.851**
	(7.464)	(8.412)	(8.216)	(10.671)
Capital–labour ratio	0.112*	0.025	0.117*	−0.001
	(2.883)	(0.743)	(2.960)	(−0.034)
Invested capital	0.440*	0.361*	0.685*	0.420*
	(9.354)	(7.724)	(15.194)	(10.657)
Worker	−0.480*	−0.414*	−0.754	−0.540*
	(−9.105)	(−8.244)	(−15.114)	(−12.240)
High growth industry		−0.285*		
		(−3.121)		
Liberalization		0.524*		1.198*
		(9.198)		(18.925)
F values	157.624*	167.350*	258.405*	366.063*
Adjusted R^2	0.926	0.940	0.953	0.968

Source: Computed by the authors.
Notes: Significance less than 1% (*), 2–10% (**); Figures inside parentheses denote t values;
Models 1 and 2 use deflated values; Models 3 and 4 use undeflated values; in Model
4 high growth industry has been excluded because of collinearity problem.

Table 2.12   Dependent variable: Value of output (Time period: 1980–2003)

Variables	Model 1	Model 2	Model 3	Model 4
Constant	2.131**	2.016**	2.341**	2.375**
	(10.277)	(9.900)	(12.752)	(12.447)
Capital–labour ratio	–0.482*	–0.478*	–0.440*	–0.441*
	(–5.606)	(–4.280)	(–3.251)	(–2.911)
Invested capital	0.812*	0.815*	0.801*	0.801*
	(52.011)	(51.612)	(54.813)	(53.645)
Labour productivity	0.810*	0.802*	0.702*	0.670*
	(35.474)	(33.358)	(35.481)	(27.978)
Liberalization		–0.028		0.027
		(–0.730)		(0.463)
F values	1,141.62*	1,124.32*	1,550.87*	1,522.60*
Adjusted R^2	0.990	0.990	0.992	0.992

Source: Computed by the authors.
Notes: Significance less than 1% (*), 2–10% (**); Figures inside parentheses denote t values; Models 1 and 2 use deflated values; Models 3 and 4 use undeflated values.

Table 2.13 Dependent variable: Number of workers (High growth industries) (Time period: 1980–2003)

Variables	Model 1	Model 2	Model 3	Model 4
Constant	–0.660*	–0.532*	–0.870*	–0.668*
	(–3.133)	(–2.531)	(–4.695)	(–3.547)
Capital–labour ratio	–0.642*	–0.653*	–0.614*	–0.614*
	(–20.371)	(–21.010)	(–19.510)	(–19.780)
Invested capital	1.030**	1.014**	1.051**	1.032**
	(56.268)	(54.60)	(60.584)	(58.354)
Labour productivity	–0.344*	–0.351*	–0.372	–0.424*
	(–7.601)	(–8.05)	(–8.850)	(–9.840)
Liberalization		0.142*		0.186*
		(3.440)		(3.918)
F values	1,421.80*	1,110.92*	1,554.31*	1,227.82*
Adjusted R^2	0.930	0.938	0.944	0.945

Source: Computed by the authors.
Notes: Significance less than 1% (*), 2–10% (**); Figures inside parentheses denote t values; Models 1 and 2 use deflated values; Models 3 and 4 use undeflated values.

Table 2.14 Dependent variable: Labour productivity (High growth industries) (Time period: 1980–2003)

Variables	Model 1	Model 2	Model 3	Model 4
Constant	0.342*	0.430*	−0.635*	−0.232*
	(1.352)	(1.694)	(−2.662)	(−0.996)
Capital–labour ratio	0.168*	0.125*	0.152*	0.078
	(2.848)	(2.124)	(2.532)	(1.397)
Invested capital	0.548*	0.558*	0.717*	0.682*
	(8.001)	(8.230)	(10.378)	(10.612)
Worker	−0.488*	−0.515*	−0.584*	−0.621*
	(−7.699)	(−7.997)	(−8.852)	(−9.843)
Liberalization		0.134*		0.378*
		(2.690)		(6.880)
F values	314.55*	240.27*	558.61*	498.88*
Adjusted R^2	0.762*	0.769	0.857	0.875

Source: Computed by the authors.
Notes: Significance less than 1% (*); Figures inside parentheses denote t values; Models 1 and 2 use deflated values; Models 3 and 4 use undeflated values; in Model 4 high growth industry has been excluded because of collinearity problem.

Table 2.15 Dependent variable: Value of output (High growth industries) (Time period: 1980–2003)

Variables	Model 1	Model 2	Model 3	Model 4
Constant	−0.644*	−0.532*	0.754*	0.379
	(−3.136)	(−2.531)	(3.266)	(1.645)
Capital–labour ratio	−0.748*	−0.654*	−0.575*	−0.580*
	(−20.374)	(−21.004)	(−14.541)	(−15.774)
Invested capital	1.028**	1.014**	0.973*	0.989*
	(56.225)	(54.688)	(43.943)	(46.565)
Labour productivity	0.655*	0.644*	0.343*	0.365*
	(14.446)	(14.378)	(6.942)	(8.766)
Liberalization		0.144*		−0.358*
		(3.441)		(−6.709)
F values	1,221.46*	943.18*	814.70*	713.83*
Adjusted R^2	0.920	0.920	0.870	0.887

Source: Computed by the authors.
Notes: Significance less than 1% (*), 2–10% (**); Figures inside parentheses denote t values; Models 1 and 2 use deflated values; Models 3 and 4 use undeflated values.

Table 2.16 Dependent variable: Number of workers (Time period: 1980–2003)

Variables	Model 1	Model 2	Model 3	Model 4
Constant	2.074**	2.014**	2.153**	2.381**
	(9.359)	(9.900)	(12.743)	(12.823)
Capital–labour ratio	–0.487*	–0.468*	–0.440*	–0.440*
	(–24.271)	(–24.281)	(–23.280)	(–23.240)
Invested capital	0.795*	0.836*	0.790*	0.802*
	(51.623)	(51.613)	(54.792)	(55.793)
Labour productivity	–0.206*	–0.218*	–0.304*	–0.302*
	(–8.284)	(–8.224)	(–15.194)	(–15.024)
High growth industry	–0.712*			–0.735*
	(–11.794)			(–14.227)
F values	934.582	949.458*	1,075.21*	1,066.22*
Adjusted R^2	0.978	0.975	0.979	0.988

Source: Computed by the authors.

Notes: Significance less than 1% (*), 2–10% (**); Figures inside parentheses denote t values; Models 1 and 2 use deflated values; Models 3 and 4 use undeflated values.

Table 2.17 Dependent variable: Labour productivity (Time period: 1980–2003)

Variables	Model 1	Model 2	Model 3	Model 4
Constant	2.3001**	2.554**	2.528**	2.851**
	(7.464)	(8.412)	(8.216)	(10.671)
Capital–labour ratio	0.112*	0.025	0.117*	–0.001
	(2.883)	(0.743)	(2.960)	(–0.034)
Invested capital	0.440*	0.361*	0.685*	0.420*
	(9.354)	(7.724)	(15.194)	(10.657)
Worker	–0.480*	–0.414*	–0.754	–0.540*
	(–9.105)	(–8.244)	(–15.114)	(–12.240)
High growth industry		–0.285*		
		(–3.121)		
Liberalization		0.524*		1.198*
		(9.198)		(18.925)
F values	157.624*	167.350*	258.405*	366.063*
Adjusted R^2	0.926	0.940	0.953	0.968

Source: Computed by the authors.

Notes: Significance less than 1% (*), 2–10% (**); Figures inside parentheses denote t values; Models 1 and 2 use deflated values; Models 3 and 4 use undeflated values; in Model 4 high growth industry has been excluded because of collinearity problem.

Table 2.18 Dependent variable: Value of output (Time period: 1980–2003)

Variables	Model 1	Model 2	Model 3	Model 4
Constant	2.131**	2.016**	2.341**	2.375**
	(10.277)	(9.900)	(12.752)	(12.447)
Capital–labour ratio	−0.482*	−0.478*	−0.440*	−0.441*
	(−25.606)	(−24.280)	(−23.251)	(−22.911)
Invested capital	0.812*	0.815*	0.801*	0.801*
	(52.011)	(51.612)	(54.813)	(53.645)
Labour productivity	0.810*	0.802*	0.702*	0.670*
	(35.474)	(33.358)	(35.481)	(27.978)
Liberalization		−0.028		0.027
		(−0.730)		(0.463)
F values	1,141.62*	1,124.32*	1,550.87*	1,522.60*
Adjusted R^2	0.990	0.990	0.992	0.992

Source: Computed by the authors.

Notes: Significance less than 1% (*), 2–10% (**); Figures inside parentheses denote t values; Models 1 and 2 use deflated values; Models 3 and 4 use undeflated values.

Table 2.19 Dependent variable: Number of workers (High growth industries) (Time period: 1980–2003)

Variables	Model 1	Model 2	Model 3	Model 4
Constant	−0.660*	−0.532*	−0.870*	−0.668*
	(−3.133)	(−2.531)	(−4.695)	(−3.547)
Capital–labour ratio	−0.642*	−0.653*	−0.614*	−0.614*
	(−20.371)	(−21.010)	(−19.510)	(−19.780)
Invested capital	1.030**	1.014**	1.051**	1.032**
	(56.268)	(54.60)	(60.584)	(58.354)
Labour productivity	−0.344*	−0.351*	−0.372	−0.424*
	(−7.601)	(−8.05)	(−8.850)	(−9.840)
Liberalization		0.142*		0.186*
		(3.440)		(3.918)
F values	1,421.80*	1,110.92*	1,554.31*	1,227.82*
Adjusted R^2	0.930	0.938	0.944	0.945

Source: Computed by the authors.

Notes: Significance less than 1% (*), 2–10% (**); Figures inside parentheses denote t values; Models 1 and 2 use deflated values; Models 3 and 4 use undeflated values.

Table 2.20   Dependent variable: Labour productivity (High growth industries) (Time period: 1980–2003)

Variables	Model 1	Model 2	Model 3	Model 4
Constant	0.342*	0.430*	–0.635*	–0.232*
	(1.352)	(1.694)	(–2.662)	(–0.996)
Capital–labour ratio	0.168*	0.125*	0.152*	0.078
	(2.848)	(2.124)	(2.532)	(1.397)
Invested capital	0.548*	0.558*	0.717*	0.682*
	(8.001)	(8.230)	(10.378)	(10.612)
Worker	–0.488*	–0.515*	–0.584*	–0.621*
	(–7.699)	(–7.997)	(–8.852)	(–9.843)
Liberalization		0.134*		0.378*
		(2.690)		(6.880)
F values	314.55*	240.27*	558.61*	498.88*
Adjusted R^2	0.762*	0.769	0.857	0.875

Source: Computed by the authors.

Notes: Significance less than 1% (*); Figures inside parentheses denote *t* values; Models 1 and 2 use deflated values; Models 3 and 4 use undeflated values; in Model 4 high growth industry has been excluded because of collinearity problem.

Table 2.21   Dependent variable: Value of output (High growth industries) (Time period: 1980–2003)

Variables	Model 1	Model 2	Model 3	Model 4
Constant	–0.644*	–0.532*	0.754*	0.379
	(–3.136)	(–2.531)	(3.266)	(1.645)
Capital–labour ratio	–0.748*	–0.654*	–0.575*	–0.580*
	(–20.374)	(–21.004)	(–14.541)	(–15.774)
Invested capital	1.028*	1.014*	0.973*	0.989*
	(56.225)	(54.688)	(43.943)	(46.565)
Labour productivity	0.655*	0.644*	0.343*	0.365*
	(14.446)	(14.378)	(6.942)	(8.766)
Liberalization		0.144*		–0.358*
		(3.441)		(–6.709)
F values	1,221.46*	943.18*	814.70*	713.83*
Adjusted R^2	0.920	0.920	0.870	0.887

Source: Computed by the authors.

Notes: Significance less than 1% (*); Figures inside parentheses denote *t* values; Models 1 and 2 use deflated values; Models 3 and 4 use undeflated values. All values are converted into natural logarithm. Liberalization denotes a dummy variable where it has a value 0 before 1991 and 1 after 1991. The effect of liberalization has been captured through this variable. Models 3 and 4 in each table refers regression using undeflated values.

Test on Corporate Firm Data—Sales, Exports, FDI

In this section, we try to find out how the corporate firms in the Indian manufacturing sector are functioning, in particular with their links to external markets in terms of exports and foreign equity holdings. Following are the tables of cross correlations based on statistics for 400 firms available in the Capital Line Database (see Tables 2.22, 2.23, 2.24 and 2.25). It may be mentioned that these firms are listed on the stock market of the country and as such the data exclude firms which are small.

We have sought to look at the interrelation between sales, value added, exports and foreign equity holdings of firms by testing the Pearson correlation coefficients. The exercise is done separately for the four years—2001, 2002, 2003 and 2004. While there exists a positive relation between sales (S) and value added (VO), we find a negative relation between exports (E) and foreign equity holdings (FII) for all four years. Both sales and value added also have a similar negative relation to exports. However, these two are positively linked to foreign equity holdings. The relations, again, hold for all four years. Comparing the correlation coefficients over the four-year period, one notices a link between exports and sales/value-added with negative coefficients which have reduced over time. Similarly foreign equity, which is positively linked to value of sales or output, has grown stronger over these four years, as can be seen from the larger positive coefficients for the second and third years as compared to the respective

Table 2.22 Correlations (Year 2001)

		S01	E01	VO01	FII01
S01	Pearson correlation	1.000	−.678*	.999*	.588*
	Sig. (2-tailed)		.000	.000	.000
	N	272	272	272	272
E01	Pearson correlation	−.678*	1.000	−.673*	−.260*
	Sig. (2-tailed)	.000		.000	.000
	N	272	272	272	272
VO01	Pearson correlation	.999*	−.673*	1.000	.591*
	Sig. (2-tailed)	.000	.000		.000
	N	272	272	272	272
FII01	Pearson correlation	.588*	−.260*	.591*	1.000
	Sig. (2-tailed)	.000	.000	.000	
	N	272	272	272	272

Source: Authors' own calculation based on Capital Line Database of Centre for Monitoring Indian Economy (CMIE) as available online.

Note: * Correlation is significant at the 1% level (2-tailed).

Table 2.23 Correlations (Year 2002)

		S02	E02	VO02	FII02
S02	Pearson correlation	1.000	−.583*	.999*	.661*
	Sig. (2-tailed)		.000	.000	.000
	N	272	272	272	272
E02	Pearson correlation	−.583*	1.000	−.570*	−.205*
	Sig. (2-tailed)	.000		.000	.001
	N	272	272	272	272
VO02	Pearson correlation	.999*	−.570*	1.000	.668*
	Sig. (2-tailed)	.000	.000		.000
	N	272	272	272	272
FII02	Pearson correlation	.661*	−.205*	.668*	1.000
	Sig. (2-tailed)	.000	.001	.000	
	N	272	272	272	272

Source: Authors' own calculation based on Capital Line Database of CMIE as available online.
Note: * Correlation is significant at the 1% level (2-tailed).

Table 2.24 Correlations (Year 2003)

		S03	E03	VO03	FII03
S03	Pearson correlation	1.000	−.372**	.999**	.786**
	Sig. (2-tailed)		.000	.000	.000
	N	272	272	272	272
E03	Pearson correlation	−.372**	1.000	−.349**	−.136*
	Sig. (2-tailed)	.000		.000	.025
	N	272	272	272	272
VO03	Pearson correlation	.999**	−.349**	1.000	.788**
	Sig. (2-tailed)	.000	.000		.000
	N	272	272	272	272
FII03	Pearson correlation	.786**	−.136*	.788**	1.000
	Sig. (2-tailed)	.000	.025	.000	
	N	272	272	272	272

Source: Authors' own calculation based on Capital Line Database of CMIE as available online.
Notes: * Correlation is significant at the 5% level (2-tailed); ** Correlation is significant at the 1% level (2-tailed).

Table 2.25 Correlations (Year 2004)

		S04	E04	VO04	FII04
S04	Pearson correlation	1.000	−.188*	.999**	.38**
	Sig. (2-tailed)		.002	.000	.000
	N	272	272	272	272

(*Table 2.25 continued*)

(Table 2.25 continued)

		S04	E04	VO04	FII04
E04	Pearson correlation	−.188*	1.000	−.172*	.004
	Sig. (2-tailed)	.002		.004	.949
	N	272	272	272	272
VO04	Pearson correlation	.999*	−.172*	1.000	.837*
	Sig. (2-tailed)	.000	.004		.000
	N	272	272	272	272
FII04	Pearson correlation	.838*	.004	.837*	1.000
	Sig. (2-tailed)	.000	.949	.000	
	N	272	272	272	272

Source: Authors' own calculation based on Capital Line Database of CMIE as available online.

Notes: * Correlation is significant at the 5% level (2-tailed); ** Correlation is significant at the 1% level (2-tailed).

Symbols used in the cross correlation tables, respectively, indicate:

S : sales
E : net exports
VO : value of output
FII : foreign equity
All values are in Indian Rupees.

preceding years. While foreign share in equity holdings do not have a positive impact on export earnings of these forms, the negative impact seems to be less over the four years.

To interpret, there seems to be an absence of a strong positive relation between exports expansions and foreign capital inflows for these corporate firms. The same applies to the links between exports/foreign equity and their value added as well as sales. Nor do we observe a links between exports and foreign share holdings in these firms. A pattern as shown here clearly fails to endorse the mainstream propositions regarding the expected sequence of trade and financial openness leading to high exports as well as output growth.

Results provided in the tables of cross correlations for the individual years 2001–04 indicate that the external transactions (net exports and foreign investment) have not been positively linked to sales or output value of these units. The pattern is rather revealing since it contests the liberalization doctrine which advocates openness of economies for growth. This also contests the much advertised plea that opening up of the Indian economy has led to higher growth in manufacturing activities. It can also be noticed that inflows of foreign capital do not seem to have a positive link to net exports from these firms. Does it indicate that much of the growth in the Indian economy is related to its home market?

Conclusion

Analysis of the economic status of labour in the organized manufacturing industries of India, as presented in this chapter, reflects a rather dismal scenario. Employment growth has generally lagged far behind output growth, both in industries with high annual average growth rates exceeding 20 per cent and low growth rates at less than 5 per cent. Fluctuations in output levels, which have been common with most industries, are matched by similar fluctuations in employment, often moving in the same direction. Volatility of employment has been prominent even in industries with negative growth rates, an aspect which indicates the extreme precariousness of the job situation. Lags in employment relative to output growth are also reflected in the stagnating wage shares to output, both for the high and the low growth industries. At the same time capital–labour ratios are in the up-trend in most industries, with tendencies to use labour displacing techniques in the Indian manufacturing industry. While the lag in employment growth is more in some of the highest growth industries, the share of high growth industry group in manufacturing sector employment is much less than the corresponding shares of the group of industries with the lowest growth rates. Thus high output growth industries not only have failed to generate employment growth at the same rate but have also continued to contributed less as their share in total industry employment, as compared to those by the low growth industries.

We notice, in terms of a set of regression results, the predominance of the rising capital–labour ratios as a determining variable for improved labour productivity. However, the above goes with a negative impact on both output and employment. Thus technological upgrading, while improving growth rates in labour productivity, failed to raise employment growth. Growth in output as took place, including those in the HG industries, resulted from higher fixed investments and the rise in labour productivity. The process has been responsible for keeping wages low as is reflected in the stagnating share of product wages in most industries.

We have also noticed that labour flexibilization, as reflected in the share of contractual labour, is high in most industries. Results from our primary survey statistics, reported in the next two chapters, reflect the prevalence of a growing number of workers with a purely temporary status.

As for the opening up of the economy, we do not find a perceptible rise in exports even in the high growth industries. Tests done on data relating to the corporate firms for 2001, 2002, 2003 and 2004 on sales, exports and FDI indicate a lack of coincidence between exports, higher sales or FDI inflows. Opening up the economy has thus contributed little to generate higher growth rates in output, sales or exports for these major manufacturing units. Our analysis unfolds the above process of structural change in the manufacturing sector of the economy.

Economic liberalization and the related reforms in the labour market in India generated an outcome where labour has less to gain in prosperity and even less in adversity. We would deal, in the next three chapters, with the qualitative aspects of labour status in these industries on the basis of data collected during our field surveys.

Notes

1. Note that at a particular digit level ASI provides information regarding a group of industries, not a single industry, included in that digit. The industries included in that digit are not exactly homogeneous but similar. They produce different products. Also, within an industry, products produced by different firms are differentiated product types. Hence, we cannot club these products as homogenous products. They constitute product groups. Moreover, ASI records groups different industries on the basis of activities like production of electrical equipments, not on the basis of commodities or products. Hence we refer to industries included at a particular digit level as an industry group classified on the basis of production activities; and not as a single industry where firms produce identical products in the typical textbook sense.
2. We use 'industry' and 'industry groups' interchangeably.

Labour under Stress: An Assessment Based on Primary Information

3

Introduction

Logic of economic reforms in India has been growth-centric which subscribes to the interest of corporate global capital. As it has been contended in mainstream economics, the spill-over effects of growth should usher in a better world by making everybody better off. It is further held that 'competitive capitalism' is the *mantra* to achieve growth as well as its spill-over, by providing an institution which links local production to the circuits of corporate global capital. Viewed from this perspective the growth-centric logic of economic reforms can be treated as a shift from the long protected non-competitive to competitive output markets which reduces the 'wasteful' utilization of resources in the output market including that of labour.

As mentioned earlier, liberalization in the Indian economy started formally in 1991 with the inception of the economic reforms. Its main tenets included *(a)* increases in the inflows of foreign capital, *(b)* strengthening of markets vis-à-vis the state and *(c)* introducing competition and efficiency in production to replace market rigidity. Economic reforms were expected to lead the Indian economy onto a higher growth path. A host of reform initiatives have been implemented since the formal launch in 1991, covering the industrial sector, fiscal and monetary management, financial institutions, trade as well as the labour market. Given the current emphasis on tracking the growth path with at least 8 per cent annual growth in the GDP, these economic reforms in different spheres of the economy are treated within and outside official circles as of paramount importance.

Competitive pressures arising from the opening up of the economy are usually expected to initiate structural shifts in the latter, from the high-profit low-output scenario of earlier years to scale expansions and low profit margins in the post-reform period. The process logically entails cost reduction, quality improvements, and productivity growth. However, at the same time, these competitive pressures are expected to weaken the implicit social contract in the economy, and especially in its formal sector. In defence of these reforms it is even held that the implicit social contract was a part of the autarchic industrialization strategies which were responsible, in the past, for slow growth in these economies.

As competitive capitalism relies on the removal of barriers to entry, the process demands exit routes both for capital and labour from what is considered as inefficient use; to more productive, cost-effective and better quality operations. These shifts in the utilization of labour and capital are thus considered as the basic prerequisites for rapid growth on a sustained basis. However, the process involves stressful adjustments, with occupational dislocation and unemployment for labour, industrial restructuring and obsolescence of capital which result in rising disparities in terms of performance between fast-growing and slow-growing industries. For political and social stability, these may necessitate cost-sharing and conflict resolution mechanisms which are also socially credible.

One should situate the status of labour in the context of the ongoing industrial restructuring and occupational dislocation in the age of economic reforms. Industrial restructuring is capable of contributing tendencies of deindustrialization in some cases and the creation of new sunrise industries in others. The status of labour should be situated in the context of industrial restructuring and occupational dislocation. The process basically is riveted around cost-cutting devices with labour as well as the less competitive industries having to bear the burden of adjustment. The channels of cost cutting adjustments across high and low growth industries include the use of (a) productivity augmenting technology and (b) labour flexibility by recruiting more labour on a contractual basis. As a consequence, both labour as well as industries which are less competitive tends to shoulder the burden of adjustment. The implications of these reforms have been far reaching for Indian labour, particularly for those employed in the organized manufacturing sector. As shown in a study (Panchmukhi et al. 2004), FDI inflows have affected the structure of Indian industries with demonstrated attempts to cope with the challenges of competitive pressure in the market by opting for labour-displacing and productivity enhancing technologies. Further, as subsidiaries of foreign firms are usually vertically integrated the additional employment effect of FDI often remains doubtful.

We recognize that information available at the secondary level from official sources does not enable an in-depth inquiry into the conditions of labour under globalization. To overcome the lacunae, we undertook a field survey of organized labour employed in manufacturing industries in a few Indian states. While at an aggregate level our analysis of secondary data, as provided in previous chapters, indicate a rather unfavourable picture for factory labour in manufacturing, it is possible to observe the qualitative dimensions of work including the wide dissimilarities in terms of wages, working hours, institutional voice representation, and skill at a disaggregated level which follows from our results of these field surveys.

The Primary Survey

We undertook a field survey of labourers in the organized manufacturing industry in selected pockets of West Bengal, Delhi, Haryana, Gujarat and Maharashtra over a period of 14 months during 2004–06. We could interview a total of 615 factory labourers. These workers were selected at random from the industrial clusters of different areas in these states. These include Mayapuri, Okhla and East Delhi in Delhi; Ghaziabad, NOIDA and NOIDA Special Economic Zone in Uttar Pradesh; Faridabad and Gurgaon in Haryana; Kolkata, Kalyani, Howrah, Hooghly and Falta Special Economic Zone in West Bengal; Surat in Gujarat; and Santa Cruz Special Economic Zone and other areas of Mumbai in Maharashtra. It may be useful to mention that the survey was also conducted in three Special Economic Zones (SEZs) of the country which include Falta in West Bengal, NOIDA in the National Capital Region of Delhi located in Uttar Pradesh and Santa Cruz at Mumbai in Maharashtra. A structured questionnaire[1] was used in these field surveys to gather information from the industrial labourers. To avoid possible biases in our sample not more than five workers were selected from a single factory. Besides in some areas a few management surveys were also conducted. As is typical in field surveys, we could not, in our interviews, easily access female workers, for various reasons. We had to contend mainly with male workers and tried to understand the plight of the women workers indirectly by talking to males. In addition to the use of questionnaires, we also had an intensive survey of workers in the labour intensive tobacco manufacturing workers (*bidi*-making) at Aurangabad in the district of Murshidabad in West Bengal.

We provide an analysis, in the following pages, of the data obtained from our surveys. This involves a grouping of the data according to one or other attributes we consider as important for analysis. These include job tenure, age, education, skill, migration, trade union membership, trade orientation and locations of industries. The device allows us to have a comparative analysis of different areas, different industries and different categories of workers as have been interviewed in the survey. The details of the exercise are provided in the following pages. Groupings of labourers as are related to the specific attributes can be used to answer the following set of questions:

1. Looking at the status of workers in terms of *job contracts*, one can distinguish between permanent and casual workers. *Does our survey indicate that the casual workers are more hard pressed than their non-casual counterparts?* As for the disparity between the workers do these relate to the nature of job tenures or job contracts?

2. *Education* plays a crucial role in skill formation. *Do the differences among the workers in our sample vary with their education level with less educated workers having been marginalized in comparison to the more educated ones?*

3. *Caste* is a social institution in Indian society which stratifies the labourers. Caste identity may be crucial for skill, education and earning levels. *Can we hypothesize that the non-general category of workers (which include scheduled castes [SC], scheduled tribes [ST] and other backward classes [OBC] and for that matter minorities) are unfavourably placed (as compared to the general category workers comprising of higher castes) in terms of wages and other amenities?*

4. *Trade orientation of industries* may matter in differentiating labour according to wages, hours of work, savings, non-wage benefits, voice representation, savings, a growing fear of losing jobs and of security levels in general. *We have introduced trade orientation as an attribute by grouping industries as exportables and importables to test the hypothesis.*

5. *Structure of industries* and their changes may also matter significantly in explaining the gaps among workers in terms of wages, working hours, voice representation, non-wage benefits, security levels as well as their fear of job loss, if any. *We have identified the labour and capital intensive industries in our sample to test the relevance of the industrial structure in terms of the above mentioned aspects.* Industries in our sample are classified according to the changes in labour/capital intensity over the post-reform period as compared to what these have been during the pre-reform years.

6. Migration of labour across different parts of the country in search of new jobs and new sources of earnings may be relevant in explaining levels of their current earnings and job insecurity. Workers who migrate are often engaged in factory jobs on contractual or casual basis while permanent regular workers show less interest to migrate unless they are offered better prospects elsewhere, or when they face a sudden deterioration in living conditions in the present locations with no immediate options available in the neighbourhood. There may be differences between the migrants and non-migrant workers concerning wage earnings and non-wage benefits, hours of work, voice representation, fear of job loss and savings. We would try to figure out whether young workers at the entry-level encounter a much more uncertain and bleak future in comparison to workers who have entered the labour force in the past. And whether the above is reflected in terms of significant divergences between the entry level workers (with age up to 25 years) and other workers who are older, in terms of wages, working hours, non-wage benefits, and voice representation. We would also like to see whether tendencies to migrate among workers are less when there are more earning members in the family of concerned labourers.

7. Globalization changes the notion of work and employment under competitive capitalism. On one hand, the so-called 'labour redundancies' warrant drastic downsizing of workforce in a factory. On the other hand, the nature of job contracts offered to labourers is often different, particularly for those who are new entrants to the job market. This is because new recruitments are increasingly on a short-duration contractual basis which hardly provides any non-wage benefits or earned leave. The scope for voice representation in trade union activities is also getting eroded day by day with the labour market reforms on anvil. These reforms legalize and institutionalize the flexible norms characterized by easy hire and fire policy of the employers.

8. *Divergent growth patterns of different industries* at the disaggregated level can influence the work pattern of labour in the respective industries. We tried to figure out if industry-specific growth patterns affect average earnings, average working hours, voice representation, and non-wage components of earnings, savings and the fear of losing jobs of workers employed therein. We have classified workers according to their employment in different industries with divergent growth rates.

9. *Workers in SEZ* seem to be more hard pressed than their non-SEZ counterparts in our survey, in terms of hourly wage levels, hours of work, savings, voice representation (union membership), fear of losing jobs, non-wage benefits such as provident fund (PF), gratuity and bonus. These SEZs are set up as enclaves where production units officially enjoy special incentives, tax concessions and the right to have flexible labour rules. It has been held that the primary concern for setting up a unit in the SEZ is the relaxation in labour laws of the land. It is also held that SEZs provide tax havens which attract many business firms. While these may be true, *our primary concern is to explore whether SEZ workers are more under duress than their non-SEZ counterparts.*

10. *Trade unions* provide ability for voice representation which had been a part of the conventional labour rights. These institutions provide an organized base to workers to vent their protests when situations demand it. But with the introduction of flexible labour norms and with shifts from Taylorist types of production processes in the post-globalization era, the significance of trade unions has rapidly eroded. With declining 'unionization', particularly among the new workers and along the new production lines (initiated by foreign capital, SEZ, and contractual casual appointments), we can meaningfully group workers according to whether they are members of trade unions or not. By doing that we can try to find if the non-members face harsh terms and conditions of work which include wages, hours of work and other relevant aspects of job contracts. Also we look into their savings propensities.

The 10 attributes mentioned here provide us the possibilities of grouping workers under the respective heads in terms of a binary classification. This will involve all 615 workers we have interviewed in different industries located in different parts of the country. We provide in the next section the results of our numerical exercise in arriving at the classification of workers in specific groups.

Grouping of Workers in Terms of the Specific Attributes

The overall picture of the surveyed areas according to state, area, work status and number of workers are provided in Appendix A in Table 3A.1.

It shows that out of the 615 workers interviewed 271 are permanent workers with tenured job contracts with a fixed age of retirement and 344 are casual or contractual on a short-term basis with temporary attachments to the current jobs. The sharp contrast between the two groups of workers is visible in the wage gaps, with the respective average hourly wages for all workers, the permanent workers and the casual ones at Rs 14.46, Rs 18.77 and Rs 11.07. The wage gap at Rs 7.70 between the permanent and casual workers is quite significant at the 1 per cent level. While 40 per cent of the 615 workers are union members, as many as 51 per cent of these are employed on a permanent basis. As can be expected, union presence is prominent among the permanent workers.[2] Workers on an average work for 9.06 hours a day, which is above the stipulated 8 hours a day. Permanent workers work for 8.58 hours a day, whereas casual workers work 9.45 hours a day. As for the educational level of workers, 90 per cent are literate or have some education with their mean schooling at five years. Among them, 40 per cent are permanent workers and 60 per cent are casual workers. Again, the incidence of migration is most pronounced among the casual workers because of the temporary nature of job contracts and earnings below the level of the minimum wages prevailing in many industries in different locations. Different social categories of workers also do matter in terms of mean hourly wage and mean hours of work. This can be witnessed for the 324 workers in general category who earn Rs 1.24 more per hour than what the 291 workers in non-general category earn on an hourly basis. Those in the general category also work 0.53 hours less on an average as compared to others, in specified social categories as SC, ST, etc.

Workers in our sample when grouped according to the specific attributes mentioned earlier, indicate their vulnerabilities, both at an aggregative level and in terms of the specificity, centred on a specific attribute within the respective groups. We provide below the details of the exercise which speaks of the differentiation among workers within each group. As already mentioned, these groupings are done according to the specific attributes of workers which include job tenures (permanent/casual), age of workers, education level (skilled/unskilled), migratory status, social background (SC, ST, OBC); and pattern of industry in terms of trade orientation (export/import intensity), factor intensity (labour/capital intensity), SEZ and finally labour absorbed in different industries. We have used here the 2-digit level of industry-classification. Workers in each group are further sub-divided, under each of the seven to eight heads, which indicate the economic status of the workers in terms of wages and other amenities. Provided below are the details of the exercise which speak of the differentiation among workers within each group.

Job contracts—permanent or casual

Table 3.1 indicates the divide across the casual and permanent workers. As it is expected, casual workers are found to be much more hard pressed than the permanent and regular workers, and in every respect of the job-related features which include wages, hours of work, PF and gratuity. They remain naturally insecure in terms of job prospects and have much less to do with union membership. These also dampen the savings propensity of these casualized workers as compared to the permanent ones.

Age-wise distribution

Our sample does not clearly indicate that the entry point workers (aged up to 25) are worse off than the workers in higher age groups in terms of wages paid (Table 3.2). In fact, workers aged below 20 years, receive higher hourly wage as compensation for working longer durations of time. But unionization among the entry group of workers is much less and they are mostly deprived of non-wage benefits like PF, gratuity and bonus.

Educational level and skills

Education plays a crucial role in skill formation. The economic status of the workers in our sample vary with their education level and as can be expected, the less educated workers who are also unskilled get marginalized in comparison to the relatively educated ones having some skill. In our survey, we found very few were completely illiterate and some had a basic level of literacy (with at least up to the level of fourth standard) among those interviewed (see Table 3.3). Of course, the skilled workers in our sample (judged in terms of education above the basic minimum) are found as better off than the unskilled workers in terms of their economic status. Possibly, the evolving post-reform industrial situation is creating more space for skill absorption and less for unskilled occupations. Again, the differences speak for the differentiated labour force, with the unskilled having less access to the basic amenities open to the skilled.

Table 3.1 Labour in terms of job tenure

		Mean hourly wage (Rs)	Mean hours of work	Saving (%)	Union membership (%)	Fear of losing job (%)	PF (%)	Gratuity (%)	Bonus (%)
Casual	Mean	11.07	9.45	19	32	43	08	0	51
	Variance	27.34	2.55	0.16	0.22	0.25	0.07	0.00	0.25
Permanent	Mean	18.77	8.58	34	51	59	91	46	66
	Variance	76.81	0.60	0.22	0.25	0.24	0.08	0.25	0.22

Casual N 344; Permanent N 271

Source: Authors' calculations based on primary data collected through questionnaire-based on field survey of 615 industrial workers in the organized manufacturing industries in some selected industrial areas of Delhi, Gujarat, Maharashtra, Uttar Pradesh and West Bengal during 2003–06.

Table 3.2 Labour in terms of age composition

		N	Mean hourly wage (Rs)	Mean hours of work	Saving (%)	Union membership (%)	Fear of losing job (%)	PF (%)	Gratuity (%)	Bonus (%)
Below 20	Mean	21	10.59	10.05	52	24	48	10	00	19
	Variance		42.18	1.85	0.26	0.19	0.26	0.09	0.00	0.16
Age 21–25	Mean	133	8.96	9.31	17	24	54	19	01	43
	Variance		20.26	1.93	0.14	0.18	0.25	0.16	0.01	0.25
Age 26–30	Mean	134	9.92	9.07	17	33	49	38	7	60
	Variance		30.70	1.78	0.14	0.22	0.25	0.24	0.07	0.24
Age 31–35	Mean	117	10.81	9.17	27	43	51	46	16	56
	Variance		31.49	2.10	0.20	0.25	0.25	0.25	0.13	0.25
Age 36–40	Mean	94	10.95	8.83	23	53	51	61	36	74
	Variance		27.16	1.67	0.18	0.25	0.25	0.24	0.23	0.19
Age 41–45	Mean	66	13.07	8.82	38	58	45	73	52	65
	Variance		34.04	1.75	0.24	0.25	0.25	0.20	0.25	0.23
Age 46–50	Mean	30	14.15	9.11	48	56	48	74	52	63
	Variance		38.96	2.33	0.26	0.26	0.26	0.20	0.26	0.24
Above 51	Mean	20	16.76	8.10	50	75	50	85	75	85
	Variance		52.91	0.09	0.26	0.20	0.26	0.13	0.20	0.13

Source: Authors' own calculations based on primary data collected through questionnaire-based field survey of 615 industrial workers in the organized manufacturing industries in some selected industrial areas of Delhi, Gujarat, Maharashtra, Uttar Pradesh and West Bengal during 2003–06.

Table 3.3 Labour in terms of education

		N	Mean hourly wage (Rs)	Mean hours of work	Saving (%)	Union membership (%)	Fear of losing job (%)	PF (%)	Gratuity (%)	Bonus (%)
Illiterate and literate	Mean	68	12.44	9.26	31	38	59	32	18	57
	Variance		47.21	2.56	0.22	0.24	0.25	0.22	0.14	0.25
Others	Mean	547	14.71	9.05	25	41	49	46	21	58
	Variance		65.25	1.79	0.19	0.24	0.25	0.25	0.17	0.24

Source: Authors' own calculations based on primary data collected through questionnaire-based field survey of 615 industrial workers in the organized manufacturing industries in some selected industrial areas of Delhi, Gujarat, Maharashtra, Uttar Pradesh and West Bengal during 2003–06.

Migration

Grouping the sample of workers according to their migratory status we find that migrant workers receive less as wages, work for more hours, are hardly unionized, and receive less of non-wage benefits as compared to workers who do not migrate (Table 3.4). It is also found that the migrant workers are mostly casual and the fear of losing job is naturally more amongst them.

Social background

Workers in our sample can further be grouped in terms of their social background which includes caste. We observe that the 'general category' workers (which include all workers except the 'others category' which includes SCs, STs and minorities) are relatively better placed (see Table 3.5). While caste did not play an important role at the time of recruitment in the private sector, SCs, STs and minorities come with a background which adversely affects their education and skill. Hence, at a time when demand for skilled labour is rising it is quite plausible that the 'others' category of workers are losing out.

Union membership

We next group the workers according to whether they are unionized or not. Our result indicates that while unionized workers put fewer hours of work per day, they also receive a lower hourly wage. It is found that for the unionized members the proportion of those with the fear of job loss is lower than for those who are non-unionized. Even in terms of non-wage benefits, the non-unionized workers are worse off than the unionized workers (Table 3.6). Thus it seems to indicate that voice representation had some effect in improving labour status for workers in the sample.

Trade orientation of industries

Trade is an integral part of the economic reform programmes in India. It has its two pronged thrusts which are on export promotion and import liberalization. The first pertains to the gaining of competitive edge for

Table 3.4 Labour in the context of migration

		N	Mean hourly wage (Rs)	Mean hours of work	Saving (%)	Union membership (%)	Fear of losing job (%)	PF (%)	Gratuity (%)	Bonus (%)
Non-migrant	Mean	308	15.32	8.75	24	47	55	48	31	65
	Variance		79.73	1.55	0.18	0.25	0.25	0.25	0.22	0.23
Migrant	Mean	307	13.60	9.39	27	34	46	41	09	51
	Variance		46.30	2.00	0.20	0.22	0.25	0.24	0.08	0.25

Source: Authors' own calculations based on primary data collected through questionnaire-based field survey of 615 industrial workers in the organized manufacturing industries in some selected industrial areas of Delhi, Gujarat, Maharashtra, Uttar Pradesh and West Bengal during 2003–06.

Table 3.5 Labour in the context of social background

		N	Mean hourly wage (Rs)	Mean hours of work	Saving (%)	Union membership (%)	Fear of losing job (%)	PF (%)	Gratuity (%)	Bonus (%)
Others	Mean	291	13.81	9.35	26	37	49	38	12	50
	Variance		57.22	2.05	0.20	0.23	0.25	0.24	0.10	0.25
General	Mean	324	15.05	8.82	25	43	52	50	28	65
	Variance		68.94	1.59	0.19	0.25	0.25	0.25	0.20	0.23

Source: Authors' own calculations based on primary data collected through questionnaire-based field survey of 615 industrial workers in the organized manufacturing industries in some selected industrial areas of Delhi, Gujarat, Maharashtra, Uttar Pradesh and West Bengal during 2003–06.

Table 3.6 Labour in terms of union membership

		N	Mean hourly wage (Rs)	Mean hours of work	Saving (%)	Fear of losing job	PF (%)	Gratuity (%)	Bonus (%)
Non-member	Mean	367	13.29	9.40	0.26	0.65	0.37	0.04	0.48
	Variance		7.10	1.51	0.44	0.48	0.48	0.20	0.50
Union member	Mean	248	16.19	8.58	0.25	0.29	0.56	0.44	0.73
	Variance		8.87	0.94	0.44	0.45	0.50	0.50	0.44

Source: Authors' own calculations based on primary data collected through questionnaire-based field survey of 615 industrial workers in the organized manufacturing industries in some selected industrial areas of Delhi, Gujarat, Maharashtra, Uttar Pradesh and West Bengal during 2003–06.

Indian goods in global markets while the second is geared to achieve cost-competitiveness for Indian industry, by permitting free imports of final goods and, especially, of inputs from abroad. Trade liberalization measures started off by the mid-1980s while FDI flows have also been made much easier since then. Indian firms with or even without foreign collaboration as well as those set up by the MNCs as subsidiaries today rely heavily on raw materials and technology, often imported from the foreign parent firms abroad. The above limits the backward linkage effects of these firms in the domestic economy (Panchmukhi et al. 2004).

With the above backdrop, we can identify certain domestic industries which compete with the finished and semi-finished products imported from abroad. Of these, those having 10 per cent or more exports as a proportion of their sale values can be called as export-oriented while industries with a share of importables at 10 per cent or more as proportion of their sale values can be called import-intensive. We have classified these industries at the 2-digit level of classification in the next two tables. As for the products of the import-competing industries, we could identify computing (30), wood (20), pharmaceuticals (35), machinery (29), furniture (36) and paper (21) as industries producing importable items.[3] Exportable industries include food and beverage (15), textiles (17), leather (19), chemicals (24), computing machinery (29) and gems plus jewellery (36) all of which export at least 20 per cent or above of their respective output. Table 3.7 delineates the conditions of labourers according to whether they work in importable or non-importable industries. While hourly wage rate happens to be relatively higher in industries producing importables, average working hours are also higher. Despite a lower percentage of unionization, workers in these industries have less fear in terms of losing jobs. Also the percentage of workers receiving non-wage benefits is lower as compared to those engaged in non-importable goods industries. On the whole workers engaged in industries producing importables seem to be marginally better off as compared to others. Possibly, these industries are better organized and more competitive as compared to others and are thus able to offer jobs at slightly better terms (Table 3.7).

As for labourers in exportable industries they are not much better off than those in non-exportable industries (Table 3.8). Export orientation of industries has not improved the lot of the labour engaged in these industries. Thus trade orientation of industries seems to have hardly an impact on the economic status of workers engaged therein. Our findings are similar to other research in the area which are based on secondary level

Table 3.7 Labour in industries producing importables

		Mean hourly wage (₹s)	Mean hours of work	Saving (%)	Union membership (%)	Fear of losing job (%)	PF (%)	Gratuity (%)	Bonus (%)
	N								
Importable	Mean	9.79	0.3	0.07	0.43	0.13	0.07	0.34	15.41
	148								
	Variance	1.90	0.21	0.06	0.25	0.12	0.07	0.22	65.93
Others	Mean	8.92	0.25	0.47	0.52	0.51	0.23	0.63	14.26
	469								
	Variance	1.74	0.18	0.25	0.25	0.25	0.18	0.23	63.04

Source: Authors' own calculations based on primary data collected through questionnaire-based field survey of 615 industrial workers in the organized manufacturing industries in some selected industrial areas of Delhi, Gujarat, Maharashtra, Uttar Pradesh and West Bengal during 2003–06.

Table 3.8 Labour in exportable industries

		N	Mean hourly wage (Rs)	Mean hours of work	Saving (%)	Union membership (%)	Fear of losing job (%)	PF (%)	Gratuity (%)	Bonus (%)
Exportable	Mean	185	14.45	8.97	34	48	42	53	32	72
	Variance		74.69	1.96	0.23	0.25	0.25	0.25	0.22	0.20
Others	Mean	430	14.47	9.11	22	37	54	41	15	52
	Variance		74.69	1.96	0.23	0.25	0.25	0.25	0.22	0.20

Source: Authors' own calculations based on primary data collected through questionnaire-based field survey of 615 industrial workers in the organized manufacturing industries in some selected industrial areas of Delhi, Gujarat, Maharashtra, Uttar Pradesh and West Bengal during 2003–06.

information (Panchmukhi and Das 1999; Panchmukhi et al. 2004) and our analysis, based upon primary sample of 615 workers, also corroborate to the conclusion drawn in those studies regarding the insignificant contribution of trade in the post-reform period on labour in trade-oriented industries vis-à-vis those in the non-trade-oriented industries.

Structure of industries

Economic reforms have significant effects on the technological structure of industries, especially in industries which are adopting labour displacing methods. This is already well evidenced in many studies (Chaudhuri 2002; Panchmukhi 2000; Panchmukhi and Das 1999; Panchmukhi et al. 2004; Sharma 2004) and it has been held that 'the surge in competitive pressures prompts enterprises to focus more and more on efficiency consideration which forces them to cut their overall costs of production. Minimization of labour costs is often a natural response in such a situation' (Panchmukhi et al. 2004). Consequently, adoption of labour displacing technologies becomes an obvious choice made by the entrepreneurs. Thus, according to Agarwala et al. (2004):

> ...if FDI inflows assume more importance, there could be an intensification of this tendency as multinationals would generally bring in technologies of this nature. Therefore, in the age of heightened consciousness for quality and competitiveness, a rise in unemployment becomes a misgiving of the modernization process.

In our analysis, we have identified two groups of industries—capital intensive and labour intensive (see Table 3.9). In terms of our estimates, an industry showing a ratio of 1.03 or more capital to labour is identified as capital intensive and the rest as labour intensive. Thus defined, capital-intensive industries, at a 2-digit level include basic metal (27), chemical (24), computing (30), paper (21), electrical (31), machinery (29), motor vehicles (34) and electronics (32) while labour intensive ones are food and beverages (15), textiles (17), wearing apparel (18), leather (19), paper (21), chemicals (24), rubber and plastic (25), non-metallic minerals (26) and fabricated metals (28). In terms of the employment pattern, roughly 30 per cent of workers are with the capital intensive industries where the wage rate on an average is relatively higher and workers put in more labour hours per day as compared to other workers employed in the labour intensive

Table 3.9 Labour in the context of structure of industry

		N	Mean hourly wage (Rs)	Mean hours of work	Saving (%)	Union membership (%)	Fear of losing job (%)	PF (%)	Gratuity (%)	Bonus (%)
Capital-intensive industries	Mean	471	14.74	9.24	27	39	49	40	17	51
	Variance		65.61	2.07	0.20	0.24	0.25	0.24	0.14	0.25
Labour intensive industries	Mean	144	13.54	8.53	21	46	56	58	33	80
	Variance		56.65	0.87	0.17	0.25	0.25	0.25	0.22	0.16

Source: Authors' own calculations based on primary data collected through questionnaire-based field survey of 615 industrial workers in the organized manufacturing industries in some selected industrial areas of Delhi, Gujarat, Maharashtra, Uttar Pradesh and West Bengal during 2003–06.

industries. The appropriation of surplus labour, therefore, takes place through both labour displacing technological changes as well as by increasing average work time. However, while labourers in the capital intensive industries receive higher wages than those in the labour intensive groups, the latter receive relatively more of the non-wage benefits, whatever these are. But in spite of a higher rate of unionization, workers in these labour intensive industries are subject to higher degrees of fear in terms of losing jobs.

It thus appears that industries which are going in for more capital intensive technologies are offering higher wages and lower non-wage benefits to their workers as compared to the labour intensive industries. The new recruitments in these industries are mostly on contractual basis and because of this the proportion of non-wage benefits are naturally lower. Capital intensive technologies require more skilled work effort and hence, wages tend to be higher in these industries in relation to wages offered in the labour intensive industries. In our sample, we find that the proportion of workers in capital intensive technologies who can save is more than what it is in the labour intensive ones, an outcome related to the wage levels in the two industries. With a large number of industries adopting capital intensive lines of production, labour content of output may tend to go down further which will create more downward pressure on labour absorption and, hence, on unemployment.

Labour in labour intensive industries

We further classify the industries in terms of changing labour use which is defined as the ratio of wages and salaries to value of output, net of wages and salaries. In a similar study the notion has been identified as an indicator of labour intensity in the liberalization period (Panchmukhi and Das 1999). We observe that the post-reform period registered declines in all industry groups in the above labour-use ratio. In our sample, all industry groups have witnessed declines in the ratio. We have identified three categories of industry groups—those which have witnessed steep declines in the ratio (SD), moderate decline (MD) and increasing (INC). As Table 3.10 indicates, hourly wage on an average has been less while working hour is more in SD as compared to those in MD. Average wage is lowest in INC where the fear of job loss is the highest. In terms of non-wage benefits, the steep declining SD group is better placed than MD and INC. However, percentage of workers with savings is highest in MD category.

Table 3.10 Labour in the context of different ratios between wage-salary component and output (Net of wages and salaries)

	N	Mean hourly wage (Rs)	Mean hours of work	Saving (%)	Union membership (%)	Fear of losing job (%)	PF (%)	Gratuity (%)	Bonus (%)
SD	511								
Mean		14.52	9.03	0.26	68	0.36	0.52	0.43	0.21
Variance		63.45	1.69	0.19	0.28	0.23	0.25	0.25	0.17
MD	48								
Mean		16.35	8.98	0.29	26	0.69	0.42	0.69	0.35
Variance		116.43	2.11	0.21	0.23	0.22	0.25	0.22	0.23
INC	56								
Mean		12.31	9.50	0.16	6	0.52	0.43	0.39	0.00
Variance		15.18	3.31	0.14	0.22	0.25	0.25	0.24	0.00

Source: Authors' own calculations based on primary data collected through questionnaire-based field survey of 615 industrial workers in the organized manufacturing industries in some selected industrial areas of Delhi, Gujarat, Maharashtra, Uttar Pradesh and West Bengal during 2003–06.

It may be noticed that the industry groups in SD are having highest union memberships among the workers in our sample. This is difficult to reconcile in the context of post-reform attempt to flexibilize labour market rules and regulations.

Labour in SEZ or other industries

As we have mentioned earlier, of the 16 areas selected for interviewing industrial labour, three were SEZs—namely, Falta in West Bengal, NOIDA in the National Capital Region of Delhi (which is actually located within the administrative jurisdiction of Uttar Pradesh) and Santa Cruz Electronics Exports Processing Zone (SEEPZ) in Mumbai, Maharashtra.[4] Of the 615 workers in our sample, 60 belong to these three SEZ areas. Industrial units set up within a SEZ need not pay the minimum wages as prevail in industries located in the neighbourhood of the SEZs. In SEZs, labour laws as well as taxation norms of the land are not applicable. Flexible hire and fire practices therefore, are easy to operate. This further deprives labour its due share of production in terms of both wage and non-wage benefits as well as other amenities as are normally available elsewhere in the country. This is reflected in Table 3.11 which is self-evident in delineating this disparity between SEZ and non-SEZ workers. The gap between average hourly wage between non-SEZ and SEZ workers is Rs 5.08 which is significant at the 1 per cent level. SEZ workers on an average work 0.48 hours more a day than their non-SEZ counterparts. Besides, the variance for the mean hours of work is more in the case of SEZ workers indicating flexible working time and very long daily working hours in the case of few workers in the sample.

As for unionization, those outside SEZs are relatively more organized as members of trade unions while a higher percentage of SEZ workers (almost three-fourth of SEZ workers in our sample) fear losing jobs and thus live with uncertain job prospects as compared to their non-SEZ counterparts. Similarly, a lower percentage of SEZ workers do receive retirement benefits in the form of PF and gratuity and earn yearly bonus. As expected under this kind of situation, only 2 per cent of SEZ workers in our sample have savings as against 28 per cent in the case of non-SEZ workers. Thus the SEZs which are supposed to be the leading enclaves of export-oriented growth in this country derive their comparative advantage by offering labour even less than what is available outside these zones. Labour processes in both SEZ and non-SEZ areas are exploitative but the degree varies, and in some cases perhaps significantly as our case studies of Falta, SEEPZ and NOIDA indicate.

Table 3.11 Labour in SEZ and non-SEZ areas

		Sample Size	Mean hourly wage (Rs)	Mean hours of work	Saving (%)	Union membership (%)	Fear of losing job (%)	PF (%)	Gratuity (%)	Bonus (%)
Non-SEZ	Mean	555	14.96	9.02	28	40	48	45	22	61
	Variance		66.24	1.78	0.20	0.24	0.25	0.25	0.17	0.24
SEZ	Mean	60	9.88	9.50	2	40	73	37	5	28
	Variance		63.68	1.88	0.19	0.24	0.25	0.25	0.16	0.24

Source: Authors' own calculations based on primary data collected through questionnaire-based field survey of 615 industrial workers in the organized manufacturing industries in some selected industrial areas of Delhi, Gujarat, Maharashtra, Uttar Pradesh and West Bengal during 2003–06.

Labour in SEZ is exploited to an extent which is comparable to the experiences of industrial labour in England at the beginning of Industrial Revolution in the 18th century. Growth as takes place on account of export initiatives of these SEZs is biased and asymmetric. Thus, welfare loss in terms of labour deprivation is not compensated by adequate welfare gain through redistribution of social surplus from the process. The plight of labour in the SEZs thus requires immediate attention of the policy makers to build up a strong social safety network as has been argued in several studies (Standing 1999: 51–53; Panchmukhi et al. 2004). In an era when labour efficiency is the buzzword of reform and development, the real test will lie in combining efficiency while safeguarding the legitimate demands and authentic interests of labour.

Labour in terms of the NIC 2-digit industrial codes

Our sample includes 16 industry groups at the ASI 2-digit codes (Table 3.12). These can be ranked in terms of their annual average growth rates (AAGR) of output over the post-reform period (1991–2003). It is interesting to observe that high growth rates do not tally with high hourly wages. For labourers the fear of job loss happens to be even higher in industries having higher growth rates. We did not find much of a correspondence between industry growth and other labour features (including union membership, fear of job loss, non-wage benefits including PF, gratuity and bonus, savings, etc.). Thus the growth-centric reform process does not seem to have much of a favourable impact on economic status of labour in our primary survey statistics.

As for the wages, the average daily working hours in the sample seem to move in tandem with hourly wage rates. This implies that labourers are paid more for working longer hours. But in many cases these high wage industries rank low in terms of their annual average growth rates. Also non-wage benefits are relatively higher in these low growth industries as compared to what these are in some of the high growth ones. Hence growth seems to have hardly any positive impact if at all, on labour status in terms of mean hourly wage rate, average hours of daily work, capacity to save, union membership, fear of job loss and non-wage benefits. In a way, our study refutes the logic that the growth-centred neo-liberal globalization process is capable of generating universal benefits including those for labour. Rather, it is possible that such growth has been the result of labour compression forced by competitive capitalism.

Table 3.12 Labour in terms of industrial groups

Industry code	AAGR (%)		N	Mean hourly wage (Rs)	Mean hours of work	Saving (%)	Union membership (%)	Fear of losing job (%)	Gratuity (%)	Bonus (%)
34	15.97	Mean	20	14.31	8.55	20	60	70	40	75
		Variance		45.16	0.26	17	25	22	25	20
36	15.70	Mean	66	13.74	10.17	39	5	41	3	32
		Variance		32.08	1.59	24	4	25	3	22
28	14.92	Mean	12	9.62	8.42	25	58	33	8	75
		Variance		28.67	0.27	21	27	24	8	21
18	14.88	Mean	56	9.54	9.50	16	52	43	0	32
		Variance		7.66	3.31	14	25	25	0	22
25	11.66	Mean	69	7.56	9.22	6	49	68	12	42
		Variance		17.07	2.58	6	25	22	10	25
26	9.31	Mean	10	11.17	8.40	20	70	40	50	100
		Variance		35.76	1.60	18	23	27	28	0
19	9.05	Mean	15	13.33	9.13	47	13	40	27	80
		Variance		32.99	1.70	27	12	26	21	17
35	8.62	Mean	20	11.64	8.15	30	65	100	40	100
		Variance		19.09	0.24	22	24	0	25	0
24	8.51	Mean	78	9.36	8.31	26	49	54	38	85
		Variance		33.69	0.48	19	25	25	24	13
17	6.96	Mean	56	10.18	9.73	45	39	25	16	48
		Variance		18.02	2.56	25	24	19	14	25

29	6.64	Mean	41	10.69	9.20	15	10	46	15	37
		Variance		55.50	1.86	13	9	26	13	24
31	6.19	Mean	64	12.75	8.48	42	42	42	25	64
		Variance		42.72	0.25	25	25	25	19	23
27	6.07	Mean	40	10.60	8.68	20	42	63	25	77
		Variance		15.60	0.33	16	25	24	19	18
21	5.85	Mean	16	6.67	9.31	0	25	63	13	50
		Variance		6.79	3.03	0	20	25	12	27
15	5.84	Mean	36	12.44	9.17	31	72	44	44	81
		Variance		57.69	2.60	22	21	25	25	16
22	2.51	Mean	16	10.29	9.00	0	19	69	0	38
		Variance		12.59	0.00	0	16	23	0	25

Source: Authors' own calculations based on primary data collected through questionnaire-based field survey of 615 industrial workers in the organized manufacturing industries in some selected industrial areas of Delhi, Gujarat, Maharashtra, Uttar Pradesh and West Bengal during 2003–06.

Conclusion

Our primary survey of selected industrial units in the organized industrial sector of the country bears testimony to the fact that labour had an unfair deal in the process of economic liberalization and reforms over the preceding decades. Contesting the trickle-down doctrine of the neoliberal policies, we find no evidence of an improved labour status during recent years in terms of employment, wages, other benefits, hours of work, job security or the ability to save. We do not find any positive impact of industrial growth, trade intensity or technological upgrading (in terms of capital intensity) on the economic status of industrial workers in our sample. Workers experiencing a migratory and/or casual status (which often results from lack of job opportunities and/or uncertain job situations), are naturally subject to worse prospects in terms of the conditions at which they work. Those with job skills as well as those who are young as compared to other workers seem to be subject to the changed work atmosphere of contractual and casualized recruitments which offer very little of the non wage benefits (PF, bonuses) or opportunities to participate in union activities. As for industries subject to higher capital intensity, the higher output growth as results are matched by longer working hours and higher wages (but less or none of other benefits) as compared to what prevails in labour intensive industries. The pattern is similar for the relatively younger workers (age less than 25) who seem to be relatively well off in terms of wages but lack opportunities in terms of non-wage benefits and trade union participation. On the whole, these are the new generation of workers, young, casualized, better paid but with no options for non-wage benefits or trade union activities. In the capital intensive industries with higher growth, labour employed is both displaced and expropriated, the latter with longer working hours. We have not seen any respite for labourers in the SEZ which in principle are supposed to initiate all-round economic progress in the country. Even in industries having higher trade-intensity, especially high export orientation, the workers are no better off.

With increased casualization under labour market flexibility, the use of labour displacing technology and enhanced work pressure on average worker in high growth industries, there appears to be a further deterioration in the well-being of labour in the age of competitive capitalism as labour bears the brunt of structural adjustments to make room for capital. Conclusions as above are not difficult to arrive at on the basis of our primary survey, despite the fact that the latter covers 16 different areas which are spread over different parts of the country with a great deal of heterogeneity in the labour conditions.

Appendix A

Table 3A.1 Distribution of sample according to state, area and worker's type

State	Area	Worker	Number
Delhi	East Delhi	Casual	5
		Permanent	9
		Total	14
	Mayapuri	Casual	11
		Permanent	30
		Total	41
	Okhla	Casual	19
		Permanent	19
		Total	38
	Total	*Casual*	*35*
		Permanent	*58*
		Total	*93*
Gujarat	Surat	Casual	64
		Total	64
Haryana	Faridabad	Casual	2
		Permanent	6
		Total	8
	Gurgaon	Permanent	11
		Total	11
	Total	*Casual*	*2*
		Permanent	*17*
		Total	*19*
Maharashtra	Mumbai	*Casual*	*25*
		Permanent	*22*
		Total	*47*
Uttar Pradesh	Ghaziabad	Casual	5
		Total	5
	NOIDA	Casual	42
		Permanent	16
		Total	58
	NOIDA SEZ	Casual	9
		Permanent	8
		Total	17

(*Table 3A.1 continued*)

(*Table 3A.1 continued*)

State	Area	Worker	Number
	Total	Casual	56
		Permanent	24
		Total	80
West Bengal	Falta SEZ	Casual	26
		Permanent	17
		Total	36
	Hooghly	Casual	3
		Permanent	16
		Total	19
	Howrah	Casual	24
		Permanent	5
		Total	29
	Kalyani	Casual	57
		Permanent	64
		Total	121
	Kolkata	Casual	52
		Permanent	48
		Total	100
	Total	Casual	162
		Permanent	150
		Total	312
All states in the sample	All areas in the sample	Casual	344
		Permanent	271
		Total	615

Appendix B

Table 3B.1 Questionnaire for Labour

Area:

Industry: Code:

Name of the Firm:

I. Personal Information

1. Name: Male ☐   Female ☐

2. Age: Years

3. Social Background: SC ☐   ST ☐   OBC ☐   Minority ☐   General ☐

4. Educational qualification: Illiterate ☐   Literate ☐   Basic Education ☐
   Secondary ☐   HS ☐   Graduate ☐   Post-Graduate and above ☐

5. Marital Status: Married ☐ Unmarried ☐

6. Number of children: ...., Son .... Daughter ....

7. Is your wife working? Yes ☐ No ☐

   If yes, where ...., When did she start? ...., Income: ....

8. When did you start working?

9. (a) Is this your first job? Yes ☐ No ☐

   (b) If no, please provide a brief job history:

Nos.	Name of firm	Duration of employment	Job status#	Reasons for changing job*	Income per month (Rs)

   * Codes: Better paying opportunity (0), Firm closure (1), Retrenchment (2), Dismissal (3), others (4), # Permanent (10), Temporary (11), Casual (12)

10. (a) Are you a migrant? Yes ☐ No ☐

    (b) From where did you migrate? District ☐ Town ☐ City ☐ Village ☐ Other ☐ state ☐

    (c) When did you migrate?

    (d) Reason for migration: Better paid job: ☐ Loss of job: ☐ Social: ☐ Better job security ☐ Skill-matching: ☐ To improve skill: ☐ Political: ☐ Others: ☐

    (e) Nature of migration: Seasonal ☐ Not-too-frequent ☐ Once-for-all ☐

11. (a) Number of dependent family members:

    Father ☐   Wife ☐
    Mother ☐   Children ☐ No ....
    Brother ☐ No ....   Others ☐ No ....
    Sister ☐ No ....

    (b) Number of earning members ....

    Wife ☐ Parents ☐ Brothers ☐ Sisters ☐ Children ☐

    (c) Do your children go to school? Yes ☐ No ☐

    (d) Are your children working ? Yes: ☐ No: ☐

    If yes, what is the type of job? ....

    How long do they work in a day?

Do they find time to study? Yes: ☐ No: ☐

If no, have they left school? Yes: ☐ No: ☐

How much do they earn in a month? Rs

II. Firm Specific Questions

1. How long have you been working in this firm?   Years
2. What are the main products produced in this firm?
3. (a) Any particular skill acquired for the job? Yes: ☐ No: ☐

   (b) If yes, how did you acquire the skill?

   On-the-job experience ☐ Special training ☐

   (c) If skill was acquired through special training, where did you get the training?

   Government Institute ☐ Private Institute ☐ Others ☐

   (d) Does your firm provide any special training? Yes: ☐ No: ☐

4. (a) How were you recruited to the firm?

   Direct recruitment ☐ Through intermediary ☐

   (b) If through intermediary then specify the nature of the intermediary:

   Labour contractor ☐ Union ☐ Friends ☐ Relatives ☐

   Other specify ....

5. Nature of job:

   Permanent ☐ Temporary ☐ Casual ☐

Notes

1. See Appendix B to this chapter for the questionnaire.
2. During the course of our survey, we got the impression that unionizing casual, contractual or temporary workers is more difficult than unionizing permanent workers as the former category of workers are footloose in nature; they frequently move from one job to another in the absence of any long term contract with their employers unlike the permanent workers.
3. The list of industries at the 2-digit level of NIC classification in which 615 workers were interviewed by us includes food and beverages (15), textiles (17), wearing apparel (18), leather (19), wood (20), paper (21), printing etc. (22), chemicals (24), rubber and plastic (25), non-metallic mineral (26), basic metals (27), fabricated metals (28), machinery (29), computing (30), electrical (31), motor vehicles (34), other transport (35) and furniture which includes gems and jewellery (36).
4. A separate profile of each one of these SEZs is provided on area profiles based on our field survey in the ICSSR–IDPAD Report (Sen and Dasgupta 2006b). See Chapter 4 of this book.

Profiles of Industry and Labour on the Basis of Field Surveys 4

Introduction

We have conducted field surveys in different parts of the country where the working conditions of labour in selected industrial units were investigated. In absence of access to resources as are needed to conduct a full-scale sample survey, we adopted a survey method choosing areas according to both their relevance as well as our accessibility to the surveyed area. Our findings are based on a survey we conducted in different Indian states over 14 months during 2004–05. With the focus of our study on globalization and labour in the organized sector of the Indian manufacturing industries, we also included in our survey a few Special Economic Zones (SEZs) which enjoy very special privileges from the state in terms of taxation, land rights and labour legislations. These units include the SEZs in NOIDA (UP), Santa Cruz (Maharashtra) and Falta (West Bengal). We also surveyed other industrial belts in different states; which include the clusters of small units in Faridabad in Haryana; Ghaziabad and NOIDA in Uttar Pradesh; Mayapuri, Okhla and East Delhi in Delhi; Gurgaon in Haryana; the industrial belts of Howrah, Hooghly, Murshidabad, Kolkata and Kalyani in West Bengal and the diamond-cutting industry of Surat in Gujarat.

Our method of survey has been on the basis of questionnaires as well as direct interviews. In our interviews we also met some managers (owners) of the industrial units surveyed, in addition to the workers employed therein.[1] We tried to obtain answers to the questionnaire prepared for the purpose. These covered the different aspects of the working conditions and well-being of the workers (see Appendix B at the end of Chapter 3 for the questionnaire).

We provide in the rest of this chapter profiles which reflect our impressions relating to economic activities and the job openings in each of the areas covered in the survey. A broad macroeconomic picture of the respective area is provided at the beginning of each section, with tables based on the area-specific employment patterns as are available in the two Census estimates of 1991 and 2001. The macroeconomic figures as are available for the individual areas at a district level, however, do not necessarily correspond to the micro-level data relating to facts observed in the individual profiles for each area. Our observations are divided into two parts, the first are our overall impressions, especially after meeting the owners/managers of the industrial units and the second, comprising the worker responses. As it can be expected, the two are not always consistent. We supplement the qualitative observations in the profiles with statistical tables which provide the quantitative information on the work status of workers in each of these surveyed areas as are gathered on the basis of our survey. Use has been made of the data to construct a set of security indices for workers in Chapter 5. These security indices are used in this chapter to supplement our analysis. We offer in the next section the profiles on the SEZs we have surveyed. This is followed by profiles of other areas in the rest of the chapter.

Export Processing Zones and Neighbouring Areas

Greater Mumbai

Mumbai, the commercial centre of India, has an image of a city of opportunities. It seems there is no dearth of job options in this city for the skilled as well as the unskilled workforce. The majority of the skilled workers are drawn from within the state and from neighbouring Gujarat. Most of the unskilled workers are migrants from Uttar Pradesh, Bihar and West Bengal. Job opportunities in textile, engineering parts, gems and jewellery and finished products seem to be abundant in the city. Some of the textile mills have remained closed which, however, did not apparently cause any dearth of jobs because of job openings in the neighbouring areas of Pune, Kalyan and Thane which have developed as big industrial centres. The development of SEEPZ seems to have helped further in creating new job avenues, particularly in the field of electronics and jewellery. SEEPZ has helped to provide some employment to workers who are both skilled and semi-skilled. In particular, those with some technical training but without much of job experience find their way in SEEPZ.

In the city of Mumbai there seems to be a big pool of workers as well as a great number of job opportunities. Employers are free to hire and fire workers any time. There is a tendency to hire workers on a temporary basis by luring them with higher compensation. Temporary workers can be fired at will by the firm. In the absence of any union to take up their cause workers find themselves at the receiving end. The cost of hiring a new worker is not very high because there is always a pool of able workers ever ready to grab an opportunity to work.

Santa Cruz Electronics Exports Processing Zone (SEEPZ)—A case study of labour under the new economy

Our field survey in Mumbai was largely concentrated to the SEEPZ area. From our interview with the firm managers in gems and jewellery and electronics units within the SEEPZ, it seems that there is a very high degree of mobility of workers across firms within the SEEPZ. As stated by the managers, workers change jobs at quick intervals. It appears easy to find alternative jobs within SEEPZ for an individual worker working therein. The above, however, is contradicted by facts we gathered from the workers interviewed in our sample who denied that such opportunities did exist. Firm managers, on their part, stated that there is not much firm loyalty on the part of the workers. However, the question of loyalty is subjective depending on various firm level internal factors, cultural as well as the inter-personal relationship at the firm level.

As we visited firms within the export zones, many firms were found producing similar products. That does not, however, mean that workers are in a position to offer matching job profiles within yards of their existing workplace. The mobility of workers from one firm to another does not amount to moving from low paid jobs to high paid jobs for most of the workers, and particularly for the unskilled. Rather, casual workers are often forced to shift from one unit to another, because they cannot continue with their jobs in the unit where they work. Firing of casual labour is easy as no labour law of the land is applicable inside SEZs. Only a handful of skilled workers, not all, are found to move from one firm to another from low paid to high paid jobs. Casualization of the workforce is rampant within the SEEPZ as that reduces the costs of engaging labour as well as firing them when desired. These are also the workers who are mobile across units.

Expectation of employers is high and demanding. Thus labour is required to put wholehearted efforts to perform on the job. Strict working hours are hardly maintained. Workers outside SEEPZ generally work beyond their stipulated time and that too without any overtime. Similar incidences of work beyond stipulated hours, even within SEEPZ are quite common. The firms, in turn, follow a strategy to remain competitive in the open economy, thus demanding a lot from their workers in terms of their skill and efficiency, long working without being adequately compensated in terms of wages and absence of other benefits. A high reserve army of labour makes the environment even more competitive for labour in terms of their survival in the industry which tends to depress wages. This is particularly true for the unskilled workers who are denied even the minimum wages as we found in our field survey results.

Incidence of casualization has been on the rise both among the skilled and unskilled workers. As for trade union membership, the institution hardly exists within the zone. This considerably brings down the bargaining power of workers. In general, workers within SEEPZ lack voice representation in terms of unionization as compared to their counterparts outside SEEPZ.

Within the SEEPZ there are both trained and untrained workers. The cost of hiring a replacement is not much with workers available, who are ready to accept job offers while having little bargaining power. Labour security (as we measure it in Chapter 5) is not higher within the SEEPZ as compared to what it is outside. Any worker can be fired any time if the situation demands that way.

There were 47 workers whom we interviewed in our sample of the SEEPZ at Mumbai (Table 4.1). Of these, 22 were permanent and as many as 25 were casual. These workers were engaged in the electronics and in the gems and jewellery industries. In terms of our calculations relating to the security level of workers, the income and job security levels for permanent workers are higher (see Chapter 5). Their security levels also vary with education (skill) levels of the workers and their migratory status. Thus, 28 workers in our sample who were migrants from other states had an overall security level which is worse than that of the non-migrant workers. As for union membership, which is rare, only eight workers happen to be union members with security levels consistently higher than those for the non-unionized workers who were interviewed by us.

The 22 permanent workers we interviewed were employed in printing (22), rubber and plastic (25), basic metal (27), fabricated metal (28), machinery (29), electrical (31) and gems and jewellery (36). Casual workers, 27 in number, were engaged in textiles (17), printing (22), chemicals (24),

Table 4.1 Profile of workers in Mumbai SEEPZ (Averages unless otherwise stated)

	Permanent	Casual	Total
Number of labourers	22	25	47
NIC code of industry groups	22, 25, 27, 28, 29, 31, 32, 36	17, 22, 24, 25, 27, 29, 31, 35, 36	
Age (Years)	29.45	31.28	30.43
Wage per month (Rs)	5,395.45	4,158.00	4,737.23
Working hours	9.00	9.00	9.00
Union membership (%)	36	0	17
Experience (years)	4.18	3.16	3.64
Minimum wage level (%)	45	24	34
Skill (%)	0.82	0.80	0.81
Special training (%)	0.55	0.36	0.45
Migration (%)	0.45	0.36	0.40
Education (years)	11.27	10.84	11.04
Average number of earning members	1.55	2.40	2.00
Asset holding (%)	18	12	15
Security index	0.53	0.37	0.45
Income security	0.50	0.23	0.35
Employment security	0.72	0.45	0.57
Job security	0.68	0.74	0.71
Work security	0.74	0.64	0.69
Skill security	0.58	0.40	0.48
Voice representation security	0.15	0.00	0.07
Financial security	0.33	0.21	0.27
Family support security	0.55	0.30	0.41

Source: Authors' calculations based on primary data collected through questionnaire-based field survey of 47 industrial workers in the organized manufacturing industries in Mumbai SEEPZ in Maharashtra during 2004–05.

Note: All percentages in this table and others relate to the share of the respective population.

rubber and plastic (25), basic metal (27), machinery (29), electrical (31), electronics (32), other transport (35) and gems and jewellery (36). There exists a perceptible wage disparity between the permanent and casual workers. Even within individual industries there are wide variations in wages between permanent and casual workers. Thus while the average monthly wage for the 12 permanent workers in gems and jewellery (NIC code 36) in our sample turned out to be Rs 4,475, the average for the six casual workers remained at Rs 3,167.67 subject to a range of Rs 1,950–3,692. Casual workers received wages on a daily basis. Generally they get work for 26 days a month. A similar pattern was visible in machinery (NIC code 29) where four permanent workers in our sample received Rs 5,750 per month on average while the mean wage of eight casual workers was only Rs 4,647.50.

It is important to point out here that in gems and jewellery (NIC code 36), in which most of our sample for SEEPZ were concentrated in Mumbai city (18 out of 47 workers belong to this industry in our sample), recruitments of workers (both permanent as well as casual) took place through intermediaries. Next is machinery (NIC code 29) in which 12 out of 47 workers in our sample were engaged. In this industry, too, most of the workers were recruited through intermediaries. The highest mean wage for a permanent worker in our sample was found in electronics at Rs 10,000 and that for the casual worker in basic metal (NIC code 27) at Rs 4,992. The lowest mean wage was observed in gems and jewellery for both permanent (at Rs 4,475) as well as for casual workers (at Rs 3,167). One can infer from this finding that wages have been consistently low in labour intensive industries like gems and jewellery (36) in comparison to capital intensive ones like basic metal or electronics (32) which require more technical skill. However, in gems and jewellery (36) the need for skilled workforce is substantially high. As a consequence, a few in this industry can earn substantially high wages (compared to those who possess craftsmanship to make sophisticated products).

Inside the SEEPZ one observes a rather exploitative labour process with labour contractors holding a superior position vis-à-vis the workers. Few labourers in Mumbai SEEPZ get paid as per the statutory norms in the country, and many are denied even the minimum wages.

NOIDA Special Economic Zone (NSEZ)—A study of labour under modern export zone conditions

The fieldwork in NSEZ was carried out with due preparations including permission from the Development Commissioner. Despite all these arrangements the biggest problem faced by us was that we were not allowed to visit the firms randomly. The office of the Development Commissioner allowed us to visit only 18 units. Though they provided the required assistance we could visit only 16 units altogether due to the absence of cooperation on part of some firm managers.

The factories and management in NSEZ

NOIDA Special Economic Zone is till now the only landlocked special economic zone in the country. It covers a large area with large numbers of units most of which are operational at the moment. The majority of firms had turnovers between Rs 60 and Rs 300 million. Apart from three units, most were producing corrugated boxes and packaging materials. These firms claimed that they are exporters with their main markets in the US, the UK and Singapore. These manufacturers of corrugated boxes and packaging material units also reported that they sell their products mostly to 100 per cent export-oriented units which are located either inside or out-side the zone. As for markets abroad, some firms reported that they are facing a recessionary trend. Most firms mentioned the existence of stiff market competition in overseas markets, mainly with suppliers from European countries and from China. Profit margins as reported by these firms show a decline over the past five years, largely due to increased cost of production with rising transportation, raw material and labour cost. Most of these firms were expecting better market conditions in 2005 when quotas on these products abroad were expected to be removed. All firm managers reported that they follow the central and state governments minimum wage policy and that they provide benefits like Employees' State Insurance (ESI) and PF to both casual as well as non-regular workers.

Firms in the NSEZ have been largely employing contractual workers. The firm managers claimed that there is no dispute between them and that the workers are happy with their work conditions. Excepting three firms, the rest had either two or three shifts. None of these firms mentioned the presence of labour unions. Interestingly, in one of the firms the management itself informed us that there exists a set of persons which include the SEZ authorities which supports employers by trying to suppress the workers demands. Firms show in their official records a small number of non-regular workers. They do not generally maintain records for the causal/temporary workers which helps them to save money on their PF and other benefits. As mentioned earlier, inside the zone the Development Commissioner also acts as the Labour Commissioner. As we questioned the firm managers/owners as to what they think about current labour policy of the government, most of them reported unhappiness over the labour policy regime which, according to them, still continues to stall and hinder the hire and fire labour policies.

Labour interviewed in NSEZ

Conditions of labour within the zone, on the basis of our interviews of workers, however, seem to be rather different. The size of employment varied from firm to firm. The proportion of non-regular to regular and male to female workers also varied, both according to the skill required for the job and their experience. Female workers, if preferred at all, were for the finishing and packaging work. Of the workers employed in the manufacturing units of electronic goods only three were professionally qualified, either as qualified engineers or with ITI diplomas, all from the same state. Wage rates of the professionally qualified workers in the electronic goods industries were higher than those in other units in the zone which was around Rs 5,000 per month. However, the rest of the workers were also with skills acquired over their work experience.

As mentioned earlier, a major problem we faced in our survey was the limited opportunity to interview the workers. We could speak only to a handful of these SEZ workers, and that too either in the evening, outside the SEZ complex or at their residence during holidays. Contacts with them were made through trade unions, to the extent these did exist in these areas. We could interview a total of 17 SEZ workers only in NOIDA, of which 13 were casual and only four were permanent. These workers were employed in industries producing wearing apparel (NIC code 18), chemical (NIC code 24), rubber and plastics (NIC code 25), basic metal (NIC code 27), fabricated material (NIC code 28), electrical machinery (NIC code 31) and gems and jewellery (NIC code 369). Of these 17 workers we interviewed, 11 were from units which we had visited earlier and we also had met the management earlier in our pilot study trip, thus trying to verify the facts given by the management to us earlier. Workers consistently reported of their bad working conditions and low wage rates. We found that in most of the units professional qualification was not a must for workers. The casual workers are paid wages which are less than the statutory minimum rates. Wage rates (for regularized as well as casual workers) varied between Rs 1,500 and Rs 3,500 per month. None are provided the benefits as are supposed to be given to the regular workers. Firms generally prefer the non-regular casual workers because of the wage differential and, because of other liabilities their units have to bear when employing them on a regular basis. Trade union leaders present in the area mentioned the problems they face in organizing the workers inside the zone, often due to the restrictions placed on movement of outsiders. They also pointed out that with the Development Commissioner acting as the Labour Commissioner, labour disputes are not being addressed separately.

In our sample of 17 workers in NSEZ, 16 happen to be migrants. Their security level (as calculated in terms of the methodology provided in Chapter 5) seems to be much lower than that of the average non-migrant worker. Permanent regular workers, as can be expected, were relatively better off in terms of security level. However, even then, their security index as calculated solely in terms of job security was lower as compared to those employed on a temporary basis, a fact which remains a paradox. Education level (which captures skill) of workers varied, from basic (up to class VIII) to graduate level with no clear correlation between the level of education and overall labour security.[2] We found 11 workers in our sample who were skilled with overall labour security levels much higher than the unskilled workers. Despite the difficulties faced by unions in organizing workers, we could find 11 of them, who were not skilled, but had membership of trade unions. Their security levels were much higher than those of non-unionized members.[3]

In the NSEZ, as elsewhere, the labour process as envisaged works as an exploitative one in terms of the underlying class process. Labour contractors who work as intermediaries receive a portion of distributed surplus in the form of commission from the capitalist owner. The degree of exploitation tends to be perceptibly high in the SEZ with wages paid much below the one statutorily fixed by the state as minimum wages (which may approximate the socially necessary labour). But within SEZ such things cannot be challenged as labour laws are much more flexible here. Despite all these privileges the entrepreneurs seem to be unhappy with the scene. Table 4.2 indicates the details of our primary survey of the NSEZ.

Falta in West Bengal—A case study of labour under duress

Falta in the district of South 24-Parganas in West Bengal epitomizes a unique case of footloose industrial labour in eastern India (see Bremen 1996).[4] Of the three SEZs studied by us, the one in Falta represents the most appalling site of immiserizing labour conditions with uncertainty and exploitation of labour to an extreme degree; a story of failed experimentation of industrialization and trade-oriented development, and with frustration moving entrepreneures away from industry.

Falta, located in the district of South 24-Parganas in West Bengal on the banks of the river Hooghly, is predominantly a rural area with agriculture and related activities as main economic activities in the area.[5] Roughly 100 kilometres away from the capital city of Kolkata in West Bengal and surrounded by some big industrial units, the majority of the population in Falta ekes their livelihood through agriculture. Falta Export Processing Zone came up in 1986 and was later converted into the Falta Special Economic Zone (FSEZ) following the official policies of converting export processing zones into SEZs.

Table 4.2 NOIDA Special Economic Zone (NSEZ)

	Permanent	Casual	Total
Number of labourers	8	9	17
NIC code of industry groups	18, 24, 31, 36	18, 25, 27, 28, 36	
Age (years)	30.50	25.33	27.76
Wage per month (Rs)	2,978.00	1,900.00	2,407.29
Working hours	9.00	9.00	9.00
Union membership (%)	0	67	35
Experience (years)	5.88	0.61	3.09
Minimum wage level (%)	25	0	12
Skill (%)	100	33	65
Special training (%)	0	0	0
Migration (%)	100	89	94
Education (years)	10.13	8.22	9.12
Average number of earning members	1.63	1.67	1.65
Asset holding (%)	0.88	0.67	0.76
Security index	0.45	0.33	0.39
Income security	0.50	0.06	0.26
Employment security	0.50	0.50	0.50
Job security	0.31	0.50	0.41
Work security	0.50	0.30	0.39
Skill security	0.67	0.33	0.49
Voice representation security	0.22	0.33	0.28
Financial security	0.63	0.37	0.49
Family support security	0.28	0.28	0.28

Source: Authors' calculations based on primary data collected through questionnaire-based field survey of 47 industrial workers in the organized manufacturing industries in Mumbai SEEPZ in Uttar Pradesh during 2004–05.

The population of Falta as per the 2001 Census was at 221,695 with a decadal growth rate of 11.69 per cent (which was below the 17.46 per cent growth rate for the entire rural areas of the district). Density of population was 1,696 per square kilometre in the district as against a figure of 1,747 for the rural area. The sex ratio of the area was 941 females per 1,000 males in 2001, rising slightly from 928 in 1991.

Table 4.3 indicates the profile of the workforce in Falta area in terms of the Census figures. These include cultivators and agricultural workers. It may again be pointed out that around 42 per cent of the total main and marginal workers were engaged in agriculture either as direct cultivators or as agricultural labourers. That means the remaining 52 per cent of the total working population was engaged in manufacturing and service related activities. In the last decade the area witnessed some growth in local services, namely trading and transport. While the main and marginal workers taken together recorded an absolute as well as relative

Table 4.3 Distribution of working and non-working population at Falta

	1991			2001		
	Persons	Male	Female	Persons	Male	Female
Main and marginal workers	61,260	54,233	7,027	73,047	62,463	10,584
	(30.68)	(52.67)	(7.36)	(32.96)	(54.68)	(9.85)
Main workers	56,394	52,631	3,763	52,409	48,255	4,154
	(28.41)	(51.12)	(3.94)	(23.64)	(42.24)	(3.87)
Marginal workers	4,866	1,602	3,264	20,638	14,208	6,430
	(2.45)	(1.56)	(3.42)	(9.31)	(12.44)	(5.98)
Cultivators*	10,296	9,703	593	7,759	6,932	827
	(16.81)	(17.89)	(8.44)	(10.62)	(11.10)	(7.81)
Agricultural labourers*	16,019	15,186	833	22,763	19,061	3,702
	(26.15)	(28.00)	(11.85)	(31.16)	(30.52)	(34.98)
Household industry workers*	2,853	2,084	769	6,397	3,919	2,478
	(4.66)	(3.84)	(10.94)	(8.76)	(6.27)	(23.41)
Non-workers	137,231	48,727	88,504	148,684	51,769	96,879
	(69.14)	(47.33)	(92.64)	(67.05)	(45.32)	(90.15)
Other workers*	27,226	25,658	1,568	36,128	32,551	3,577
	(44.44)	(47.31)	(22.31)	(49.46)	(52.11)	(33.80)

Source: Census of India, Government of India, 2001.

Notes: Figures in the parentheses indicate percentage of the particular category in the total population of the area unless otherwise stated.
*Figures in parentheses for these rows indicate the percentage of the concerned category in total main and marginal working population.

increase, there was a *decline* in the number and percentage of main workers since 1991. One can postulate that manufacturing workers would fall under the main worker category. The significant drop in the number of main workers during the 1991–2001 period, as indicated in terms of the Census figure of 2001, in a way, testifies to the decline of industrial activities, most of which were riveted around FSEZ. The process of de-industrialization was imminent during our survey as workers losing factory jobs were inclined to take to agricultural work or some menial work in the government sponsored poverty alleviation/rural employment schemes. The process can best be understood as an inverse transfer of labour from industry to agriculture which negates the claims of labour absorption as propounded in the Lewis type of development model. In fact, such inverse migration goes against all the models of development based on the so-called dual economy structure.[6]

It can be seen from Table 4.3 that there has been a significant jump in the proportion of 'other workers', who neither have principal agricultural jobs nor industrial activities as are reported in terms of the Census figures for total main and marginal workers between 1991 and 2001. It signifies the increase in the number of people taking to menial and temporary works in rural employment schemes (say, for construction of rural roads) or in agricultural fields (providing seasonal labour) or even digging in the brick fields on a daily wage basis. These constitute a significant increase in informal activity in the area, with wages rather low (around Rs 20–25 daily with no other benefits) and work conditions characterized by occupational hazards.

The Falta SEZ (FSEZ)

The SEZ in Falta comprises an area of approximately 20 square kilometres which can accommodate around 300 industrial units catering to foreign markets. As per official records on the website, there are 90 operating units. During our survey we found that only 30–35 units were actually operational.

Our field trip to the FSEZ took place in the second round of survey during July–August 2005. Earlier in December 2003 we went there to conduct a pilot study. We interviewed 44 factory labourers and also talked to the labourers associated with loading and unloading activities at the zone. On the basis of information collected from there we had the following observations:

The factories and management: A few industrial units (about 30–35) were operating within the zone at the time of our survey. The important industries within the zone were plastics and textiles, and a few engineering units. These industries happened to be mostly labour intensive. It seems the existence of a large army of cheap labour was the main reason for the setting up of this zone, besides the geographical advantage of its proximity to the port.

As for the surrounding area of FSEZ, one can mention the village Kasipur which is one among the major villages, located within one kilometre radius of the zone. It has no electricity and as for water only two tube wells remain to serve around 100 households as the sole source of portable water. One evening we were chatting with the villagers at a tea stall sitting in the dark. But that meeting could not last long due to the intervention of a local village head-type individual, who was very influential and enjoyed political clout in that locality. He did not like us talking to the villagers regarding the factory jobs and our other related queries regarding their economic, social and cultural life. Hence, the meeting ended abruptly.

The Falta area as a whole is predominantly rural. People generally prefer to do farming and combine non-factory jobs on a daily basis as they find the terms of factory jobs comparatively less attractive in terms of both wages and working hours. Thus, when they take up factory jobs it is only as the last option for their subsistence. There are many people in the village Kasipur (which we visited), who left factory jobs and got back to farming and other menial jobs, mostly in the brickfields. Most of the workers work for not less than 12 hours a day and earn on an average a meagre sum which is between Rs 30 and Rs 40 per day. The gap between male and female wage rate is around Rs 10 on an average, with females getting around Rs 20 to Rs 30 on an average.

The labourers: As for the employment pattern a very small percentage of total workers as are employed in a unit are shown as actuals and recorded in the factory account book. For example, in a shoe factory there are about 600 workers, but only 30 names are recorded in the factory register. Those, whose names do not appear in the factory book, can under no circumstances claim their labour status in the particular factory in which they are engaged, a fact which benefits the employers.

There are very few permanent workers in these units. The differences between permanent and non-permanent workers are thus non-existent. Wages are pathetically low and mostly below the minimum wage rate. The average wage of the unskilled workers ranges between Rs 30 and Rs 40 per day with workers who get even less. Wages paid are mostly on a no-work-no-pay basis, even when employed on a permanent basis. Labourers in turn are recruited mostly from local areas in the nearby villages where they live. The neighbourhood still remains rather under-developed without any proper road connectivity and some of the villages, located within a radius of 2 kilometre of the SEZ, are without power as is the case with the village of Kasipur mentioned earlier. Labourers are recruited mainly through contractors who, in turn, are affiliated to political parties and their affiliated labour unions. These bodies play a big role in labour management. Industrial units rely on them by delegating to these contract-ors the task of labour recruitment. Labourers were generally afraid of giving us time for interviews as they were terribly scared of the contractors and the local union leaders.

One can think of a chain of surveillance and dominance which is as: labourers → union and/or contractors → employers. Among the labourers only a few are at a supervisory level. But there is hardly any difference between supervisory and other labour in terms of the job actu-ally performed. However, it could be the case that these supervisors in some cases were close to the contractors/unions. We found a case where a woman with a supervisory job in a plastic firm (who was appointed through a contractor) was denied a renewal of ESI by the company, and she complained to the union of which she was a member. This news was leaked to the contractor, who recruited her. Later she was not allowed to work although she was given the wages. But she feared that after some time she would lose her job permanently and would not get any job in other units in the zone due to the strong network of unions and contractors.

Firms in the zone usually pay the contractors, who make payments to workers after retaining their shares. Workers do not know how much the contractors are retaining. However, as for the unions, workers make payments to the union directly as and when the need arises. Also, there is membership payment, which can be paid in instalments. Workers not committed to unions generally do not want to come to the union office because they want to avoid meeting union leaders. However, the control of the contractors over workers is absolute in every sense of the term, with a nexus between union leaders, contractors and local ruling party leaders.

As for the permanent workers, very few have PF facilities and that too despite the fact that payment of PF is now compulsory in terms of the recently amended legal provisions. We did not find a single case where gratuity is provided. There is generally no concept of retirement age. Leave rules exist for permanent workers—15 days in a year which include leave for health-related purposes. No maternity leave exists for women and no leave exists for workers appointed through contractors.

There are a few skilled workers who have come from outside—mostly technical hands—and ITI trainees. Their condition is slightly better in terms of salary and facilities (including accommodation). The incidence of in-migration is very low. The same is true about out-migration due to the lack of adequate skills. We came across a case where the individual returned from Gujarat to his home in Falta when it was developed. But after five to six years of service in Falta he now regrets that he is in a situation worse than before.

It is, however, noticeable that despite poverty every child goes to the school in this area. The proportion of school children completing basic education (say up to class VIII) is probably not only high but also rising, thanks to the mid-day meal facilities. The area has got few primary schools, one primary health centre and one hospital at the sub-divisional town nearby.

Most of the population in FSEZ and in surrounding areas is unbanked. They are also not in a position to have any savings. Rather, they take loans from local moneylenders and relatives/friends—sources which are distant from institutional sources. The major reasons for their indebtedness include weddings, illnesses and house repair. We observed that local people wanted to share their sorrows and grievances with us whenever they got a chance and particularly when they were away from the union office and/or the contractors whom they did not trust and were afraid of.

Finally, it was not the case that all the casual and contractual workers listed in the factory rolls necessarily got a job. Every morning they assembled at the factory gates in the SEZ and in some cases workers had to travel by foot for one hour or more as they do not even have a bicycle. Table 4.4 shows the main findings of our primary survey at FSEZ which we have already described.

Wage disparity is significant between male and female workers. In many cases, male members of the family do not take up factory jobs and those taken up by female members are often their last preference. This is because the male members in many instances are found to prefer working

Table 4.4 Falta Special Economic Zone (FSEZ)

	Permanent	Casual	Total
Number of labourers	17	26	43
NIC code of industry groups	19, 21, 25, 31	19, 21, 25	
Age (years)	31.47	30.88	31.12
Wage per month (Rs)	3,092.71	1,919.04	2,383.05
Working hours	9.18	10.04	9.70
Union membership (%)	29	50	42
Experience (years)	5.06	4.27	4.58
Minimum wage level (%)	41	12	23
Skill (%)	100	96	98
Special training (%)	24	0	9
Migration (%)	47	8	23
Education (years)	10.06	7.77	8.67
Average number of earning members	1.24	1.08	1.14
Asset holding (%)	6	15	12
Security index	0.47	0.30	0.37
Income security	0.45	0.07	0.22
Employment security	0.71	0.48	0.57
Job security	0.32	0.13	0.21
Work security	0.59	0.39	0.47
Skill security	0.71	0.37	0.50
Voice representation security	0.10	0.18	0.15
Financial security	0.27	0.13	0.19
Family support security	0.57	0.65	31.12

Source: Authors' calculations based on primary data collected through questionnaire-based field survey of 43 industrial workers in the organized manufacturing industries in Falta Special Economic Zone in West Bengal during 2003–06.

in the agricultural field or in digging works under different rural-based government programmes to factory jobs.

As for our interviews with workers, they talked to us more freely when we met them at the factory gate individually. This probably makes our survey unbiased by having equal access to different sections of labourers. Also, in regard to the relation of workers to the unions, our survey remains relatively unbiased. This is because we were only permitted to formally interview workers at the union office in the presence of union leaders as desired by these leaders. But such reporting in the presence of the leaders could be biased as the workers did not want to divulge many facts in presence of the leaders. This was avoided when we could talk to them outside the factory gate in the street.

Profiles of Other Areas under Survey

West Bengal: Kolkata—A case study of labour under transformation

Kolkata is the third largest metropolitan city in India (after Mumbai and Delhi) inhabited by more than 4.5 million persons as per the 2001 Census which increased from a little less than 4.4 million persons in terms of the 1991 Census. The city has an area of 185 square kilometres with a population density of 24,218 per square kilometre. In 2001.The sex ratio of the city at 829 improved as compared to 1991 when it was at 799.

Calcutta, being the capital of the British Raj till 1912 used to be the major centre of modern industries in the colonial period. Industries prominent till today include jute, engineering, textile, chemical and leather. Our field survey of Kolkata, carried out during 2004–05, covered a number of labourers in the industrial units of the city. It concentrated on a few industrial pockets covering a population of 0.891 million as per the 2001 Census. Of these 0.479 million were males and 0.411 million females. Industries (at NIC 2-digit level of coding) covered in our survey included food and beverages (NIC code 15), textiles (NIC code 17), wearing apparel (NIC code 18), leather (NIC code 19), paper (NIC code 21), chemicals (NIC code 24), rubber and plastic (NIC code 25), non-metallic minerals (NIC code 26), machinery (NIC code 29), electrical machinery (NIC code 31), motor vehicles (NIC code 34), other transport (NIC code 35) and furniture (NIC code 36).

Table 4.5 gives a macro overview of the working population in the city. Of the total population, 33 per cent constitutes the category of main and marginal workers according to the 2001 Census. During 1991–2001, there has been a perceptible rise in female participation in the workforce which now stands at 10 per cent of the total female population in the area. As in other surveys, our sample includes only the male members, as female workers showed their reluctance to talk to us especially due to their fear of possible reprisals by the management.

Table 4.5 Distribution of working and non-working population at Kolkata

	1991			2001		
	Persons	*Male*	*Female*	*Persons*	*Male*	*Female*
Main and marginal workers	248,530	227,528	21,002	297,837	256,127	41,710
	(30.04)	(49.94)	(5.65)	(33.41)	(53.41)	(10.13)
Main workers	245,909	225,711	20,198	278,713	242,643	36,070
	(29.72)	(49.54)	(5.48)	(31.27)	(50.60)	(8.76)
Marginal workers	9,017	6,687	2,330	114,486	77,041	37,445
	(1.09)	(1.47)	(0.63)	(12.80)	(16.10)	(9.09)
Cultivators*	52	51	1	885	512	373
	(0.02)	(0.02)	(0.001)	(0.30)	(0.20)	(0.89)
Agricultural labourers*	268	266	2	620	489	131
	(0.11)	(0.12)	(0.01)	(0.21)	(0.19)	(0.31)
Household industry workers*	1,437	1,228	209	7,334	4,898	2436
	(0.58)	(0.54)	(1.00)	(2.46)	(1.91)	(5.84)
Non-workers	663,795	258,002	405,793	673,271	249,954	423,317
	(80.20)	(56.60)		(75.50)	(52.10)	
Other workers*	282,479	259,518	22,961	349,369	301,167	48,202
	(97.91)	(98.15)	(95.58)	(97.20)	(97.81)	(93.51)

Source: Census of India, Government of India, 2001.
Notes: Figures in parentheses indicate percentage of the particular category in the total population of the area unless otherwise stated.
*Figures in the parentheses indicate the percentage of the concerned category in the total main and marginal working population.

We interviewed 100 labourers; of whom 48 were permanent and 52 casual. All of them were factory workers offering their labour on a time wage basis.[7] About 40 per cent of the workers in our sample were union members who were all permanent. Union presence among the casual workers is thin and the trade union leaders we met expressed their difficulties in mobilizing casual workers because of their high turnover ratio. Table 4.6 narrates the major findings of our primary survey in Kolkata.

Of late, labour processes in the organized manufacturing units of the city seem to be in a process of transformation. Enterprises find it profitable

Table 4.6 Kolkata: Industrial structure and labour

	Permanent	Casual	Total
Number of labourers	48	52	100
Industry group code	15, 17, 19, 21, 24, 25, 26, 29, 31, 34, 35, 36	15, 17, 18, 19, 21, 24, 25, 26, 29, 31, 35, 36	
Age (years)	42.08	29.94	35.77
Wage per month (Rs)	4,820.21	1,973.23	3,339.78
Working hours	7.98	9.25	8.64
Union membership (%)	77	6	40
Experience (years)	20.03	4.52	12.04
Minimum wage level (%)	79	6	41
Skill (%)	65	79	72
Special training (%)	48	17	32
Migration (%)	13	29	21
Education (years)	10.33	9.08	9.68
Average number of earning members	1.40	1.81	1.61
Asset holding (%)	0.27	0.15	0.21
Security index	0.71	0.38	0.54
Income security	0.92	0.21	0.56
Employment security	0.58	0.49	0.54
Job security	0.93	0.66	0.79
Work security	0.64	0.49	0.56
Skill security	0.97	0.53	0.74
Voice representation security	0.49	0.07	0.27
Financial security	0.48	0.20	0.33
Family support security	0.63	0.41	0.52

Source: Authors' calculations based on primary data collected through questionnaire-based field survey of 100 industrial workers in the organized manufacturing industries in Kolkata in West Bengal during 2003–06.

in this age of competitive capitalism to employ casual workers and also to outsource in-house jobs, which earlier used to be done within the factory premises using factory-based labour, to households. Both help in cost cutting by avoiding the fixed costs of employing labour which include the provident fund and other benefits normally offered to permanent workers. Recruitment of casual workers is done through agencies which include the contractor. In most cases the latter carry the double mantle of the local union leaders or political bosses. A process of 'informalization'—a term used in the literature is distinctly visible with growing casualization of factory labour and the pushing of wages below the statutory minimum leaving no bargaining power for labour (Papola 1992).

The impression, we got as we talked to the labourers, is that although it is not easy to retrench a permanent worker (which is not the case with casual workers) many had to lose their jobs due to sudden closures of small and medium units. In many cases, permanent workers had to take up casual jobs in other factories or had to resort to informal services as street-vendors or hawkers after losing their jobs in the closed units. Some became self-employed as household workers who did the factory work from home as these were outsourced to them. All of these suggest a pattern of *de facto* labour flexibility which is on the rise despite the absence of any *de jure* changes in existing labour laws, in particular changes in the existing Chapter VB of Industrial Disputes Act (last amended in 1976) and the Contract Labour Act. In recent times, there has been a significant drop in the number of strikes and labour agitation and the trade unions in many cases are hard pressed by the political parties to which they are affiliated to, to adopt capital-friendly strategies in this age of globalization, and not to contest strongly emerging labour flexibility in the organized manufacturing. The political pressure on trade unions to avoid strikes and cease work or any kind of labour agitation is based on the perceived apprehension of the political parties in India (all of whom when at power adhere to the similar path of Fund-Bank prescribed economic liberalization programme unleashed in 1991 by the then Congress Government at the Centre) that strikes, cease work, or labour agitation of any kind would deter the entry of foreign capital (see Dutt 2003: 121–29).[8] The present liberalization programme is based on the premise that foreign investment would replace domestic investment and would trigger higher growth and development. Hence, aversion to labour militancy remains the *mantra* encouraging foreign investments by foreign enterprises in India in these days of privatization, liberalization and globalization.

The factories, we visited in Kolkata, are owned by local entrepreneurs and all those firms were small in size. Participation of foreign capital seemed to be a remote possibility in these enterprises at the time of our survey. Yet, the general enthusiasm in the country with respect to foreign direct investment in India, which also prevails in West Bengal, forces the trade unions to adhere to moderate positions even vis-à-vis the locally owned enterprises.

In West Bengal the projection of a capital-friendly labour has been very much on the agenda of the trade unions which still remain the major arms of handling organized labour in the country. A significant wage disparity could be observed between the permanent (or regular) workforce and casual workers in the case of most units we surveyed. A gender disparity in wages is also discernible. As we found in our construction of labour security index in Chapter 5, the gap between permanent and casual workers is phenomenal when one looks at the income security level of these two categories of workers. Thus the level of social security, almost non-existent for the casual workers, is substantial for the permanent workers. However, labour security does not seem to be on the agenda of the economic policies, which is being pursued since 1991 under the name of economic reforms. Closures of jute mills, engineering units, textile mills, etc., in this state over the past two decades have rendered the position of many factory workers vulnerable to the point of absolute poverty. Large units like Dunlop Rubber Factory in Sahagunj (Hooghly) have closed down. A majority of the retrenched workers had to take refuge in informal works like vending, rickshaw pulling, small household jobs, etc. With massive deindustrialization in the city in recent times there has been a process of sectoral transfer of working population from manufacturing to non-manufacturing (including informal and low-return household works) which has taken away jobs of many in the factory space.

The above is a story of unfurling misery for many workers on several grounds. First of all, persons who are forced to live on mere subsistence with the closure of these industries are devoid of finding alternative jobs with vertical mobility due to lack of access to proper skill and credit on their part. Second, they add to the number of the working poor without any social support from the state and with very little or none from the family. Thus they are deprived of some basic amenities of life like medical care and education for the family, which some of them used to enjoy earlier as regular factory employees. Third, they are forced to encounter a state of growing uncertainty even in terms of their daily subsistence, given the fact that their earnings from providing labour in the informal segment of the economy are abysmally lower than they would have been in formal employment in the organized sector.

In an interview with a soft luggage manufacturing unit owner of the city (whose product has become a brand name over the last decade) we came to know how outsourcing of in-house jobs helped him to reduce costs and increase profitability in the face of fierce competition from his rivals, and particularly from the other global brands in soft luggage which entered into the local market after 1991. The owner of the unit claimed that the factory workers are actually receiving higher income after their conversion as household workers. The workers, however, provided us contrary evidence and indicated that they were rather happy with regular factory jobs, which used to fetch them certainty of earnings at the end of the month, and which had disappeared now with the growing tendency of outsourcing of in-house jobs.

It can be noticed further, at an aggregate level, that the number of household level workers in the area as a whole has actually increased over the last decade (see Table 4.5). The gender dimension of exploitation can be inferred as female participation in household work has also increased significantly. As we have found in the course of our interviewing the male members of the family, a woman when forced to take up a job outside home does, in many instances shoulder the double burden of work and her surplus labour (beyond what is necessary labour which she gets as subsistence) is also appropriated by male members of the household. So, with female participation we need to explore much more carefully than what is usually done in the literature on feminization of labour.

At end of our analysis, it can be held that the story of Kolkata is no different than what it is in other parts of the country, with competitive pressures and job cuts, casualization and withdrawal of security benefits. Despite the presence of trade unions and their political activism, labour today is facing a challenge to meet the burden of adjustment, even in organized manufacturing. A process of transformation is thus underway in the labour markets, which has relocated the informal space occupied by labour to the charity of the international aid agencies and civil societies in days to come. In the process the retreat of the state vis-à-vis the market has been quite evident.

Howrah—A case study of labour under stress

Howrah is an old traditional industrial area in West Bengal. The history of industrial development in the city goes back to the colonial period with jute mills, light engineering enterprises (notable among them are the foundry units) and even chemical industries which came up over the years. Howrah covers a geographical area of 51.74 square kilometres with a population of 1.007 million in 2001 which went up from 0.950 million in 1991. The density of population is quite high (and comparable to Kolkata) with 19,473 persons per square kilometre. The sex ratio in 2001 at 842 moved up from 799 in 1991.

The glory of Bengal as the premier industrial region of undivided India was in large part due to Howrah which, however, has faded with time. There remain now only a few industrial pockets in Howrah which accommodate some foundry units, metal industries, units producing mechanical gadgets, jute mills (on the bank of the river Hooghly) and chemical industries. Of late, the state government has taken some initiatives to set up new industrial zones in the Howrah district (notable among them the Uluberia cluster) with the help of foreign capital. Nonetheless, the story of Howrah remains one of faded glory and industries which still survive are out-of-date in terms of their technological levels, production processes as well as organizational set-ups. Lack of credit to the small and medium enterprises as well as inadequate demand seems to be one of the reasons for this decay. These units face stiff competition from similar units in Coimbatore and the demand from public sector units like Indian Railways has shifted from these units to other areas like Coimbatore.

Table 4.7 provides a general macro overview of the working and non-working population of Howrah. The number of household level workers has gone up in recent times, indicating a shift from factory-level jobs to the category of self-employed industrial workers. The female participation rate in the workforce has also increased in the recent past, too. There is a slight drop in the other category of workers over the last two census decades.

As for our survey, a total number of 29 factory workers were interviewed in Howrah out of which five were permanent and the rest were casual. Incidence of causalization is perhaps greater in Howrah than in its twin

Table 4.7 Distribution of working and non-working population at Howrah

	1991			2001		
	Persons	*Male*	*Female*	*Persons*	*Male*	*Female*
Main and marginal	301,592	285,638	15,954	346,984	313,413	33,571
workers	(31.73)	(54.06)	(3.78)	(34.44)	(57.29)	(7.29)
Main workers	299,970	284,476	15,494	330,648	301,836	28,812
	(31.56)	(53.84)	(3.67)	(31.82)	(55.17)	(6.26)
Marginal workers	1,622	1,162	460	16,336	11,577	4,759
	(0.17)	(0.22)	(0.11)	(1.62)	(2.12)	(1.03)
Cultivators*	811	664	147	754	444	310
	(0.27)	(0.23)	(0.92)	(0.22)	(0.14)	(0.92)
Agricultural	1,187	1,122	65	521	425	96
labourers*	(0.39)	(0.39)	(0.41)	(0.15)	(0.14)	(0.29)
Household industry	4,319	3,983	336	9,190	6,940	2,250
workers*	(1.43)	(1.39)	(2.11)	(2.65)	(2.21)	(6.70)
Non-workers	648,843	242,758	406,085	660,548	233,655	426,893
	(68.27)	(45.94)	(65.56)	(65.56)	(42.71)	(92.71)
Other workers*	293,653	278,707	14,946	336,519	305,604	30,915
	(97.37)	(97.57)	(93.68)	(96.98)	(97.51)	(92.09)

Source: Census of India, Government of India, 2001.

Notes: Figures in the parentheses indicate percentage of the particular category in the total population of the area unless otherwise stated.

*Figures in the parentheses indicate the percentage of the concerned category in the total main and marginal working population.

city, Kolkata. Permanent workers enjoy much higher levels of income and job security (as discussed in Chapter 5) as compared to casual workers who are placed at the bottom rung in terms of these attributes. An important feature of the Howrah industrial belt is the influx of labourers from the neighbouring states, namely Bihar and Jharkhand. In our sample of 29 workers, there were 10 migrant workers whose security level (as calculated in Chapter 5) is much lower than those of their non-migrant counterparts. Table 4.8 indicates the major findings of our survey in Howrah.

Local foundry units in Howrah have witnessed stiff competition in recent times from Coimbatore and other places and also from China where production is based on modern technology. Closures of existing units have been frequent with no interest of establishing new industrial plants at the Howrah belt. In Howrah, as in Kolkata, the process of informalization

Table 4.8 Howrah: Industrial structure and labour

	Permanent	Casual	Total
Number of labourers	5	24	29
NIC code of industry groups	27, 35	25, 26, 27, 34, 35	
Age (years)	40.40	27.37	29.62
Wage per month (Rs)	3,824.40	2,142.50	2,432.48
Working hours	8.00	9.08	8.90
Union membership (%)	100	21	34
Experience (years)	18.40	4.58	6.97
Minimum wage level (%)	60	8	17
Skill (%)	100	67	72
Special training (%)	0	33	28
Migration (%)	0	42	34
Education (years)	9.60	8.13	8.38
Average number of earning members	1.20	1.96	1.83
Asset holding (%)	20	17	17
Security index	0.63	0.36	0.41
Income security	0.73	0.24	0.32
Employment security	0.65	0.46	0.49
Job security	0.80	0.60	0.64
Work security	0.48	0.49	0.49
Skill security	1.00	0.51	0.60
Voice representation security	0.25	0.07	0.10
Financial security	0.40	0.11	0.16
Family support security	0.75	0.42	0.47

Source: Authors' calculations based on primary data collected through questionnaire-based field survey of 29 industrial workers in the organized manufacturing industries in Howrah in West Bengal during 2003–06.

within the formal factory space is discernible with a growing number of casual workers who are bereft of any social benefits and are often earning below the basic minimum wage. The labour process here is exploitative with performers of surplus labour getting low wages as necessary labour and the appropriation of surplus labour on the part of the capitalist owner. Wages in many units are actually less than even the statutory minimum wages. If we accept that minimum wages constitute what can be treated as the socially necessary accepted basket of commodities for a labourer, then labourers in many instances are receiving much less than that.

The economic plight of the workers can best be described as those pertaining to 'working poor'—a term often used by many official agencies including the World Bank in the context of the poverty of Third World. The underlying labour process prohibits vertical social movements which demands better education and healthcare facilities for the factory workers which they cannot purchase from the market for obvious reasons. The end result is a huge army of reserve labour who are forced to resort to informal occupations and self-employment as household workers. The utter destitution at the level of their families compels the female members of the households to take to low-paid household jobs without any social dignity. Thus the female members of their household enter the job market out of compulsion, which forces them to accept low-paid jobs in the informal segment of the economy. The double burden of paid jobs and unpaid household works stands for a double exploitation for them with the gender-labour process turning exploitative. Howrah, therefore, testifies a case of labour under stress under competitive capitalism.

Hooghly—A case study of labour under strain

Like Howrah, Hooghly is an old industrial belt, known for jute mills, car production (the only car manufacturing unit of the state is located here), engineering units, textile mills and chemical industries.[9] The total urban area of the district is 198.81 square kilometres of which the survey was conducted in an area of 59.01 square kilometres only which comprise the main industrial areas of the district like Rishra, Serampore, Chinsurah, Konnagar, Uttarpara, Hind Motor and Belur (henceforth, referred to as Hooghly areas). The population of the area was 0.703 million in 2001, which increased from 0.555 million in 1991. The density of the area is 11,929 persons per square kilometre, which is much higher than the district wise density of the urban areas. The sex ratio in 2001 was 895, which rose from 855 in 1991.

We provide in Table 4.9 a macro overview of the working and non-working population in the surveyed areas. It can be seen from the table that there has been a rise in the proportion of the main and marginal workers in the Hooghly district, which in turn is primarily due to the increase in the proportion of marginal workers. Most of the latter are family members of the workers of closed factories who, under strain, have taken to part-time occupations to support the basic need of their families.

Hooghly is unique in the state and elsewhere in India in terms of a fall in the proportion of other categories of workers and non-workers. Female participation as main workers exhibited noticeable increases between 1991 and 2001. There has also been an absolute increase in the household category, of self-employed workforce although they constitute only 1.89 per cent of the main and marginal categories of workers. The reason behind this is the outsourcing of factory jobs and closure of many old enterprises including a number of jute mills, textile mills and the Dunlop Rubber Factory. Among the household workers female percentage has gone up significantly, thus indicating a higher labour force participation rate for women.

Table 4.9 Distribution of working and non-working population at Hooghly

	1991			2001		
	Persons	Male	Female	Persons	Male	Female
Main and marginal workers	161,843 (29.15)	148,696 (49.68)	13,147 (5.14)	234,108 (33.26)	200,123 (53.87)	33,985 (10.22)
Main workers	161,389 (29.07)	148,373 (49.58)	13,016 (5.09)	216,843 (30.81)	188,668 (50.79)	28,175 (8.48)
Marginal workers	454 (0.08)	323 (0.11)	131 (0.05)	17,265 (2.45)	11,455 (3.08)	5,810 (1.75)
Cultivators*	41 (0.03)	39 (0.03)	2 (0.015)	474 (0.20)	290 (0.14)	184 (0.54)
Agricultural labourers*	50 (0.03)	43 (0.03)	7 (0.053)	370 (0.16)	266 (0.16)	104 (0.31)
Household industry workers*	279 (0.17)	213 (0.14)	66 (0.50)	4,416 (1.89)	2,414 (1.21)	2,002 (5.89)
Non-workers	393,274 (70.85)	150,586 (50.32)	242,688 (94.86)	469,800 (66.74)	171,374 (46.13)	298,426 (89.78)
Other workers*	161,017 (99.49)	148,077 (99.58)	12,940 (98.43)	228,541 (97.62)	196,915 (98.40)	31,626 (93.06)

Source: Census of India, Government of India, 2001.

Notes: Figures in the parentheses indicate percentage of the particular category in the total population of the area unless otherwise stated.
*Figures in the parentheses indicate the percentage of the concerned category in the total main and marginal working population.

We interviewed 19 workers in our survey of the Hooghly area. Of these, 16 are permanent and three casual. These workers are engaged in the food and beverages industry (NIC code 15), chemical (NIC code 24) and motor vehicle industry (NIC code 34). The incidence of casualization is generally high here as well although in our sample we had very few casual workers. Due to the dominance of permanent workers in our sample Hooghly was ahead of other areas in terms of the ranking of labour security, and in particular of income security. But disparity has been quite significant between permanent and casual workers even within this rather biased sample. We provide in Table 4.10 the major findings of our survey of the Hooghly district.

In Hooghly district a major closure of industry took place with the closing down of Dunlop India Limited which was the biggest tyre factory of Asia providing employment to more than 4,000 workers.[10] A sample survey of 100 retrenched workers in a separate study indicates that the workers losing jobs took to informal activities like vending, rickshaw pulling and

Table 4.10 Hooghly: Industrial structure and labour

	Permanent	*Casual*	*Total*
Number of labourers	16	3	19
NIC code of industry groups	15, 24, 34	24	
Age (years)	37.81	24.67	35.74
Wage per month (Rs)	4,545.31	1,950.00	4,135.53
Working hours	8.13	8.67	8.21
Union membership (%)	100	0	84
Experience (years)	18.06	3.33	15.74
Minimum wage level (%)	87	0	74
Skill (%)	81	67	79
Special training (%)	13	33	16
Migration (%)	0	0	0
Education (years)	10.31	10.67	10.37
Average number of earning members	1.56	2.33	1.68
Asset holding (%)	13	0	11
Security index	0.69	0.31	0.63
Income security	0.94	0.17	0.82
Employment security	0.66	0.50	0.63
Job security	0.87	0.50	0.82
Work security	0.53	0.60	0.54
Skill security	0.98	0.56	0.91
Voice representation security	0.59	0.00	0.50
Financial security	0.38	0.11	0.33
Family support security	0.56	0.08	0.49

Source: Authors' calculations based on the information gathered through primary survey during 2004–05.

low-paid household work (Basu unpublished). While workers blamed incompetent management for the closure of this giant tyre factory in Asia, the management put the blame on rigidity of the trade unions in accepting the proposals of the management.[11] But as noted by Dutt (2003), '...it was the incompetent management which was responsible for the sad state of affairs of the company. The company declared a lockout to cover its inefficiency as also to bring about downsizing of the labour force' (p. 175). Increased female participation in non-wage jobs, pertaining mainly to the household type, was visible in their distress. The sufferings may increase further as Hind Motor, a big car manufacturing unit in the area, has already decided to shift its production base to the automobile cluster of Gurgaon in North India.

Of the 19 workers interviewed, five had basic education (up to class VII), seven had secondary level, six intermediary level and one graduate levels of education. In terms of this specific sample, education explains the gap between workers in terms of income security levels. Of workers in our sample fifteen were skilled and they enjoyed higher income security than their unskilled counterparts. We did not have a single migrant worker in our sample even though the area is full of migrant workers from the neighbouring states of Bihar and Jharkhand. Sixteen workers in our sample were union members and the gap between unionized and non-unionized worker in terms of our income security index is also quite high (see Chapter 5 of this book for details).

A major finding of this survey and especially in the context of Dunlop India Limited corroborates the fact that conditions of the retrenched workers have turned out to be vulnerable due to the ratchet effect which is visible in their consumption spending. Thus their income has gone down without their consumption coming down commensurately. Some of them even have negative average savings. These workers neither have a fixed employer–employee relationship nor can they obtain statutory social security benefits. Nor do they have bargaining power, with the lack of voice representation and the ineffectiveness of trade unions in the process. They live and work in an unhygienic condition. Persistent poverty, insecurity, uncertainty and disease syndromes have pushed families to all kinds of informal jobs after the loss of formal employment in factories. Also it has led them to indebtedness to meet their day-to-day contingencies.

The emerging pattern of informal economic activities witnessed in the area are characterized by the following features: small scale of operation in terms of these activities, reliance on family members and informal sources of credit at onerous terms, low endowment of capital, use of labour intensive technology, limited barriers to entry, high degrees of competition and low skill formation due to lack of financial resources. The strain continues and gets amplified further as there are more closures, outsourcing and casualization.

Kalyani—A case study of labour under deindustrialization

Kalyani, located 50 kilometres north-east of Kolkata, was developed as an industrial township by the first elected state government after independence in 1947. The area of the township now covers 21.91 square kilometres with a population of 8.23 million as per the 2001 Census which rose from 5.55 million in 1991. The density stands at 3,749 persons per square kilometre with the sex ratio being 957 in 2001 increasing from 927 in 1991.

Table 4.11 provides a macro overview of the town concerning its working population as can be found in the Census for 2001. Of its population 32 per cent constitutes the main and marginal workforce which includes the 46.31 per cent of the total male population and 12.15 per cent of the

Table 4.11 **Distribution of working and non-working population at Kalyani**

	1991			2001		
	Persons	Male	Female	Persons	Male	Female
Main and marginal	15,231	13,245	2,076	26,571	20,748	5,823
workers	(27.57)	(45.92)	(7.76)	(32.35)	(49.44)	(14.50)
Main workers	15,264	13,225	2,039	24,315	19,434	4,881
	(27.46)	(45.85)	(7.63)	(29.60)	(46.31)	(12.15)
Marginal workers	57	20	37	2,256	1,314	942
	(0.10)	(0.07)	(0.14)	(2.75)	(3.13)	(2.35)
Cultivators*	367	326	41	99	64	35
	(2.40)	(2.46)	(1.97)	(0.37)	(0.31)	(0.60)
Agricultural	2,176	1,999	177	340	287	53
labourers*	(14.20)	(15.09)	(8.53)	(1.28)	(1.38)	(0.91)
Household industry	325	259	66	471	260	211
workers*	(2.12)	(1.96)	(3.18)	(1.77)	(1.25)	(3.62)
Non-workers	40,258	15,598	24,660	55,564	21,218	34,346
	(72.43)	(54.08)	(92.24)	(67.75)	(50.56)	(85.50)
Other workers*	12,396	10,641	1,755	25,661	20,137	5,524
	(80.91)	(80.34)	(84.54)	(96.58)	(97.06)	(94.87)

Source: Census of India, Government of India, 2001.

Notes: Figures in the parentheses indicate percentage of the particular category in the total population of the area unless otherwise stated.

*Figures in the parentheses indicate the percentage of the concerned category in the total main and marginal working population.

female population. There has been a marginal rise in male workforce since the Census in 1991. Almost 97 per cent of the total main and marginal workforce belongs to the other worker category implying the diversity of odd jobs they take to eke out their daily livelihood. Over the last decade there has not been any perceptible change in the share for the household category of workers. A significant number of household workers and dislocated factory workers are with informal services, which include rickshaw pulling, vending by males and paid household jobs of non-wage type by females.

Kalyani is one of the few planned townships in the state which was developed just after Independence. As indicated earlier, it was built in the decade of the 1950s as a model industrial hub in proximity to Kolkata. However, the story of Kalyani as an industrial township remained a failure as the project never took off to the heights as was envisaged, largely due to poor infrastructural facilities including a lack of proper transportation. By the time we went for the survey only a handful of industrial units, including a prominent beer manufacturing unit, were operational and other industries had already left. Industrial estates today resemble the picture of a ghost town or a war-ravaged place which is abandoned by their occupiers, only to be used by social hoodlums.

As Table 4.11 indicates, the proportion of main and marginal workers in Kalyani went up during 1991–2001 as per the Census findings with the rise being most prominent among the female population entering the labour force. Note that during this period there has been a significant drop in cultivators and agricultural labourers as a proportion of main and marginal workers in the area. The major aspiration of the labour force in the area has been, from the beginning, to find jobs in factories. However, even household workers as a proportion of the main and marginal workers has gone down, which is unlike what it is in other areas of our survey. But closures of prominent factories in the area have reduced the scope for employment in factories as well, especially for entry-level workers—a fact which we came across in the course of our casual chatting with the young population and union activists in the area. Uncertainty, especially in terms of the high probability of losing permanent factory jobs, looms large among those who are in employment in these factories over a considerable period of time. As a result of these factors, there has been a significant increase in *other* workers as proportion of total main and marginal workers in the area. These include workers engaged in services, apart from the regular and casual factory-based workers.

Table 4.12 indicates the major findings of our survey at Kalyani, which are discussed in the following.

Table 4.12 Kalyani: Industrial structure and labour

	Permanent	Casual	Total
Number of labourers	34	57	121
NIC code of industry groups	15, 17, 21, 24, 25, 26, 27, 28, 29, 31	15, 21, 24, 25, 27, 31	
Age (years)	41.06	31.56	36.59
Wage per month (Rs)	4,069.50	1,965.33	3,078.28
Working hours	8.25	8.56	8.40
Union membership (%)	0.95	0.32	0.65
Experience (years)	16.73	5.56	11.47
Minimum wage level (%)	55	2	30
Skill (%)	91	75	83
Special training (%)	0.08	0.05	0.07
Migration (%)	31	18	25
Education (years)	8.27	9.18	8.69
Average number of earning members	1.44	1.72	1.57
Asset holding (%)	33	18	26
Security index	0.65	0.44	0.55
Income security	0.81	0.29	0.56
Employment security	0.54	0.44	0.49
Job security	0.84	0.65	0.75
Work security	0.44	0.44	0.44
Skill security	0.94	0.80	0.87
Voice representation security	0.56	0.21	0.40
Financial security	0.55	0.23	0.40
Family support security	0.54	0.43	0.49

Source: Authors' Calculations based on the information gathered through primary survey during 2004–05.

Not more than 100 small and tiny units were operational when we went for the survey during 2004–05. Altogether we interviewed 121 factory workers engaged in 20 different units including the beer factory we mentioned earlier. One of the main reasons of setting up the township in Kalyani, which is now famous because of a state-level university, was the availability of cheap labour from the nearby rural hinterland. Besides, the town today has large numbers of immigrants from Bangladesh.

Of the 121 labourers in our sample, 63 had basic education, 22 had secondary and 12 intermediary-level education, eight were graduates, 15 just literate and one completely illiterate. As for skill, 101 persons had some skill, having access to special training and on-the-job training, while the remaining 20 were totally unskilled. Thirty were migrant labourers and the rest non-migrants. In Kalyani, migrant labourers have fared well in terms of all the categories of securities—income, job, skill and social, which is not the case elsewhere in our field study. Possibly the reason behind this lies in the fact that the migrant labourers here are all skilled and the demand for skilled labour in the industrial units is also high. The above possibly explains the fact that migrant workers fare relatively well as compared to their non-migrant counterparts. Of the 121 labourers in our sample, 79 were union members who belonged to the major central trade union in the state. The presence of other trade unions in the area is quite thin but at the same time it is found that unionized workers were relatively better off than their non-unionized counterparts.

As stated in the beginning, Kalyani remains a story of an unfulfilled project with the dream of an industrial township. Industries which came initially started leaving way back in the 1970s. One major reason cited by many trade unionists and firm managements in our interview was the fact that many industrial units were set up at Kalyani to take advantage of certain governmental policy packages including easy availability of bank credit. Prior to the concept of export processing or SEZs the government had certain policy packages for setting up industries in industrial estates like Kalyani. Entrepreneurs took advantage of those subsidies and availed of cheap credit. Later, they took similar advantage of the Board of Industrial Finance and Restructuring (BIFR) route by declaring their units as sick. By this device they could transfer the finance elsewhere (and in most cases outside the state). Firm management, however, cited labour militancy as the major reason for industries closing down in Kalyani during the 1970s and 1980s. However, records of local labour organizations indicate that incidences of militant labour agitations and strikes were quite nominal in the area since the inception of the Kalyani Industrial Estate in the 1950s. The fact, however, remains that many enterprises used the BIFR route to escape and make money, thus leaving the local labour in jeopardy. Investment in the area came in search of capital accumulation but accumulated capital was withdrawn from the place thus denying reinvestment. Outward flight of invested capital in manufacturing activities in the area resulted in significant sectoral shifts of labour from manufacturing to non-manufacturing activities which fetched them much lower earnings. The reasons for such withdrawals, however, were not confined to labour problems alone.

Kalyani industrial estate today remains a story of deindustrialization of diverse modern manufacturing units, which were set up and later followed by the fleeing of capital. Capital accumulated was never re-invested while even the original capital abandoned the site. As a consequence the status of the working population also changed from industrial wage labour to the ranks of a reserve army of labour, who mostly adhered to informal occupations as 'self-employed'. The category, found in official databases, actually misrepresents the true plight of the labouring person by super-ficially dignifying the labour status of the workers.

In our total sample for Kalyani, 57 were casual workers and 64 were permanent. The permanent workers fared better in terms of income, job, skill reproduction and social security as compared to the casual workers. As elsewhere in the country, the phenomenon of casualization has struck the industrial units in Kalyani. Many small units, facing stiff competition from low-priced imported goods under the import liberalization policies of the 1990s found it difficult to compete. While the need for technological improvements was felt widely, bank finance was not easily available to meet the cost of technological upgrading. (The above has particularly been the case with the introduction of the new Basel capital adequacy norms in Indian banks since 1998 [Sen and Ghosh 2005].) Also technological improvement with cost-effective increases in labour productivity entails less job creation and it is the local labour that bears the brunt. Factories which fail to go for technological upgradation in order to withstand foreign or domestic competition (from large firms enjoying economies of scale) either close down or shift their activities elsewhere and in other production lines. Availability of institutional finance along with better infrastructural facilities might have saved the situation. Even with recent government initiatives for industrial revival of the state, new enterprises are not showing ample interest in Kalyani. So, in the end Kalyani remains a lost story—a case of unique deindustrialization, paving the way for rising social and economic problems in the area. One way the interest of the area and that of the workers could have been protected was if the foreign companies with whom the State Government was negotiating to attract FDI in the state, could have been told to set up their ventures in Kalyani and as a location close to Kolkata (only 50 kilometres away and with space and infrastructure necessary for industries already existing), many foreign or domestic companies might show interest.[12] That would, otherwise, avoid impending eviction of farming people from their farmland and place of habitation.

Murshidabad (*bidi* or tobacco manufacture) industry—A case study of labour under super-exploitation

The field survey in this area is based on the information gathered for *bidi*-making in a tiny town called Aurangabad in the district of Murshidabad.

Aurangabad is a small town with a geographical area of 2.77 square kilometres only. There are around 100 factories in this town, and the largest occupation has been *bidi*-making. The population of this town as per the 2001 Census is 32,148, which rose from 25,861 in 1991 with a decadal growth rate of 24.31 per cent. The male and female populations are evenly distributed with male population at 16,024 and the female population at 16,124. The sex ratio is high with 1,006 females per 1,000 males. Murshidabad is one of the few districts in the country where the sex ratio is quite high, possibly due to the skill the girls acquire at an early age as *bidi* workers, a skill considered valuable by the industry.

Almost 90 per cent of the population in Aurangabad are engaged directly and indirectly for their livelihood on *bidi*-making. *Bidi*-making in the district of Murshidabad of West Bengal has evolved through the last one hundred years as the most predominant industrial activity of the area. In terms of a rough estimate around 2.0 million people are engaged in *bidi*-making which is largely an unorganized activity. Only a part of the final processing takes place within factory space.

Bidi-making entails a special type of labour process which is worth pinpointing. We will deal with the salient features of the labour process in an effort to understand the underlying class process which sets the dynamics of appropriation and distribution of the surplus labour.

As in other sections of this chapter, we start with a macro view of the working population in Table 4.13. As is evident from the table, there is a high incidence of household industry workers in the area which constitutes 75 per cent of the total main and marginal workers. Out of this, the female participation as household workers constitutes 95 per cent of the total female main and marginal workforce. The point merits attention as we can see in the context of the significance of female labour in the *bidi*-making' labour process of the area.

We provide, in the Appendix to this chapter, the details relating to the structure of the *bidi* industry in Murshidabad. These include the stages of the production process, the underlying labour process, the appropriation of surpluses by different agents, etc.

Details as are provided in the Appendix on the *bidi*-making process from the point of view of performance and appropriation of surplus labour, à la Marx, generate the following observations:

1. Payments towards the socially necessary accepted labour time (SNALT) for the majority of the household workers, who happen to be female, are mostly below the official rate. Thus, a worker does

Table 4.13 Distribution of working and non-working
population at Murshidabad

	1991			2001		
	Persons	Male	Female	Persons	Male	Female
Main and marginal	10,889	6,475	4,414	15,722	8,198	7,524
workers	(42.11)	(49.75)	(34.99)	(48.91)	(51.16)	(46.66)
Main workers	10,227	6,450	3,777	13,617	7,636	5,981
	(39.55)	(49.38)	(29.51)	(42.36)	(47.65)	(37.09)
Marginal workers	662	25	637	2,105	562	1,543
	(2.56)	(0.19)	(4.98)	(6.55)	(3.51)	(9.57)
Cultivators*	62	60	2	10	8	2
	(0.57)	(0.93)	(0.05)	(0.06)	(0.10)	(0.03)
Agricultural	226	218	8	15	10	5
labourers*	(2.06)	(3.37)	(0.18)	(0.10)	(0.12)	(0.07)
Household industry	4,786	2,427	2,359	11,940	4,736	7,204
workers*	(43.95)	(37.48)	(53.44)	(75.94)	(57.77)	(95.75)
Non-workers	14,972	6,587	8,385	16,426	7,826	8,600
	(57.89)	(50.43)	(65.51)	(51.09)	(48.24)	(53.34)
Other workers*	5,153	3,745	1,408	3,757	3,444	313
	(47.32)	(57.84)	(31.90)	(23.90)	(42.01)	(4.16)

Source: Census of India, Government of India, 2001.
Notes: Figures in the parentheses indicate percentage of the particular category in the total population of the area unless otherwise stated.
*Figures in the parentheses indicate the percentage of the concerned category in the total main and marginal working population.

not even receive the return for her necessary labour, which is at par with the statutory fixation of the minimum wages by the state. This indicates super-exploitation in the labour process.

2. From the Appendix one can identify the different stages in the distribution of the surplus generated by the production process. These include *(a)* the performer who is usually the female worker within the households receiving the entire payments from the *munshi*s or the intermediaries; *(b)* the male household member who receives and hence appropriates the surplus under patriarchy; *(c)* the intermediaries or the *munshi*s who provide the necessary conditions of existence to the producers. It is possible for a *munshi* to occupy another subsumed class position too as a merchant, as he often sells *bidi*s directly to the market. This is possible as he retains all the rejected *bidi*s from the direct producers (the household labourers). He receives commission from the capitalist owner and also, can make some surplus out of the quality control exercise

mentioned earlier; *(d)* the factory owner who extends the size of the surplus appropriated from production by misrepresenting the liabilities as PF and other fiscal dues.

3. The gender process occupies an important position in *bidi*-making. There is even a social conditioning in terms of which marriage can be ensured when girls are proficient in good quality *bidi*-making. Of course no such qualification is needed for the grooms. Besides, the double burden of female household workers is a case in point. The result is a gendered-labour process which is intertwined in the *bidi*-making town of Aurangabad. This also probably explains the relatively better sex ratio in this district.

4. The distribution of surplus labour takes place at different levels. The stakeholders include the state[13] (in the form of cess, excise duties, etc.) to provide the necessary law and order conditions to the owners; the intermediaries (the *munshis*) who organize production at households; other finance capitalists which include banks and moneylenders to provide necessary finance for production; and lastly, those who provide raw materials on credit. There is a huge accumulation of surplus by the owners, a fragment of which goes as distribution of social surplus to sustain the exploitative labour process and further accumulation of surplus. Distribution of social surplus occurs in different forms. But the most prominent and pronounced one is for a religious cause in building mosques or temples, and catering to the religious needs of the area. Thus religion and surplus labour generation process in a sense are linked as religiosity demands loyalty to the masters. Owners also distribute a portion of the social surplus for buildings and maintaining schools, hospitals and charitable medical units. All these help them to build a social base in their kingdom for control over their subjects—the direct producers.

National Capital Region of Delhi—A case study of labour under a globalized environment

In the National Capital Region of Delhi seven industrial areas were surveyed (excluding the NSEZ) and a total of 175 workers were interviewed. The areas include East Delhi, Mayapuri and Okhla in Delhi, Faridabad and Gurgaon in Haryana and Ghaziabad and NOIDA (Greater) in Uttar Pradesh.

Of the areas surveyed, Mayapuri, Okhla and East Delhi are the old industrial areas of Delhi whereas Gurgaon, Faridabad and NOIDA are the new ones. The main focus of the survey was to investigate the inter-relations between market demand and the competitive pressure faced by the firms, their sales, profits and technical changes experienced in the recent past and the changes in the labour processes in terms of wage and labour contracts and work conditions. Table 4.14 indicates the area-wise break-up of total number and category of workers surveyed in different industries. In our sample, we have a higher proportion of permanent workers than that of casual workers. However, during our survey we also observed that casualization is very common in these areas.

Table 4.14 National Capital Region of Delhi: Industrial structure and labour

Area	Total Workers Surveyed	Permanent	Casual	NIC Code of Industry Groups
Gurgaon	11	11		15, 18, 24, 25, 34
Faridabad	8	6	2	18, 19, 24, 27, 28
Ghaziabad	5	5		31
NOIDA	58	16	42	17, 18, 19, 21, 24, 25, 31, 34
Mayapuri	41	30	11	17, 18, 22, 24, 25, 27, 28, 29, 31, 34, 36
Okhla	38	19	19	18, 21, 22, 24, 25, 31, 34
East Delhi	14	9	5	15, 18, 22, 25, 27, 28, 31, 34
Total	175	122	53	

Source: Authors' calculations based on primary data collected through questionnaire-based field survey of 29 industrial workers in the organized manufacturing industries in Delhi (including NOIDA) during 2003–06.

NOIDA (Greater)

In the NOIDA area 58 workers had been interviewed of which 16 were permanent and 42 were casual. We visited 16 factories. Turnovers of these units ranged from an annual Rs 60 million to Rs 440 million. Information provided by the firm management, as can be expected, varied from what we obtained from the workers. Casualization was common with firms showing clear preferences for casual recruitments. Garments and home furnishing units employed large proportions of workers on a non-regular basis, a regular supply of which was provided by labour contractors. Wage rates reported by the casual workers were below the minimum wage rates of the area in the respective industries. Existence of a large reserve army of labour even in this urban area seems to be the main reason for a visible wage depression in the area. Because of mass unemployment and non-availability of alternative means of survival, these workers are ready to work at wages below the statutory minimum rate and the female workers receive even less, as compared to their male counterparts. Piece rate wage payment system was in vogue in some units. Casual workers obtained their payments from the firm through their respective contractors. Companies also pay commission to the labour contractors on these recruitments and companies maintained no records for the non-regular workers. During our survey we met some non-regular workers who were carrying identity cards provided by the labour contractor. That card however, did not bear any information about the labour contractor or the firm. It carried only personal information of the workers. Most of the workers were migrants from Eastern UP, Bihar and West Bengal. In our sample, there were 52 migrant labourers and their security level, in terms of our calculation is found to be significantly lower than those for their non-migrant counterparts, who are six in number in our sample.

Table 4.15 NOIDA: Industrial structure and labour

	Permanent	Casual	Total
Number of labourers	16	42	58
NIC code of industry groups	17, 18, 19, 21, 24, 31, 34	17, 18, 19, 21, 24, 25, 31, 34	
Age (years)	27.31	26.83	26.97
Wage per month (Rs)	4,759.88	2,480.55	3,109.33
Working hours	9.00	9.00	9.00
Union membership (%)	0	81	59
Experience (years)	4.28	2.15	2.74
Minimum wage level (%)	63	7	22
Skill (%)	94	74	79
Special training (%)	19	12	14
Migration (%)	94	88	90
Education (years)	9.44	9.64	9.59
Average number of earning members	1.50	1.64	1.60
Asset holding (%)	56	29	36
Security index	0.46	0.34	0.37
Income security	0.60	0.13	0.26
Employment security	0.50	0.50	0.50
Job security	0.25	0.50	0.43
Work security	0.54	0.48	0.49
Skill security	0.67	0.33	0.43
Voice representation security	0.13	0.27	0.23
Financial security	0.60	0.21	0.32
Family support security	0.38	0.27	0.30

Source: Authors' calculations based on primary data collected through questionnaire-based field survey of 29 industrial workers in the organized manufacturing industries in NOIDA in Uttar Pradesh during 2005.

Note: All percentages in this table relate to the share of respective population.

Trade unions have some degree of presence in the area. However, the rate of unionization happens to be low as workers fear that they will lose their jobs if they are members of a union, which differs from the situation prevailing in West Bengal. Of the 58 workers we had interviewed, 34 were union members and their job security is more than the non-union members, although with a much lower income security.

The fundamental class process here, as elsewhere, is exploitative with surplus labour being appropriated by the owner and labour contractor holding the subsumed class position for providing the arrangements for the creation of surpluses for the owner. Labourers, who are the direct producers, receive low wages which are even below the statutory level of minimum wages in the case of casual labour.

Delhi

Survey areas in Delhi covered East Delhi, Mayapuri and Okhla—all of which are old industrial belts. The impact of globalization, however, is very much visible in the area with new garment units, set up in large numbers, catering to the export markets. However, in recent times many units have shifted their production base to neighbouring states with relatively favourable cost conditions which arise from favourable state government policies.

We interviewed a total of 93 workers in the Delhi area who had been working in diverse industries (Tables 4.16A, 4.16B and 4.16C). Casualization has been a common phenomenon here. These non-regular workers are employed by a labour contractor or recruited directly on a temporary basis for a specific time period. Firms generally re-employ casual workers after giving them a break every six months, thus saving money. Wage payments are made on a monthly basis, daily basis or on a piece rate basis. No increment in wages has been made in the recent past, and only some revision in wages seems to have been done. Non-regular workers receive wages which are even below the minimum wage rates in the area. Permanent workers are also not happy with their work conditions and wage payments which have not been subject to any increment in recent times. Wage rates varied between Rs 1,500 and Rs 3,600 per month across firms for permanent workers. Workers, both regular and non-regular, were migrants from eastern Uttar Pradesh, Bihar and West Bengal. Of the 93 workers in our sample as many as 89 were migrants. As for union membership, only 33 workers were members of some union or the other. But these unionized workers appeared to fare better on security scoring over the non-unionized members.

Table 4.16A   East Delhi: Industrial structure and labour

	Permanent	Casual	Total
Number of labourers	9	5	14
NIC code of industry groups	15, 28, 22, 27, 34	15, 25, 28, 31	
Age (years)	33.78	27.80	31.64
Wage per month (Rs)	2,716.22	2,160.00	2,517.57
Working hours	9.00	9.00	9.00
Union membership (%)	44	80	0.57
Experience (years)	9.94	4.05	7.84
Minimum wage level (%)	22	0	14
Skill (%)	89	60	79
Special training (%)	0	00	0
Migration (%)	1.00	100	100
Education (years)	7.11	6.80	7.00
Average number of earning members	1.56	1.60	1.57
Asset holding (%)	22	20	21
Security index	0.37	0.33	0.36
Income security	0.57	0.07	0.39
Employment security	0.50	0.50	0.50
Job security	0.22	0.50	0.32
Work security	0.37	0.30	0.34
Skill security	0.67	0.33	0.55
Voice representation security	0.17	0.35	0.23
Financial security	0.15	0.27	0.19
Family support security	0.33	0.30	0.32

Source: Authors' calculations based on primary data collected through questionnaire-based field survey of 14 industrial workers in the organized manufacturing industries in East Delhi industrial area in Delhi during 2004.

Faridabad

Faridabad is a new industrial area in the National Capital Region. The workers we could interview were engaged in wearing apparel (NIC code 18), leather (19), chemicals (24), basic metal (27) and fabricated metal (28) (Table 4.17). Faridabad is a place where the industries cater to both domestic as well as the international market with a large number of new industries coming up. A major factor behind, apart from the infrastructural facilities, is the availability of cheap migrant labour.

In Faridabad we could only survey two industrial units producing footwear. With respective annual turnovers of Rs 220 million and Rs 450 million the number of workers employed varied between the two firms, with the first engaging 260 workers and the second 600. Wages in the first firm, as reported by the managers, were between Rs 3,286 and Rs 4,825 per month for skilled workers and Rs 2,860 for the unskilled. For the second firm

Table 4.16B   Mayapuri: Industrial structure and labour

	Permanent	Casual	Total
Number of labourers	30	11	41
NIC code of industry groups	22, 24, 27, 28,	17, 18, 22,	
	29, 31, 34	25, 27, 36	
Age (years)	35.20	30.36	33.90
Wage per month (Rs)	3,128.90	2,274.82	2,899.76
Working hours	9.00	9.00	9.00
Union membership (%)	0	45	12
Experience (years)	12.38	2.66	9.77
Minimum wage level (%)	30	18	27
Skill (%)	93	91	93
Special training (%)	0	0	0
Migration (%)	90	100	93
Education (years)	9.03	8.64	8.93
Average number of earning members	1.53	1.82	1.61
Asset holding (%)	43	18	37
Security index	0.40	0.29	0.37
Income security	0.56	0.17	0.45
Employment security	0.50	0.50	0.50
Job security	0.23	0.50	0.30
Work security	0.44	0.43	0.44
Skill security	0.67	0.33	0.58
Voice representation security	0.11	0.16	0.12
Financial security	0.32	0.12	0.27
Family support security	0.35	0.14	0.29

Source: Authors' calculations based on primary data collected through questionnaire-based field survey of 41 industrial workers in the organized manufacturing industries in Mayapuri in Delhi during 2005.

with 600 workers wages were paid on a daily basis, both for the skilled and the unskilled. As reported by managers in both units, non-regular workers were very few in number. There were hardly any professionally qualified workers in either firm and female labour was employed only for packaging and final processing. As for the presence of trade unions the managers indicated that these do exist but there seemed to be no problem in terms of labour disputes. They also reported that the workers seem to be happy with working conditions. Also, the benefits (PF, bonus, etc.) are paid on an equal basis to both temporary and casual workers. However, the owner–managers mentioned the increased competition they were facing with liberalization.

In Faridabad we could interview only eight workers. This was due to the difficulties which were typical in these interviews. The workers were

Table 4.16C   Okhla: Industrial structure and labour

	Permanent	Casual	Total
Number of labourers	19	19	38
NIC code of industry groups	28, 22, 24, 31, 34	18, 21, 25, 31	
Age (years)	33.84	29.32	31.58
Wage per month (Rs)	3,345.00	2,913.84	3,129.42
Working hours	9.00	9.00	9.00
Union membership (%)	5	100	53
Experience (years)	7.42	1.49	4.45
Minimum wage level (%)	47	37	42
Skill (%)	68	74	71
Special training (%)	11	0	5
Migration (%)	100	95	97
Education (years)	9.53	8.95	9.24
Average number of earning members	1.63	1.63	1.63
Asset holding (%)	84	89	87
Security index	0.45	0.39	0.42
Income security	0.53	0.08	0.30
Employment security	0.50	0.50	0.50
Job security	0.26	0.50	0.38
Work security	0.46	0.40	0.43
Skill security	0.67	0.33	0.50
Voice representation security	0.22	0.47	0.35
Financial security	0.65	0.60	0.62
Family support security	0.28	0.28	0.28

Source: Authors' calculations based on primary data collected through questionnaire-based field survey of 41 industrial workers in the organized manufacturing industries in the Okhla industrial belt in Delhi during 2004.

reluctant to talk to our team out of fear. Moreover, when the team reached the spots they were constantly under watch by the firm managements so that the workers could hardly talk to us. We could somehow manage to speak to eight workers outside the factories in the absence of both firm managers and union leaders. The education levels of the workers varied from basic to graduate level which, in terms of our calculation, affected their security levels as well. Five workers in our sample were migrants and their security levels were lower than those for non-migrant workers in the sample. Two workers in our sample were union members and enjoyed a higher job security than the non-unionized members.

We got the impression that working conditions were bad, from the few labourers we could interview. The labour process here is exploitative to a degree which is quite high with a denial of even the basic minimum wages in many cases.

Table 4.17 Faridabad: Industrial structure and labour

	Permanent	Casual	Total
Number of labourers	6	2	8
NIC code of industry groups	18, 19, 24, 27	27, 28	
Age (years)	36.00	35.50	35.88
Wage per month (Rs)	5,733.33	3,550.00	5,187.50
Working hours	9.00	9.00	9.00
Union membership (%)	0	100	25
Experience (years)	11.00	5.50	9.63
Minimum wage level (%)	83	50	75
Skill (%)	100	100	100
Special training (%)	17	0	13
Migration (%)	67	50	63
Education (years)	10.83	9.00	10.38
Average number of earning members	1.33	1.50	1.38
Asset holding (%)	0.67	1.00	0.75
Security index	0.51	0.41	0.48
Income security	0.64	0.08	0.50
Employment security	0.50	0.50	0.50
Job security	0.25	0.50	0.31
Work security	0.60	0.45	0.56
Skill security	0.67	0.33	0.58
Voice representation security	0.13	0.50	0.22
Financial security	0.72	0.67	0.71
Family support security	0.54	0.25	0.47

Source: Authors' calculations based on primary data collected through questionnaire-based field survey of 41 industrial workers in the organized manufacturing industries in the Faridabad industrial belt in Uttar Pradesh during 2005.

Gurgaon

In Gurgaon we surveyed 10 industrial units at random (Table 4.18). But for three units, all others had annual turnovers between Rs 10 and Rs 850 million. Of the latter, the manufactured leather garments units, which also were 100 per cent export-oriented, had established markets in USA and Europe. Firms here encounter stable market conditions while employing varied proportions of non-regular to regular workers. However, increased market competition was reported due to new entries of firms in both domestic as well as in foreign markets, especially with Chinese exporters as their main competitor. Cost of production was found rising with the increasing costs of raw material, transportation and electricity. The firms here reported stable market conditions while employing varied proportions of regular to non-regular workers; the latter recruited through

Table 4.18   Gurgaon: Industrial structure and labour

	Permanent	Casual	Total
Number of labourers	11		11
NIC code of industry groups	15, 18, 24, 25, 34		
Age (years)	28.73		28.73
Wage per month (Rs)	4,717.18		4,717.18
Working hours	9.00		9.00
Union membership (%)	0.00		0
Experience (years)	4.05		4.05
Minimum wage level (%)	64		64
Skill (%)	45		45
Special training (%)	27		27
Migration (%)	27		27
Education (years)	11.00		11.00
Average number of earning members	1.18		1.18
Asset holding (%)	64		64
Security index	0.49		0.49
Income security	0.59		0.59
Employment security	0.50		0.50
Job security	0.27		0.27
Work security	0.54		0.54
Skill security	0.67		0.67
Voice representation security	0.16		0.16
Financial security	0.55		0.55
Family support security			

Source: Authors' calculations based on primary data collected through questionnaire-based
field survey of 11 industrial workers in the organized manufacturing industries in
Gurgaon in Haryana during 2005–06.

contractors or through local contacts. Wages are set according to the skill differentials and job experience. All firms in the automobile hub employed large numbers of professionally qualified diploma engineers or ITI diploma holders with wage rates varying between Rs 6,000 and Rs 13,000 per month, both for permanent and casual workers. Wage rates for non-professional workers, generally employed for packaging work, were between Rs 2,500 and Rs 3,500 per month. Female workers, non-existent in the automobile units, are employed in small numbers only in leather goods manufacturing units. ESI, PF and bonuses are provided to all the workers and extra benefits like gratuity, earned leave and casual leave, were also granted to the permanent workers. Working conditions, as reported by managers, remained the same for both regular and non-regular workers.

In Gurgaon, altogether 11 workers were interviewed who were spread over five different industries. These include food and beverages (NIC code 15), wearing apparel (18), chemical (24), rubber and plastic (25) and motor vehicles (34). Wage rates in automobile industries had been relatively higher than what it was in other industries for skilled workers. Industries, other than automobiles, pay below minimum wage rates to casual and female workers. Three workers in our sample had basic education, four had secondary education, one had higher secondary education and three were graduates. The security levels, as we have calculated, varied according to education level. Skilled workers enjoy a higher level of security. Three workers in our sample were migrants with lower security levels.

None of the members in our sample is a union member. However, union presence in the large automobile industry is quite strong, as the labour agitation in the Hero Honda factory in 2005 against casualization of the workforce and increase in working hours, indicates. Perhaps, this remained so far the largest labour agitation in the organized manufacturing sector and that too in a multinational company in the post-reform years, which reflects the dissent within the labouring community, particularly those who are in organized manufacturing, regarding growing labour flexibility and throttling of labour rights. In fact, labour flexibility in large units, domestic or foreign, is on the rise since 1991 at a rapid pace. The system is exploitative with casual workers who most of the times are denied even the minimum wages, and also with space for permanent employment getting squeezed day by day.

Ghaziabad

Ghaziabad is an old industrial belt of the northern state of Uttar Pradesh. Due to the proximity of the area to NOIDA and Delhi, new industries—in the garment sector in particular—are coming up. We could interview five workers in this area, all in one unit of an electrical machinery producing unit (Table 4.19). Industries here have access to both domestic and foreign markets. Of late, increased competition from Chinese exports has adversely affected exports from units here.

One large manufacturing unit we visited was producing galvanized steel and steel rolling strips. It employed 800 workers of whom only 200 were permanent. All workers were reported as skilled. Wage rates for these permanent workers vary between Rs 15,000 and Rs 20,000 per month, which was quite high as compared to what it was in other areas. The remaining workers were casual with wages at Rs 123 per day which too is reasonable if not high. Work is carried out generally in three shifts. Benefits like ESI and PF are given both to permanent as well as casual workers.

Table 4.19 Ghaziabad: Industrial structure and labour

	Permanent	Casual	Total
Number of labourers		5	5
NIC code of industry groups		31	
Age (years)		32.20	32.20
Wage per month (Rs)		2,860.00	2,860.00
Working hours		9.00	9.00
Union membership (%)		40	40
Experience (years)		1.30	1.30
Minimum wage level (%)		40	40
Skill (%)		100	100
Special training (%)		0	0
Migration (%)		100	100
Education (years)		11.60	11.60
Average number of earning members		1.60	1.60
Asset holding (%)		0	0
Security index		0.33	0.33
Income security		0.23	0.23
Employment security		0.50	0.50
Job security		0.50	0.50
Work security		0.58	0.58
Skill security		0.33	0.33
Voice representation security		0.10	0.10
Financial security		0.07	0.07
Family support security		0.30	0.30

Source: Authors' calculations based on primary data collected through questionnaire-based field survey of five industrial workers in the organized manufacturing industries in Ghaziabad in Uttar Pradesh during 2005–06.

Permanent workers are provided extra benefits like medical facilities, earned leave, casual leave, bonus and gratuity.

We also visited an assembly unit manufacturing escalators. The unit had an average turnover of Rs 20 million. Established in the year 2003 it already had manufacturing units in other states. The management reported that it was facing growing market conditions and claimed that it ranked fifth in India in terms of production of escalators. It employed 113 workers. Of these 100 were permanent and 13 were contractual with one-year contracts. Labour contractors provided the non-regular workers and were paid commissions for that by the firm. All permanent workers were qualified mechanical engineers. Wage rates for permanent workers claimed by the firm varied between Rs 6,000 and Rs 10,000. Wage rates for the contractual workers varied between Rs 2,500 and Rs 4,000 per month. Casual as well as permanent workers were provided with benefits like ESI, PF and bonus.

We also interviewed five contractual workers from this assembly unit and found out that wages which were actually provided to these workers varied between Rs 2,000 to Rs 2,500 per month, which are much below the minimum wage rates in the area, which is fixed at around Rs 4,000 by the state government. Workers repeatedly reported their unhappiness with their work conditions as well as wage rates. In our sample, three workers had around 10–12 years of experience. They also mentioned that the existing labour rules and regulations along with minimum wage rules in reality are not paid heed to by the local enterprises. Thus all of these workers work beyond the statuary working hours and receive only a fixed sum of Rs 500 for overtime work for the whole month. The firms do not follow government's overtime payment rules as per labour law of the country.

All five workers we interviewed were migrants and, hence, their income security level was considerably low as expected. In our sample two out of five workers were union members and enjoyed higher job security than the remaining workers in the sample. Ghaziabad has prospered as an industrial area for the last three decades. However, as far as the condition of labour is concerned, we found degree of exploitation quote high in Ghaziabad. Most of the workers, we interviewed, were hardly getting any non-wage benefits. Furthermore, even statutory minimum wages were denied to them in most cases. The modern development of the area has percolated very little, if at all, to the labouring people in terms of raising their standard of living. The local growth process of the area thus remains exclusively oriented to the category of people as described earlier. The story elsewhere remains the same in recent times with high growth rates around 8–9 per cent, which has neither reduced absolute poverty nor relative poverty significantly. On the other hand, it has increased the gap between rich and poor, non-labour and labour class, farmers and industrialists. In aggregate income inequality has increased.[14]

Surat—A case study of diamond industry workers under the neo-liberal regime

In Surat, the diamond-cutting industry occupies a special place in the Saurashtra region, both as a major foreign exchange earner and as a provider of jobs to workers from the region. The diamond-cutting industry comes under the category of cottage and small-scale industries. It is highly export-oriented and its import intensity is also very high. This industry uses raw diamonds as its raw material. They use a major machine called 'ole'. Generally four workers work on one ole. The price of one 'ole' lies within the range of Rs 20,000–30,000, thus raising the capital intensity of production. The scale of operation can increase only with increases in the number of 'ole'.

We interviewed 64 workers in Surat some of whom did not occupy any permanent position (see Table 4.20). They enjoy a very low level of social security with security levels varying according to their education (skill) levels. Of all workers in our sample, 53 were skilled, who enjoyed better security levels as compared to the unskilled workers in our sample.

Wages in this industry are not directly paid to workers. These are paid on a monthly basis, on the basis of piece rate as per work done in a month and as ascertained by the managers employed in the units. The rate paid to workers varies between Rs 8 and Rs 13 which varies from

Table 4.20 Surat: Industrial structure and labour

	Permanent	*Casual*	*Total*
Number of labourers		64	64
NIC code of industry groups		17, 29, 36	
Age (years)		28.89	28.89
Wage per month (Rs)		4,349.84	4,349.84
Working hours		11.19	11.19
Union membership (%)		0	0
Experience (years)		2.56	2.56
Minimum wage level (%)		48	48
Skill (%)		83	83
Special training (%)		22	22
Migration (%)		73	73
Education (years)		8.34	8.34
Average number of earning members		1.69	1.69
Asset holding (%)		52	52
Security index		0.34	0.34
Income security		0.18	0.18
Employment security		0.26	0.26
Job security		0.52	0.52
Work security		0.47	0.47
Skill security		0.10	0.10
Voice representation security		0.00	0.00
Financial security		0.55	0.55
Family support security		0.59	0.59

Source: Authors' calculations based on primary data collected through questionnaire-based field survey of 11 industrial workers in the organized manufacturing industries in Surat in Gujarat during 2006.

factory to factory. A major factor for variation in the wage rate is the size of diamond. For larger size of diamonds the rate is higher. The workers usually work 10–12 hours in a day. All of these are casual having no job contracts. The attrition rate in this industry is high. But there is no fear of being unemployed even for a single day as getting a new job is quite easy, especially for skilled people. The smaller factories generally do not give any benefits like PF and ESI. But some of the big companies provide it. Most of the companies do not provide any medical facility to the workers. But there are exceptions. We observed a dispensary for the workers in one of the units. Recently the association of diamond exporters had started an insurance scheme for the workers.

The workers do not face much of physical search procedure at the entry or exit of the factory. The system works on trust which is taken care of at the time of recruitment. Thus, no worker can get a job in any factory without a proper reference. There is no union for workers, or at least workers are not aware of its existence while they are keen to have one. But no one wants to initiate the process, especially in big factories, where they have a constant fear of being thrown out or even getting physically assaulted. Not a single worker we interviewed happened to be a member of trade unions. But in terms of the records maintained by a major central trade union operating in Surat, there are 350,000 diamond workers in Surat but they only have 5,000 memberships out of these workers. The unions also run a co-operative of workers in the diamond-cutting industry. But the President of this union is an office bearer of the productivity council, which is an association, primarily of factory owners. The factory owners are very organized and have an active association. Even the Labour Department officials in the state (at the Assistant Labour Commissioner level) fear the diamond factory owners, which works as a very powerful political lobby in the Gujarat state power structure. The official bodies in the labour department are thus not very successful in implementing the provisions of labour law in the diamond-cutting factories.

There are three layers of employees in a diamond-cutting factory. These include (a) the workers, (b) managers and (c) the owner (called the *Seth*). The production process has the following sequence: (a) the manager provides raw diamonds to a worker; (b) the worker removes the waste from the diamond at a preliminary level and makes a tentative size of the diamond; (c) then it goes to the workers in 'ole'. Their duty is to polish the different sides of the diamonds and finally (d) it goes back to the manager as a final product.

Conclusion

Our survey of industrial units and workers in different parts of the country offers some startling revelations which relate to the exploitative pattern of labour use in these concerns. We have witnessed the tendencies on part of employers both to pay wages at levels which are as low as possible, and to make use of additional labour hours without much compensation. We also notice that a large number among those employed are unskilled and migrants which tends to depress the wages and other terms of employment in their place of work. These are the masses of casualized labourers who are constantly under the threat of going back to the huge reserve army of unemployed labourers. No amount of legal safeguards offered by the government or even by unionized bargaining are found to be effective in ameliorating the state of the unskilled, casualized workers who seem to be on the verge of destitution. Skill for some does pay, at least in creating a distinct wage barrier which, however, often fails to deliver what skill should command as wages. Location seems to be important in settling the destiny of workers. Thus the sub-contractees in *bidi* factories of remote Aurangabad town in West Bengal have less to expect from their jobs than those in the National Capital Region (NCR) of Delhi, a fact which indicates that proximity to power and prosperity does matter to some extent.

In India the neo-liberal logic of growth-oriented manual unfurls the Marxian law of capital accumulation (M–C–M) which seeks a cost-cutting route to compete under global capitalism. In the process the burden of adjustment (say closures, technological upgrading, etc.) is ultimately borne by the direct producers, which is labour. Labour remains the ultimate victim of such a process, a fact which goes in the name of labour efficiency and skill-oriented productivity growth.

The class processes underneath also depress necessary labour for generation of more and more surplus labour. The process of informalization (casualization) helps the process by lowering wages and other benefits, often below the subsistence minimum. Also within the factory space positions are occupied by subsumed class groups as managers and supervisors which appropriate another layer of the surplus and the direct producers (labour) work in an informal capacity with no record of them in the factory book.[15] Finally there remain the capitalist owners of these industrial concerns who have enough ammunition to maximize their share of the surplus, which is achieved by exploiting labour directly and also by deceiving the state of the revenue which could cut into these surpluses.

An account, as discussed in this chapter, of the expropriation of industrial surpluses at the cost of labour raises questions which relate to the validity of the neo-liberal economic logic, of achieving growth via efficiency in liberalized regimes. We pursue such questions in the next chapter, by looking into the security of labour in terms of attributes (say income, jobs, etc.), which are supposed to improve with labour market flexibility as per the neo-liberal logic.

Appendix

The production process and the appropriation of surplus labour in the *bidi* manufacturing industry of Murshidabad

To offer a detailed profile of the production process in the *bidi* industry we need to point out that family labour is extensively involved in the making of raw *bidi*. Mostly women, and of all ages, are usually engaged in raw *bidi*-making. The production process from raw to final *bidi* entails a unique structure with one part of the job being performed by family labour in the unorganized or informal segment of the economy and other part carried out in the formal organized factory segment. The link between family labour and the factories is established through the intermediaries, who in local parlance, are called *munshis*. The latter are supplied with raw materials by the factory which, in turn, is supplied by the *munshis* to the final producers in households, the labourers. So, family labour does not have any formal direct link with the factory which processes the final goods.

To make 1,000 raw *bidi* sticks as per the official norm, 110 *kendu* leaves, 300 grams of piled tobacco and two bundles of coloured threads are required. Factories provide the raw materials to their respective *munshis* to pass on to the labourers. The labourers hand over the raw *bidi* made with these raw materials to the *munshis*. When labourers give their produced stuff to the *munshis* the latter make stringent checking of the quality of the *bidi*. Only 'good' quality stuff is retained and the rest is rejected. The rejected stuff is known in local parlance as *chhat* (rejected). The intermediaries (*munshis*) retain the *chhats* without making payment for them to the labourers. This means labourers get payments only for the part which is accepted by the *munshis*. (For example, suppose a labourer makes 1,000 raw *bidi*s in a day and at the end of day's work comes to her *munshi* to hand over her produced stuff. And the *munshi* after verifying them for their quality finds, as per own norms, only 50 per cent of the lot as acceptable, which implies the labourer will receive payment for 500 *bidi*s accepted by the *munshi*. If the wage is Rs 40 for 1,000 *bidi*s, then this labourer will receive only Rs 20 and the rejected 500 *bidi*s will be retained by the *munshi* himself.)

An important point, which should not be missed here, is the fact that while most of the family labour to make raw *bidi* is performed by women, the *munshis* are all males. This raises two important points. First, that there is no standardized norm for *bidi* checking for quality control. It all depends on the whims and fancies of the *munshis*. Second, it often is the case that a labourer gets less input in terms of the quantity of raw materials as are required to produce 1,000 raw *bidi* sticks. Quite often she may get less than 110 leaves and 300 grams of tobacco which are the needed inputs to roll 1,000 raw *bidis*. Almost always she gets one instead of two coloured threads, which are required to make 1,000 *bidis*. In this case, she has to procure the rest of the *tendu* leaves, tobacco and thread herself and at market prices. If she fails to do that and supplies less than 1,000 *bidis*, the *munshi* will deduct the proportionate value of the raw materials from her payment. For example, if she supplies 700 *bidis* by using say 210 grams of tobacco and 80 leaves (which she received from the *munshi*) then the market value of the 90 grams of tobacco and 30 leaves will be deducted from her wages. This is so because the *munshi* always records that he has been providing the stipulated quantity of tobacco and leaves to make 1,000 *bidis*, despite supplying less than the required amount for 1,000 *bidis*. And in addition, there is the additional profit the *munshi* enjoys by using the raw materials that remain with him. There is no way that a labourer, who is also a woman, can challenge the quantity actually supplied to her by the *munshi*.

At the next stage of the production process raw *bidis* are supplied to factories by the *munshis*. The production process at the factory level starts with the same quality control exercise, known as checking, which the *munshi* performs with the labourers in the factory. This time the *munshi* remains at the receiving end of expropriation. Once again there is no standardized norm for quality control and there are only a handful of labourers at the factory, who check the *bidis* brought by the *munshi*. In the process, the *chhats* this time are retained by the factory and not returned to the *munshi*. The next stage follows after the checking exercise when those *bidis* are baked in charcoal fire set in iron furnace (known as *jaal* in local parlance). The baking process is supervised by one supervisor, who is known as 'jaal master' in local parlance. There are a few tasters who taste the final *bidi*. It should be noted here that the quality control mechanism in this industry is very stringent. It first starts with the checking of raw sticks by the intermediaries (*munshis*) and ends with tasting of the final *bidi* at the factory level. Since there is a large overseas as well as domestic market for *bidis*, quality control has to be very important for the branded *bidi*. Each brand carries a unique taste as per the preference of the particular consumers of specific regions.

We can see a process above with the mechanism through which super surplus is generated at different layers in the industry, enjoyed by the capitalist owners as well as the intermediaries. Further, the owners of factories as well as the intermediaries have super surplus by retaining the rejected sticks, which they sell in the market as unbranded or with new brand names. For the rejected (*chhat*) sticks the actual producers do not receive any payment. Hence, the realized surplus is more for the *chhat bidis* which enter the local market either in the names of some new brands or without any brand name. Also the companies do not pay any excise or cess payments to the government for these *bidis*.

At end of baking the final *bidis* are packed in single packets of 25 *bidis* and the market price of the final *bidi* is on the basis of how the pack is rated. These packs are then put together in cartons and then packed in bigger jute sacks, which are transported to the wholesalers at different parts of the country. *Bidis* produced in Aurangabad mostly go to the North Indian market and to Kolkata and few are exported abroad. At the time of independence the main market of Aurangabad was Assam and the entire North East. The tea garden workers were the main consumers of *bidis* of Aurangabad. However, with the political disturbance in North East and the setting up of local factories there, this market gradually dried up. Few *bidi* companies, mainly Pataka, have an overseas market as alternative destinations.

To complete our story of expropriation in this industry we need to describe the different categories of workers. First, there are checkers, who are senior workers with dominant positions among others in the factory. Then, there are bakers, who bake the *bidis*. And, lastly there are packers and labellers, who pack and label the *bidis*. At each level there are supervisors, who supervise and monitor the checking, baking and packing process and also co-ordinate between the different activities. Supervisors are called *sardars*. There is also child labour, to do the packing and labelling jobs. *Bidi*-making is very hazardous and most workers engaged in the baking process suffer from health hazards. Also, those who pile raw tobacco suffer in terms of health. We did not find any female worker in the factories. As for timing there is no fixed peak season or off-season for *bidi*-making and the work can continue round the year. However, there are periods when companies slow down the production due to various reasons, which are not very explicit. Often they do so to run down their inventories. Sometimes they slow down the pace of production to create pressures on the workers so that even their legitimate demands can be refused. For instance, in August 2005 production ceased for several days as the large factories were not ready to accept the revised minimum wage rate for the *bidi* workers as was agreed upon between them and the trade unions.

As for wages paid to workers at various levels within the industry while the factory workers receive fixed monthly wages (with casual workers getting paid on a daily basis), family labour (processing raw *bidis*) are paid by *munshis* on a piece rate basis. Generally, when there is large volume of work, family labour gets orders for 3–4 days a week. And on an average one person makes no less than 1,000 *bidis* a day. As per the last wage revision enacted following bipartite negotiation in July 2005 between the Bidi Merchants Association (BMA) and the Trade Unions, the official wage per 1,000 *bidi* stands out at Rs 41, a rate which has been revised upward from Rs 37. If family labour would get full payments with no *chhat*, the payment per day or week should be respectively at least Rs 41 and Rs 120–160. But in reality this was hardly the case. In the BMA office in Aurangabad, we found a poster of the BMA—the producers' organization—calling for strike in the industry against wage hike! The 'Minimum Wages for the Bidi Workers Act' came into existence way back in 1967. However, in Aurangabad the minimum wages are hardly paid. Only those workers, who are making branded *bidis* for the well known companies like the Pataka Group of Industries, receive minimum wages. Those, who are involved in unbranded *bidi*-making, were getting much below the minimum wages. Often, they got Rs 20–25 per 1,000 *bidis*.

Coming to the remuneration the *munshis* were paid, it was a commission of Rs 2.50 per thousand sticks of *bidi* paid by the factories. The *bidi*-making activity however is spread almost all over the district, with Aurangabad as the centre of the activity. In places distant from the centre, wages were even lower and we did not come across any single evidence of a worker earning above the minimum rate. In places like Dhulian, the average wage was not more than Rs 25 per 1,000 *bidis*. Most of the large factories in these areas were closed and no order was placed for *fresh bidis* as company owners were not willing to pay the revised rate which came in August 2005. It is quite paradoxical because these companies, as members of the BMA, were also part of the agreement signed in July 2005! Those, who check and bake *bidis*, are mostly permanent staff while the packers and labellers are mostly casual. A significant portion of packing and labelling staff comprises of male children in Aurangabad. They are paid as little as Rs 15 on a daily basis.

As for social security benefits in the recent past, provident fund has been made mandatory for the unorganized workers. As unorganized sector workers, *bidi* workers are now entitled to PF facility like their organized counterparts elsewhere in the country. Hence, from a worker's wage of Rs 41 per 1,000 *bidi* sticks, Rs 4.10 is deducted at the rate of 10 per cent. A matching grant has to be made by the companies. But we found that even the matching amount was deducted from the wages of the workers. Hence, in effect a worker receives Rs 32.80 instead of Rs 36.90 to make 1,000 *bidis*. These PF contributions are collected by the *munshis* which they give to the companies to put in the workers' PF fund. There are cases of manipulations in this regard by *munshis* as well as by the factories. As the workers are mostly illiterate, they find it quite difficult to manage their PF fund and other official formalities with the government staff and bureaucracy. Some middlemen interfere in the process and they retain the amount of their cut backs from the workers' PF receipts. There are instances of irregular PF receipts and we also found that in some cases PF accounts are opened in some one else's name, someone who is not the actual worker. Companies openly exhibit their reluctance in providing the PF benefits. As workers are not recorded in the factory account and they are dealt with directly by the *munshis*, many workers fail to get themselves registered for this benefit. When we interviewed a few factory managers, they indicated that the PF benefits for the workers have created a burden for their companies and it is actually imposed upon them by the government. This, however, is despite the fact that companies in reality were not bearing the burden as the matching PF contribution is also taken from the worker's payment. A rough estimate provided by the Secretary of the BMA indicates that 0.35–0.4 million workers get the PF facility in the district, comprising around 25 per cent of the total workforce engaged in *bidi*-making in the industry. What reaches them on a net basis however, is subject to questioning.

Recognizing the fact that *bidi*-making is a hazardous activity, the government levied a cess of Rs 2 per 1,000 *bidi*s on the companies. With this fund, a health corpus fund is created to address their health related problems of workers and a hospital has been set up at Dhulian, especially for the workers. This cess payment is supposed to be made by the companies to the government. However, even this cess is actually contributed by the workers from their wages which is totally illegal. Therefore, a typical worker, assuming that she gets the minimum wage, receives Rs 30.80 instead of Rs 32.80 (net of PF deductions) for producing 1,000 *bidi*s a day!

As mentioned earlier, those who are making unbranded *bidi*s receive wages which are even lower as compared to the minimum rate. In general, their wages vary in the range of Rs 20–25. As unbranded *bidi* manufacturers evade excise payments, they do not have to bother about registering the workers for the PF benefits and also, they do not have to make cess payment. So, the unbranded *bidi*-making workers are automatically denied the PF benefits while they just get the wages which are much below the official rate. Even those who are paid as per the official rate, most of the time receive wages at par with the unbranded *bidi* wages due to the generation of *chhat* at the time of checking by the *munshi*s mentioned earlier and also, due to the provision of lower quantity of raw materials by the *munshi*s.

There is no explicit benefit like bonus or *ex gratia* for the *bidi* workers. They rely on the owners' mercy for some relief at the time of distress like flood and draught, and social need like daughter's marriage or children's education. Some companies have their charitable trusts for free medical treatment of the workers and their families. In Pataka Company, those, who bake and taste raw *bidi*s, are given milk to compensate for their health hazard. Benefits received in kind may take several forms which depends on the benevolence of the employers. It ultimately helps them to control the social base of their production process.

As for the social conditions of production a strong gender bias as mentioned earlier, is observed in the *bidi*-making process. About 70 per cent of the total workforce engaged in *bidi*-making is female. While the family labour for making raw *bidi* is mostly performed by the women of all ages, factory labour including the occupation of *munshi* is meant for the male members. Child labour is rampant both at the family and factory level. At the factory level, they are preferred to adult workers as they can be paid much below the minimum rate. Second, social demand for family labour is so strongly biased towards the female that at the time of marriage negotiation, irrespective of caste, creed and religion, the would-be bride must know the art of 'good' *bidi*-making. The 'good' *bidi* is adjudged not only in terms of the quality but also in terms of the speed of *bidi*-making. Hence, a girl, who can make good quality *bidi* swiftly, will stand a better chance to find a matching groom than one who is not socially acknowledged as a 'good' *bidi* maker and thus is neglected!

We were told that generally in Hindu families female members make *bidi*s while in a Muslim family apart from the female members, males are also involved.

But the male head of the family does most of the supervision and monitoring job and they also maintain the contact with the *munshis*. So, it is the male head of the family, who receives the payments from the *munshis* on behalf of the actual labourers, who are mostly female. Male members of the family may be engaged in other occupations simultaneously like rickshaw pulling, vending, fishing, etc. Female workers also may depend on other sources of earning as house-maids, in order to sustain the continuous flow of earnings for their families. Income from *bidi*-making remains very volatile even after concerted efforts by the trade unions and government over years to rationalize the wage structure and also to introduce some of the benefits, which only the organized manufacturing workers are entitled to till today in this age of globalization with labour flexibility!

As for taxes and cess payments to the government, excise duties are exempted up to the production of 1.6 million sticks of branded *bidis*. Accordingly it has become a general practice that companies sell 1.6 million sticks in one name and another 1.6 million in another name. Sometimes branded *bidi* manufacturers market their products avoiding brand name to evade taxes and other payments to the government. Although not explicitly mentioned, unbranded *bidis* are automatically exempted from any excise payment to the government. Thus, for producing unbranded *bidis* the state does not receive anything either in the form of excise tax or in the form of cess. Pataka *bidi* pays Rs 50 million every year as cess. This does not cover 60 per cent of the total *bidi* production in the district, which includes unbranded sticks.

Rather unusual for similarly organized industries, trade unions are active in the region. Almost all the national trade unions have their presence in the area. The periodic revision of wages has been a consequence of trade union activism in the area. Nonetheless, the main issue in the Aurangabad *bidi*-making labour process remains the recognition of a household worker (especially women) as the legally recognized worker of a factory who can claim PF and other social security benefits. The above is still missing from the agenda of the trade unions active in the area.

Notes

1. However, it must be noted here that we could interview only a handful of firm managers, not all, in units where a labour survey took place. This was because of their reluctance to give us time to interview them.
2. See Chapter 5 for the different notions of labour security.
3. It is to be noted here that in a SEZ trade union rights are not recognized. Hence, employers did not recognize the presence of unions at the time of our field survey. But a few central trade unions are trying to organize these workers outside the SEZ campus. We came to know about the presence of unions among a few workers in the NSEZ in this manner at the time of interviewing the workers, and hence 11 out of 17 workers in our sample were unionized workers.

4. The term 'footloose labour' was coined by Jan Bremen in his book.
5. As per Census of India figures, the geographical area of Falta is 130.68 square kilometres, being classified as rural and constituting 1.34 per cent of the total rural area of the district.
6. In the Lewis and later in the Harris–Todaro and Ranis–Fei framework economic development means development of the 'modern' industrial sector which would shift labour away from 'backward' agriculture or primary activities and such a transfer is permanent as development of the 'modern' sector is perceived to be an irreversible process. A counter claim can be made here with our experiences at Falta.
7. In our sample we do not have any evidence of piece rate wages. But that does not mean work on the piece rate basis is non-existent. Rather, there are many firms which are now outsourcing their factory jobs to household workers in the informal segment of the economy, which is unorganized, on piece rate basis and the incidence of such cases is on the rise in recent time.
8. As elsewhere in the country, major trade unions in Kolkata are mostly attached to the principal political parties of the state. There is a common belief at the level of industry and bureaucracy that due to high presence of unions and their militancy many industries have left the state and manufacturing production has suffered. However, a study by Dutt (2003) indicates otherwise. Instead of high incidences of strikes and disputes caused by labourers, because of high incidences of lockouts and closures by managements for a variety of reasons (labour-related problems being just one among them) manufacturing production has suffered.
9. A new car-manufacturing unit was proposed to be set up at a place called Singur in the district of Hooghly close to Kolkata by Tata Motors as per the initiative taken by the West Bengal Government for drawing additional private investment in the state. It was supposed to produce low-cost passenger car and was expected to generate, as per the claim of the Government of West Bengal and the Tata group of industries, a good number of employment opportunities in the area, not only in the newly created factory but also in the downstream units which were expected to come up with the setting of the unit in the locality. However, the critiques of the project pointed out that it would fail to generate sufficient employment for all those who had been evicted and were directly or indirectly related to the land where the firm was to be set up. Hence, as per their arguments new job opportunities would fall short of the number of people who became unemployed due to eviction. As a result of political agitation the project could not take off and finally, Tata Motors had to abandon it. But the political agitation brought to the fore one of the key issues related with current type of industrialization-led development process. The latter is based on the typical mainstream Lewisian development model, which defines development as transfer of labour from so-called 'subsistence' agriculture to the so-called 'modern sector', that is, industry. Agricultural land is acquired for setting new industries by the state. And people dependent on farmland directly as well as indirectly lose their livelihood. The question, however, remains as to whether these new industries are able to absorb all those who are displaced in adequate numbers and with a reasonable earning capacity. The problem is not unique to Singur. It is the case in every part of the country where agricultural land had been taken away for setting new industries and it remains the major dilemma associated with the current industrialization-led development process. One of the major reasons for the new industries failing to generate adequate employment, which is far short of what is required or warranted, given the unemployment scenario, is their extensive use

of labour-saving technologies so as to garner higher level of factor productivity including labour—the point which we have already discussed in Chapter 2.

10. Dunlop India Limited remained under lockout from 7 February 1998 to 12 March 2000—for a period of over two years. Irregular supply of raw materials, lack of working capital and incompetent management were given as the principal reasons, by the labour force, for the lockout. The company has a big contingent of 4,150 workers who, due to the lockout extending over 764 days, suffered great hardship. The total loss of man-days during the entire period of lockout works out to be 3.17 million—a colossal figure indeed. Many workers died due to economic hardship aggravated by old age and disease. The management did not reduce the number of workers, but their non-availability either due to death or migration to native states led to a reduction of workers to 3,900 after lockout. Quoted from Dutt (2003: 146, Box 3.5).

11. INTUC and CITU were the two principal unions at Dunlop India Limited.

12. In February 2008, the Government of West Bengal announced that preferences will be given to places like Kalyani, Durgapure–Asansole (which were developed after independence as industrial townships and are now facing the scourge of deindustrialization due to the closure or shifting of many prominent industrial units, many of which are public sector enterprises. This is reported in the State Development Report of the Government of West Bengal [2008], which was prepared by the Institute of Development Studies, Kolkata under the guidance of Professor Amiya Kumar Bagchi) for setting up new industrial units by foreign or domestic companies, and attempts would be made to avoid locations which are mainly farm land and where population density is very high so that eviction does not take place.

13. Following payments are made to Central and State Governments as taxes and duties per thousand sticks of *bidis*:

    (i)   CENVAT (Central Value Added Tax):   Rs 4.60
    (ii) Additional duty to the State Governments: Rs 1.40
    (iii) NCCB: Re 1.00
    (iv) Cess: Rs 4.00
    (v) Education Cess: Re 0.22
    TOTAL: Rs 11.22 per 1,000 *bidi* sticks.

14. As per *Forbes* magazine in 2007 India had 100 billionaires which is one of the highest numbers for any country. These billionaires are the product of a neo-liberal regime. In contrast, one-fourth of India's population lives in abject poverty as per Planning Commission estimates, with less than US$ 1 earning a day, the international standard of measuring poverty. Now, with growing casualization and denial of minimum wages and suppressive wages in the informal activities the benefits of high growth hardly reach the direct producers. Rather, the current 'growthmanship' thrives on this growing inequality, for which labour flexibility is a necessary first order condition, as noted by Professor Amit Bhaduri in a TV interview on 16 February 2008 on a national channel—*Loksabha*.

15. As shown by Karl Marx in *The Capital* (Volume I), the rate of exploitation (measured as the ratio of surplus value, s over variable capital, v) increases in this process. It increases more, à la Marx, in cases of piece wage payments as well. Similarly, it increases when regular occupations are converted into irregular casual ones.

Labour Security in Indian Organized Manufacturing Industries 5

Introduction

Of late, labour market flexibility has made it important to discuss issues concerning the security aspect of labour. The notion dwells on aspects affecting their livelihood which include, first and foremost, their job status, both current as well as what can be expected over time. Second, the terms of the job contracts which relates only to workers with permanent jobs. Terms of job contract include wages as well as other benefits/costs related to these jobs. The above includes bonuses, housing, medical facilities, transport facilities, leave rules, tenure of jobs and similar other benefits which affect the well-being of labour. Third, there remains the economic and social status of labour which in essence defines their security. This is influenced by the available support system, from the state and/or from the social support network which includes the family. For labourers without firm jobs social support remains the sole means of survival.

Labour in employment can be differentiated between those engaged in the organized sector of the economy and others who are with the unorganized activities. These activities include agriculture, a sizeable part of manufacturing and most of the services sector.

Our study, as mentioned earlier, deals with labour in the organized manufacturing sector of the Indian economy. Thus we have chosen a small segment of labour employed in the economy, notwithstanding the fact it covers as little as 1.6 per cent of the total labour force in the country.[1] However, the choice demands an explanation as to why we decided to deal with such a small segment of labour. In our judgement, the organized sector of industry still provides a test case for judging the impact of labour market flexibility in the country. This is due to the existence of a number of large-scale and old industries in this sector where labour has a tradition of being better organized and labour legislation is relatively adhered to.

Above all, this is the only sector in the country where labourers enjoy some element of labour security. Finally, this remains the sector which is better integrated with the rest of world in terms of the trade links as well as the destination of FDI, both of which are likely to have a mark on the relative position of labour vis-à-vis capital in the domestic economy. In our judgement, a study of organized sector labour in the manufacturing sector, as the present one, is expected to throw light on what we have observed as the dwindling status of labour under the new regime of market-led changes with flexibilization of the labour market in India.

As for the data sources, in our judgement the variables at the macro level as are available in the official data set are not exhaustive enough to permit an analysis of the security level of the labour force in employment. As mentioned in the earlier chapters, this has prompted us to do a primary field survey of industrial workers in select regions. We have used the primary data set to arrive at a more meaningful observation relating to the level of security/insecurity for a representative set of workers in industrial units we have interviewed in our field survey.

The present chapter proceeds as follows: The first section offers the conceptual basis of the notion of labour security under globalization and labour flexibility; the second section analyzes the major impact of labour flexibility in India under globalization; the third section discusses the methodology of construction of the labour security index; the fourth section discusses the empirical results and the fifth section concludes with a summing up of the major findings of the study.

The Notion of Labour Security

The notion of labour security rejects the conventional position of the neo-classical economists on labour issues, used widely as a manual for labour market reforms in developing countries. In terms of neo-classical theory, labour can be viewed just as any other commodity in the market which is used in the production process.

In our view, a position as above undermines the social relevance of labour as an organic component of the economy and society. It ignores the important fact that the remuneration of labour needs to cover its well-being and sustenance in the short and the long run. This is often not fulfilled in terms of the payments made out to labour, which falls even short of the value of output contributed by labour. It needs to be recognized that the so-called market for labourers is essentially a social institution, an aspect which is hardly recognized in terms of a traditional neo-classical position.

A distinction, as earlier, between the orthodox mainstream position on labour and the more general humane approach which governs our research is particularly important in the context of the sweeping reforms as have engulfed most economies including those in the developing area. While we go by the Marxian position which views labour in its alienated capacity under capitalism, we also follow Polyani in viewing labour as a cog in the wheel of 'social transformation' in which globalization is the current stage (Munck 2003: 9–10). This relates to the stage of social transformation where capital takes within its fold labour under exploitative conditions.

In recent years one witnesses a new pattern of production relations which contrasts the earlier decades of Fordism in Western Europe when expansions in the workforce went hand in hand with mass production of goods from factories at the level of nation states. With capital now free and willing to move across countries, export platforms are continually set up in developing countries where labour can now be utilized at terms which suits capital better. The labour processes used by these units were replicated in other production centres in the host economies. The mode of employing labour in developing countries has been very different from what has been the case with workers in advanced countries, not just in terms of low wages but also with the mode of work and the related benefits. Labour flexibility, which opened up possibilities of parcelling out jobs at cheaper rates, have created new modes of employment which has gradually replaced the earlier pattern of tenured jobs. Norms are set in the process for using flexible and casualized labour in these developing economies, which proved convenient for capital, both domestic and of foreign origin. In India the changes, as pointed out later in this chapter, had far-reaching effects on the socio-economic status of labour vis-à-vis capital, which defines labour security.

The notion of labour-security goes back to the post-war era of welfare state and the days of socialism in the Soviet Union and Eastern Europe both of which are now passé in the era of today's market-led capitalism. Norms were set in these earlier forms of state for a minimal security of the 'labouring man', as an individual, and as a collective.

While in state-run socialism some benefits were provided to people by the state which compensated for low wages paid to labour, in welfare states institutions were provided by the government itself to administer redistributive justice. In advanced countries the measures instituted by the state also protected capitalism from a realization crisis, by providing a market for wage goods commanded by labour. However, such institutions have tended to disappear as the market-dominated forces have advanced in both sets of these countries. A similar pattern is visible in the developing countries where the state has given way to market capitalism.

In the literature, the failure of the welfare state in the West has often been attributed to globalization and the opening of markets, especially with free movement of factors of production which include capital (Munck 2003: 56; also see Wood 1994). However, the generality of such positions can be questioned, especially when we look at the developing region where degrees of mobility had been much smaller for both labour and capital. As for movements of labour, one should point out that under globalization the labour market is hardly global except for a small group of professionals. As a result, labour often has turned out to be a global reserve army. The above gets reflected in the dwindling labour security or its total absence (which amounts to insecurity) which can be easily observed (Standing 1999: 51–53).

In the present chapter we have tried to quantify the nature as well as the extent of insecurity among workers who were interviewed in course of our field survey. The method of our quantification of security dwells heavily on the work of Guy Standing (1999, 2004). Our exercise, however, is situated with a perspective which relies on a set of variables as have relevance in terms of the socio-economic background of a Third World country. We have used the quantitative as well as the qualitative information which have been gathered on the basis of our personal interviews of the firm managers, workers, union leaders and people associated with factory activities. The pattern of the interviews has been structured by following the questionnaire which is appended to Chapter 3.

One can view labour flexibility and the absence of labour security from two interrelated angles. The first one relates to the precarious existence of individual labourers in terms of their current status. The above affects the social reproduction of the labourer, which provides the social and bio-logical environment, which also makes it possible for the worker to survive and perform. These are determined by the level of income earned, by work environment and job contracts and above all the dignity with which the labourer works, as can be judged by the security level related to the job.

Second, it is often noticed that the security level of the labourers is not only actual but also tends to be prospective. Thus, a tenured job is not only a source of satisfaction to the person who holds it but also to some extent sort of a guarantee to future prospects, of jobs and additional benefits, both social and economic (for example, borrowing status) which can provide the person a sense of security over a period. Aspects as discussed here which define labour security thus dwell upon the present as well the future well-being of a labourer.

Labour Flexibility and Insecurity in India—The Major Compulsions under Globalization

Economic reforms in India which started in full swing in the year 1991 prepared the ground for the introduction of labour market flexibility. It changed, in particular, the pattern of labour–capital relations in the economy which has gone through a major upheaval in the following years. Pressures mounted up in the country to dismantle the existing labour laws which so long had some relevance, at least for organized industries including the public sector where labour was relatively protected. Rationalizing labour flexibility by the need to achieve market-driven competitive efficiency, labour rights in its different forms continued to be suppressed in the country (Deshpande et al. 2004: 39–41). Large-scale privatization in the country gave a further push to introduction of these reforms in the direction of labour flexibility.

Different political regimes in the country as have come up as ruling powers since the launching of reforms in 1991 have been more or less unanimous in accepting the demands of big capital, especially of foreign origin, for implementing labour flexibility. Changes in labour laws were introduced which permitted 'hire and fire', particularly in the FDI controlled units and in SEZ units. Other industrial units in the country welcomed the opportunity of employing labour on a casual basis, which exonerated the employers from expenses related to the usual benefits normally enjoyed by labour with a permanent job. With this device the risks of having business with export markets in overseas markets could be transferred to labourers by simply firing them when goods could not be sold. Labour under free markets thus turned out as a 'risk bearing factor of production' as pointed out elsewhere in the literature (Johnsson 1978).

In India such a position was officially endorsed in the Report of the National Commission on Labour (2002) which was set up by the government. In terms of the recommendations of the commission, contract labour was justified in view of the uncertain demand from global markets. However, the committee at the same time recommended adequate social safety nets which remain hard to be implemented. We will deal in more detail the recommendations of the National Labour Commission in Chapter 6.

We find the following eight aspects as of crucial significance in determining labour security:

1. *Income security:* A crucial indicator of welfare for an individual worker which in turn is conditioned by the following five aspects:

    (i) Income as received by an individual worker from the current job which is at least equal to the institutionally fixed statutory minimum wage in the country. In India minimum wages have not been revised as regularly as is desirable.[2] These wage rates are often below the level which is compatible with the prevailing prices and the cost of living of labourers. A worker earning less than even the institutionally fixed minimum wage naturally lives in a vulnerable state with considerable stress and strain. Absence of revisions in minimum wages is also indicative of a weakened bargaining strength for workers in the industry as a whole under labour market flexibility. Income security also relates to the non-wage benefits like PF, gratuity, etc., which can be received by the workers with a permanent job status. These are the benefits which also constitute part of the income earned by an individual worker in the organized manufacturing sector when they have a permanent job status. Income security ensures the current economic status of labour.

    (ii) Facilities of on-the-job skill-formation which enhances future income can also be counted under this head.

    (iii) The possibility that the worker can get the wages on a regular basis which affects the level of income security for the worker. Irregular payments, which adversely affect the purchasing capacity of workers also affects their sustenance in terms of attaining a minimum level of consumption.

    (iv) The record of wage revisions in recent past (which ideally should be at par with the general rise in the price level) can also be treated as an indicator of income security. This is because if these revisions are done on a regular basis, it helps to maintain the real income of workers over time. It also signifies the presence of firm-level collective voice representation at the level of trade unions.

(*v*) Income security is affected not only by the availability of non-wage benefits (PF, gratuity, paid medical leave, annual bonus, etc.) but also by the access the worker has to these benefits. This is because an access to these benefits safeguards a worker's earning prospect during and at end of the working life. Also, an access to these payments can be a support in meeting expenses during emergencies which is otherwise difficult to meet from the regular wage income.

2. *Employment security:* In the Indian context it stands for continuity in the present job till superannuation without any fear of losing it.[3] The notion is partly subjective as it depends on the individual worker's perception of the present job including (*a*) whether there is a fear of dismissal from the job and if it has increased in the recent past; (*b*) chances of having an alternative employment and (*c*) whether the worker is confident of keeping the present job over the next 12 months. The last factor to some extent tends to objectify the reality of the worker's fear. Employment security is also a function of the nature of the job contract—which can be long-term/regular or short-term/casual. It ensures tenured employment with protection from unwarranted dismissals in terms of hire and fire strategies. The issue of employment security becomes particularly relevant with the opening up of domestic markets under globalization, and the related changes in technology, labour laws as well as in demand—all three of which contribute to uncertain product markets. With labour market flexibility the impact of uncertainty is often shifted to the labour market, making job prospects uncertain for labour.

3. *Workplace security:* It provides insurance against work-related accidents, payments against leave on medical grounds, payments for overtime and protection of women in night shifts. Insurance cover for those eventualities does not usually exist in India except in a few large industrial concerns. Work security also demands protection against work beyond normal working hours as are stipulated by law. The norm of fixed working hours has been shelved aside in India with the advances of economic liberalization since 1991. Given the prevailing labour legislations, work security in India can be judged by (*a*) whether the worker enjoys the benefits of ESI which entitles the worker free medical benefits and (*b*) whether the worker works for normal working hours of eight hours a day or more.

4. *Security in terms of trade union representation:* It refers to the worker's ability to express his/her protest as a collective voice through trade unions. An indirect way of assessing this brand of security can be by considering the union membership status of the worker. However, just by being a union member the worker does not always get an opportunity to air a collective voice in an organization. This has been more so with the strength of collective bargaining through union membership having eroded in recent time.

5. *Security in terms of family and community support:* It remains vital for workers in the Indian context. This is because unlike in the advanced Western societies, family plays a big role in India in protecting its members in the face of uncertainties and distress, especially when the state has already taken a back-seat in offering social security. However, with the steady breakdown of the extended family-based social structure it now has become increasingly difficult for a lone earner in a nucleus family, and especially, with a migrant status, to get support from the family network. To judge the extent of family support security we can consider *(a)* whether the concerned worker is the single earning member and *(b)* how many members of the family are financially dependent on the earning member. The number of dependents, if large, makes it even more difficult for the worker to save for the future or even to survive. Family support is often negatively impacted by labour migration or even by income disparities and aspiration gaps among labourers. Also poverty in its abject form may, in extreme cases, make it difficult to sustain a community spirit.

6. *Job security:* Distinct from employment security, job security indicates the level of an individual's mobility within the job. A person at the same position in a job (in absence of any opportunity for upward mobility) faces hurdles in terms of achieving remuneration as is proportionate to his/her capabilities. As an example consider two different individuals working in the same organization possessing identical skills, education and experience. It may so happen that one moves up while the other remains at the same level. This affects the second person's attachment to the job. The above, with monotony of work and lack of incentives finally affect the level of efficiency. While talking to workers on our field trip, we observed that the relationship of individual workers with their supervisors is an important factor for judging their job security.

7. *Skill reproduction security:* This is important on two grounds: first, because skill helps to fetch better paid jobs and second, it also

opens up alternative employment opportunities in case of a job loss. Skill is also relevant in terms of the vertical mobility of individuals. Basic education, access to skill formation and special training are important inputs for acquiring this skill-related security. Thus an illiterate worker is ill-equipped as compared to one having basic education in accessing skill and special training. However one should bear in mind that skill alone is never sufficient for vertical mobility and/or higher pay. From the above angle, it can be stated that the role of skill remains over-rated in the neo-liberal supply-side view of the economy.

8. *Financial security:* It remains important for an average worker in a country like India, especially in absence of any social safety-net or social security measures from the state. Financial security, in terms of savings, possession of bank accounts and holding of other assets, if any, can be used as safety-nets at times of distress and old age, an aspect which is important in situations that prevail in India.

We would enquire into the eight aspects of labour security mentioned here in the context of the workers we have met and interviewed. However, there remains another aspect of labour security which has relevance in terms of the social structure as prevails in India. Regular employment with job and income security provides a person with a social standing, which a worker on a casual and temporary job generally does not enjoy. This contributes in a significant way to a person's access to markets, including those for credit. The perception of a labourer as above was earlier common in India with the emergence of organized factory-based jobs that had a permanent status with the job-related benefits. A class of workers thus emerged with a dignified social status. The steady erosion in the status of labourers, especially for those employed with a casual status, therefore, can be viewed as the sliding down of these workers in the social hierarchy as compared to what they used to command in organized industries.

Construction of Labour Security Index—The Methodology

While the idea of constructing a labour security index in this study originated from the work by Standing on similar lines, there is a basic difference between the approach of Standing and ours in defining labour security (Standing 2004). Thus Standing measured labour security at the aggregate country level, and ours is an attempt to do the same at a micro-level. Standing relied on the broad macro parameters of labour security which are articulated in terms of different state policies and institutions. Our analysis is based upon micro-level information in which macro-level policy articulation and institutional effects also have a role. We provide in the Appendix to this chapter the detailed methodology used in framing our labour security index, henceforth referred to as composite labour security index (CLSI).

The construction of a security index essentially involves one's subjective views on a range of issues, as there can be no predetermined methodology available in the making of such an index. In our construction of the index we have adopted an ad hoc procedure which makes use of the insights we had from what we observed in the field studies. We have chosen to calculate the eight different types of security, namely, income, employment, workplace, non-wage benefits, voice representation, family support, job security and financial security as in Standing and in addition, family support as an additional security indicator. We have relied on the set of parameters based on the responses of workers in our field surveys. These parameters are arranged in a binary set-up where values 0 and 1 are assigned for the respective values above and below a defined threshold/cut-off point.[4] High values of the index would naturally indicate high levels of security and vice versa.

The CLSI for an average Indian labourer is constructed by assigning equal weights to each of the eight components mentioned earlier. The CLSI thus constructed is the simple arithmetic average of those eight component security indices. The index of each individual security components are calculated by the same method as that of the overall CLSI which is as follows:

$$I_{\text{Index}} = \frac{1}{8}\sum_{i=1}^{8} I_i$$

where I_i represents the i-th index component of the CLSI indicated by I_{Index}.

Empirical Findings

The present section discusses the main empirical observations on the security level of workers as are based on our field survey in the selected industrial clusters of Delhi, Gujarat, Haryana, Mumbai, Uttar Pradesh and

West Bengal. The workers we had interviewed in these areas were all based in small and medium factories in different industries. These units provide a homogenous sample of factory-based wage labour. However, heterogeneity among them can be noticed in terms of different work conditions, mode of wage payments, education and skill levels, social groupings, etc.

Since the survey in each area was carried out at a point of time and not over time, our analysis provides only cross-sectional data and not time-series analysis. We offer in Table 5.1 the area-wise CLSIs of the respective areas by following the method outlined here. The indices are arranged in a descending order.

Table 5.1 Area-wise assessment of worker's composite labour security index (CLSI)

$(N = 615)$

Area	CLSI
Hooghly	0.63
Kalyani	0.55
Kolkata	0.54
Gurgaon	0.49
Faridabad	0.48
Mumbai	0.45
Okhla	0.42
Howrah	0.41
NOIDA SEZ	0.39
Mayapuri	0.37
NOIDA	0.37
Falta SEZ	0.37
East Delhi	0.36
Surat	0.34
Ghaziabad	0.33

Source: Authors' own calculations based on primary data collected through questionnaire-based field survey of 615 industrial workers in the organized manufacturing industries in some selected industrial areas of Delhi, Gujarat, Maharashtra, Uttar Pradesh and West Bengal during 2003–06.

It is possible to observe differences in the CLSIs constructed for different regions. The indices provide a multi-faceted dimension, with the index arrived at for the individual regions often dominated by one or the other particular component of the security index. Our grading of individual areas in terms of their CLSIs goes by the following score table:

1. 0.75–1.00: very high
2. 0.50–0.75: just above average
3. 0.25–0.50: critical
4. 0.00–0.25: worst

As can be seen from Table 5.1, none of the areas we have surveyed come under the very high category of the CLSI and only three out of the 15 areas surveyed are at just above average level. These are Hooghly (0.63), Kalyani (0.55) and Kolkata (0.54). Incidentally, all of these are in the same state of West Bengal. For the remaining 12 areas, CLSIs are at critical levels and despite the fact that some of these areas have witnessed spurts of activities in new industries in recent times, and are specially geared to the export market while attracting foreign capital.[5] These areas include Gurgaon, Surat, NOIDA and Ghaziabad. We also notice that the three areas under SEZ have been at their worst in providing labour security.

However, CLSI values of different areas are found to be different from each other even from within a single state.[6] Spatial variations as such may be ascribed to *(a)* the nature of industries and *(b)* the political, economic and cultural aspects relating to the particular location. One of the reasons why the CLSIs tend to differ across industries is the fact that the statutory minimum wages which are historically determined may differ across industries. In addition, the regional pattern of economic growth and development, the level of trade union activism in particular areas and even the socio-cultural ambience of the area may contribute to explain these spatial differences in labour security. One also needs to look at the spatial-temporal evolution of factors, such as minimum wages, savings habit, trade union activities as well as local political dynamics, family bondage and socio-cultural ethos influencing labour processes to come close to an explanation of these differences, especially in a country like India (see Chakrabarti and Cullenberg 2003).[7] We will deal with the industry-specific security indices later in this chapter.

In the field trip we had covered three SEZs which included Falta (West Bengal), NOIDA (UP) and Santa Cruz (Mumbai). As the relative rankings indicate, barring Santa Cruz, workers in the SEZ areas were generally worse off than the non-SEZ workers when judged by the respective CLSIs. As we will point out later, income security levels are found to be abysmally low in both areas while it is not substantially higher in Santa Cruz either.

We now disaggregate the composite security index by looking at its individual components for each area in Tables 5.2A to 5.2H. As for income security, if we arrange the areas in a descending order, we find that Hooghly has the highest (and 'very high') income security level at 0.82. But the gap between Hooghly and the rest of the areas, both within and across states seems to be rather high. Even Gurgaon, an industrial area, which ranks second in terms of income security (and fourth in terms of CLSI)

Table 5.2A   Area-wise assessment of worker's income security

(N = 615)

Area	Income security
Hooghly	0.82
Gurgaon	0.59
Kalyani	0.57
Kolkata	0.56
Faridabad	0.50
Mayapuri	0.45
East Delhi	0.39
Mumbai	0.36
Howrah	0.32
Okhla	0.30
NOIDA SEZ	0.27
NOIDA	0.26
Ghaziabad	0.23
Falta SEZ	0.22
Surat	0.19

Source: Authors' own calculations based on primary data collected through questionnaire-based field survey of 615 industrial workers in the organized manufacturing industries in some selected industrial areas of Delhi, Gujarat, Maharashtra, Uttar Pradesh and West Bengal during 2003–06.

Table 5.2B   Area-wise assessment of worker's employment security

(N = 615)

Area	Employment security
Hooghly	0.63
Mumbai	0.57
Falta SEZ	0.57
Kolkata	0.54
East Delhi	0.50
Mayapuri	0.50
Okhla	0.50
Faridabad	0.50
Gurgaon	0.50
Ghaziabad	0.50
NOIDA	0.50
NOIDA SEZ	0.50
Howrah	0.49
Kalyani	0.49
Surat	0.26

Source: Authors' own calculations based on primary data collected through questionnaire-based field survey of 615 industrial workers in the organized manufacturing industries in some selected industrial areas of Delhi, Gujarat, Maharashtra, Uttar Pradesh and West Bengal during 2003–06.

Table 5.2C   Area-wise assessment of worker's job security

(N = 615)

Area	Job security
Hooghly	0.82
Kolkata	0.79
Kalyani	0.75
Mumbai	0.71
Howrah	0.64
Surat	0.52
Ghaziabad	0.50
NOIDA	0.43
NOIDA SEZ	0.41
Okhla	0.38
East Delhi	0.32
Faridabad	0.31
Mayapuri	0.30
Gurgaon	0.27
Falta SEZ	0.21

Source: Authors' own calculations based on primary data collected through questionnaire-based field survey of 615 industrial workers in the organized manufacturing industries in some selected industrial areas of Delhi, Gujarat, Maharashtra, Uttar Pradesh and West Bengal during 2003–06.

Table 5.2D   Area-wise assessment of worker's skill reproduction security

(N = 615)

Area	Skill reproduction security
Mumbai	0.69
Ghaziabad	0.58
Faridabad	0.56
Kolkata	0.56
Gurgaon	0.54
Hooghly	0.54
NOIDA	0.49
Howrah	0.49
Surat	0.47
Falta SEZ	0.47
Mayapuri	0.44
Kalyani	0.44
Okhla	0.43
NOIDA SEZ	0.39
East Delhi	0.34

Source: Authors' own calculations based on primary data collected through questionnaire-based field survey of 615 industrial workers in the organized manufacturing industries in some selected industrial areas of Delhi, Gujarat, Maharashtra, Uttar Pradesh and West Bengal during 2003–06.

Table 5.2E   Area-wise assessment of worker's work security

(N = 615)

Area	Work security index
Hooghly	0.91
Kalyani	0.87
Kolkata	0.74
Gurgaon	0.67
Howrah	0.60
Mayapuri	0.58
Faridabad	0.58
East Delhi	0.55
Okhla	0.50
Falta SEZ	0.50
NOIDA SEZ	0.49
Mumbai	0.48
NOIDA	0.43
Ghaziabad	0.33
Surat	0.10

Source: Authors' own calculations based on primary data collected through questionnaire-based field survey of 615 industrial workers in the organized manufacturing industries in some selected industrial areas of Delhi, Gujarat, Maharashtra, Uttar Pradesh and West Bengal during 2003–06.

Table 5.2F   Area-wise assessment of worker's voice representation security

(N = 615)

Area	Voice representation security
Hooghly	0.50
Kalyani	0.40
Okhla	0.35
NOIDA SEZ	0.28
Kolkata	0.27
East Delhi	0.23
NOIDA	0.23
Faridabad	0.22
Gurgaon	0.16
Falta SEZ	0.15
Mayapuri	0.12
Ghaziabad	0.10
Howrah	0.10
Mumbai	0.07
Surat	0.00

Source: Authors' own calculations based on primary data collected through questionnaire-based field survey of 615 industrial workers in the organized manufacturing industries in some selected industrial areas of Delhi, Gujarat, Maharashtra, Uttar Pradesh and West Bengal during 2003–06.

Table 5.2G   Area-wise assessment of worker's financial security

$(N = 615)$

Area	Financial security
Faridabad	0.71
Okhla	0.62
Surat	0.55
Gurgaon	0.55
NOIDA SEZ	0.49
Kalyani	0.40
Hooghly	0.33
Kolkata	0.33
NOIDA	0.32
Mayapuri	0.27
Mumbai	0.27
East Delhi	0.19
Falta SEZ	0.19
Howrah	0.16
Ghaziabad	0.07

Source: Authors' own calculations based on primary data collected through questionnaire-based field survey of 615 industrial workers in the organized manufacturing industries in some selected industrial areas of Delhi, Gujarat, Maharashtra, Uttar Pradesh and West Bengal during 2003–06.

Table 5.2H   Area-wise assessment of worker's family support index

$(N = 615)$

Area	Family support index
Gurgaon	0.66
Falta SEZ	0.62
Surat	0.59
Kolkata	0.52
Hooghly	0.49
Kalyani	0.49
Faridabad	0.47
Howrah	0.47
Mumbai	0.42
East Delhi	0.32
Ghaziabad	0.30
NOIDA	0.30
Mayapuri	0.29
Okhla	0.28
NOIDA SEZ	0.28

Source: Authors' own calculations based on primary data collected through questionnaire-based field survey of 615 industrial workers in the organized manufacturing industries in some selected industrial areas of Delhi, Gujarat, Maharashtra, Uttar Pradesh and West Bengal during 2003–06.

has income security at 0.59. Of the 15 areas only four have income security at 'above average' (which is between 0.50 and 0.75) and one (that is, Hooghly) very high income security. These include Hooghly, Gurgaon, Kalyani, Kolkata and Faridabad. As pointed out earlier, three of these (Hooghly, Kalyani and Kolkata) are located in the same region and so are Gurgaon and Faridabad. Worst scoring in this regard of income security is recorded for three areas—Ghaziabad, Falta SEZ and Surat. As already mentioned, this has been the case despite the fact that industries in some of these areas are oriented for the export market. None of the SEZ areas in our study recorded a good income security index value. *It may be a safe guess that export growth in recent times is facilitated by cheap labour which is easy to avail of in terms of the norms of flexible labour policy by depressing wage income.*

Looking at the employment security of different areas, Hooghly tops the list when ranked in a descending order of the respective indices. But for Surat, Howrah and Kalyani, all other areas have around 0.50 as the score (which is 'just above average'). Even Howrah and Kalyani are very close to the above level. The index for employment security as constructed here seeks to assess the level of uncertainty the workers currently face in retaining their present job and also, in terms of finding an alternative job in case of losing the present one. Somehow, we got the impression during our survey that unless the factory is closed down or the market condition turns too bad for business to continue, firms generally do not fire their workers, and even their casual workers. With time some degree of personal bondage gets established between the workers and the firm owners. Nevertheless, with employment security score just above average, it does explain the fact that large numbers of workers in these areas also fear losing their present jobs and that they are facing a great deal of uncertainty with regard to their future prospects in terms of getting a comparable job within the same area. A similar picture prevail among the SEZ workers in Falta and NOIDA, workers in Surat (who possess the skill of diamond making alone), workers in Ghaziabad and Howrah (where in recent times, large-scale closing down of factories is common).

Rating of an area in terms of one particular component of labour security (say, income) need not fare well or too badly in terms of other components of the CLSI (for example, employment). We try to check by looking at the correlation between income and employment security which turns out to be only 0.316 and is not even statistically significant.

We now consider the ratings of different areas in terms of job security. It refers to an individual worker's position within the present job in terms of inter-personal relationship with supervisors and also in terms of the chances as remains of vertical mobility. Hooghly again is at the top with very good scoring (0.82) and quite close are Kolkata and Kalyani. But within the same state of West Bengal, the Falta SEZ stands at the bottom of the list with worst kind of job security (0.21). This again reflects on the poor status of workers in the export-oriented industries. As for other areas, three out of the 15 surveyed areas had good scoring while four other areas including the export-oriented areas of Santa Cruz EPZ and even the diamond-cutting industries in Surat recorded scorings at just above average. Wide variations are noticed in job security across regions which again are difficult to explain. It is possible that the evolution of spatial-temporal factors like socio-cultural environment of the region, nature of organizations in different regions, etc., can be treated as explanatory factors.

Arranging the areas in terms of the respective skill reproduction security, we find Mumbai is at the top of the list with close to 'very high' scores. In addition five more areas have skill reproduction scores at 0.50 or above which is above average. And four more areas are close to that level of scores. We also notice that the high skill reproduction index for industrial areas like Mumbai, Ghaziabad and Faridabad do not match high values of income security. Again, the correlation coefficient between income and skill reproduction security is quite low (0.205), which implies a surprising lack of any association between high skill orientation and high earnings from an individual worker's perspective in our sample. Most workers in our sample had basic education. They also had some special training in acquiring the skill. *Yet, what we found was that their skill, in most cases, was not adequately rewarded in terms of wages, which is reflected in their relatively low levels of income security. Is it related to the widely practised policies of labour flexibility?*

We need to point out here an anomaly which we notice in the security levels of workers as is connected with education levels.[8] CLSIs for interviewed workers exhibit a positive trend with levels of education when we view the illiterates at the bottom of the scale. Paradoxically, the highest composite index value was obtained for workers who have attained the secondary level of education and not for those with higher levels of education and skill. Lack of demand for these workers in the manufacturing sector is possibly a major explanation for this paradox. With this 'mismatch' between skill (education) and labour demand there is also an aspiration gap, with graduates aspiring for a better paid and high-skilled job as compared to what is worth a secondary level of education. Lack of such employment opportunities (particularly for the educated youth at entry point) forces them in many instances to accept factory jobs which contributes to low levels of job security as compared to those for workers with less qualifications. Also the young educated youth generally have higher expectations and aspirations regarding income and standard of life as well as social status which a factory-based low-skilled job may not ensure under the prevailing conditions of the Indian labour market. Moreover, the enterprises we visited showed their reluctance in employing graduates as factory workers unless there is some compulsion when they try to put them into supervisory jobs. Given the nature of the skill-mismatch, the highly qualified ones sometimes have no other option than taking on factory jobs.

A related issue which crops up in testing the validity of the neo-liberal prescriptions for the labour market relates to their faith in skill-formation as a supply-side solution to unemployment. We can differentiate the workers between two categories, with category I separating the skilled and unskilled[9] and category II differentiating workers with special training and those without special training. The CLSI level of the skilled and unskilled workers in our exercise are found to be at par. This may be due to the way skill is defined (both in terms of mean education and special training) in our study. But we get a different picture when we categorize the workers in terms of special training. Those with a special training from some professional or technical institutions have CLSIs which are higher as compared to others. In other words, it is not skill as such which helps workers to attain more security. Rather, it is skill appropriate for a particular job accessed through special training (often at the job) and which does matter to find better placement in the job market. *The supply-side argument on skill formation in general (and not with reference to specialization) misses out the links between jobs and skill as such.*

The view on above held by the neo-classicals as can be mentioned here is faulty for two reasons. First, that there is no automatic mechanism in the market, nor any 'invisible hand' which on its own would guarantee employment and protection to an individual worker on the basis of his/her skill, defined in terms of basic education or above. And second, the demand for skill (rather for 'exact skill') which is suitable for a particular factory job is equally, if not more, important for job creation and security. *Thus, we reject here the neo-classical supply side view of skill formation as such as an agenda for job creation which ignores the demand aspect in the job market.*

Workplace security in our study stands for protection in terms of ESI benefits and the normal working hours of eight hours a day. This can be treated as passé in the context of the current labour reforms. As with the income and employment security indices, Hooghly here tops the list. Also Kalyani and Kolkata, all from the same state, have high scores. Variations as observed across different areas reflect the differences in the evolution of work culture between different regions of the country. We also notice a clustering of areas within regions in terms of workplace security. However, there exists a high correlation between workplace security and income security which is what can be expected.

For voice representation security (via trade unions), the maximum score was only in the range of 0.50. This indicates how limited trade union representation had been as an effective tool to defend the rights of the organized workers. Voice representation index in Surat takes a toll with a value at 0 which is followed by Mumbai (Santacruz SEZ) with a similar low value. The fact, that in 10 out of 15 areas witness the 'worst' level of scoring brings home the inadequacy of voice representation for most workers in our sample. The consistently low values of this index results from the presence of workers who are not unionized in our sample and also to some extent, the passive attitude of workers towards the trade union activities.[10] Does it pay an individual worker in terms of deriving more security by being able to collectively register their voice? Probably so, since we find that unionized workers attained a higher level of composite security (CLSI 0.55) in every respect than the non-unionized workers (CLSI 0.39). However, such observations do not speak much with the growing tendency of casualization, and falling union memberships. Unionizing a casual worker turns out to be difficult because of the frequent changes they go through in terms of jobs and places.[11]

We now look at the financial security index of workers, which is defined in terms of the savings habit, possession of assets and related aspects. It can have an important role in supporting a worker to meet situations of unwarranted exigencies and distress. Financial security of workers has become increasingly important in India with the disappearance of social security benefits that used to be run by the state and also by the growing financial exclusion of poor borrowers by banks which today go by the Basel norms of credit rated lendings (Sen and Ghosh 2005). Arranging in terms of the financial security index, we find Faridabad at top of the list, followed by Okhla, Gurgaon and Surat which also have high or above average scores. We notice that three of these are old industrial townships with a long history of trade and industrial activity. One also can observe a spatial pattern in terms of the financial security availed of by the workers. Thus Kalyani, Hooghly and Kolkata in West Bengal (which excludes

Falta SEZ and Howrah, the decaying industrial belt); and Faridabad, Okhla and Gurgaon in North India have values of the index which are close to one another. As in the case of other security indices, we need to fall back on the spatial-temporal factors in this case, as explanations of the savings habit and asset holding of workers in different areas. This is probably more so when we notice that the correlation coefficient between financial security and income security index are at very low levels. *High income security obviously does not go in tandem with high savings or the savings habit and asset holding of workers. The latter are probably more influenced by the socio-cultural backdrops in which an individual worker is placed.*[12]

Family as a social institution provides a significant backup to its individual members in a country like India. In our calculation, Gurgaon is at the top of the list of the family support security index, and is followed by Falta, Surat, Kolkata and Hooghly. We notice that family support is high and important either in old industrial areas like Kolkata, Hooghly and Surat or in areas close to the rural set-up like Gurgaon and Falta. As a contrast, it is low in cosmopolitan areas like Mumbai, NOIDA, Delhi (which includes Mayapuri and Okhla) where workers with a migrant status are far from their hometowns or villages. This index, however, has very low degree of association with income security or employment security which define the current economic status of the individual worker. *The above tells us more about the role of family support as an alternate institution which tries to compensate (to the extent it is possible) the withering away of state level social security in India in terms of economic reforms.*

Contesting the Neo-liberal Prescriptions—A Dialogue

Observations as offered in the previous section and earlier in Chapter 3, can be used to verify and contest the principles as well as policies as originate from neo-liberal growth and development theories. This can be done by opening up a dialogue which critically views the policies as follow from these doctrines, especially from the angle of the much needed security of workers.

Let us pose here a set of questions which follow from the neo-classical paradigm. One of these relates to the difference in the perception of security among workers who belong to different age groups, which the neo-classical paradigm of perfect markets chooses to ignore. We have already pointed out in earlier chapters that workers in our sample are differentiated in terms of their age. We have found that the new recruits among workers who are at the entry-point feel more insecure than the old timers who are at the exit point. (In terms of the Indian condition individual workers up to 25 years of age are taken as entry point workers since they start looking for jobs from the age of 15–16 years and continue job searching till they are 25 or even more. On the other hand, workers above 50 years of age whose working life usually comes to an end when they reach 55–60 years are considered as exit point workers.)

We now pose a similar question which relates to the relative position of workers in terms of security according to their education and skill. In other words, does education (treated as skill by us) play an important role in providing labour security, as is expected from the supply side point of view of mainstream doctrines? And does individual skill of the workers matter in explaining security differentials among them? To check this we can go back to Table 5.2D and the low correlations between income and skill level security of different regions. We notice that the regions recording higher skill do not necessarily deliver high income security levels for workers. We thus observe that in terms of our sample, education level (and skill) at industrial units in different regions did not match the respective levels of income security, which is contrary to what is expected from the neo-classical framework.

Migration, in terms of mainstream doctrines, should not bifurcate the labour force in terms of their remuneration, etc. Rather migration is considered to level off the differences, if any, amongst them. Our data, however, is contrary, as pointed out in Chapter 3. Again, social background (castes, religious minorities), family support and union membership are not supposed to have any role in explaining labour status (or security in the present context) in terms of the mainstream neo-classical approach, which treats labour as a mass of homogeneous input in the production process. Our analysis contests all these, as pointed out earlier in this chapter. In our judgement social background should be recognized as an important criterion in judging labour security. We believe that an individual worker's social background (namely, caste and religion as a social institution in the Indian context) does play some determining roles with regard to their income, education, skill and job. We define here social categories as per the official norm on the basis of caste and religious minorities. We observe that the general category is placed at the top of the social hierarchy (CLSI 0.48), and is followed by religious minorities and SCs and STs (both having CLSI 0.44) and Other Backward Classes (OBCs, CLSI 0.38). Our findings vindicate our hypothesis that the more lowly a labourer is placed in the social hierarchy of caste and religion (in the sense of minority in the Indian context), the less is the labour security the person can achieve.[13] However, we do notice that differences among workers in terms of their social background are not robust enough to put a strong claim in this regard. Thus the composite value (CLSI) for the general social category of workers is significantly higher than the respective values of the indices only for OBC, SC and ST and (religious) minorities as a social group. However, the voice representation index, financial index and family support index for the general category are marginally lower than those of minorities—a point worth noticing here. They are also better placed in the labour market in terms of income security, employment security, job security and work security (see Tables 5.2F–5.2H, and also Chapter 3 of this book).

Industrial growth in neo-liberal doctrines is likely to have a trickle-down impact in terms of income, employment and other indicators of labour welfare. In absence of area-specific growth rates of different industries we have used the aggregate industry growth rates at 2-digit levels and then related these to the components as well as the composite security level of workers in the respective industries. The pattern of industry-wise diversity in labour security is self-evident from the statistics presented in Table 5.3 which offers both the components as well as the composite security index at the industry-specific levels.[14]

The data set presented in Table 5.3 seem to indicate that the industry-specific growth rates hardly had much of an impact on levels of specific and composite labour security. The latter is indicated by the low value of rank correlation coefficient (–0.094) between industry growth rates and the respective CLSIs. A similar absence of co-relation between the industry-specific individual security levels is self-evident in the table. *In general one does not observe any association between high growth rates and the specific security levels in different industries in terms of our data from primary surveys. The result tallies with the observation, made earlier in Chapter 2, using macro-level industry data from secondary sources.* Tables 5.3 and 5.4 provide some basic features of the industries in our sample which include the annual average growth rates of output at constant prices, wages, employment, capital–labour ratios and labour productivity. The data helps us to relate industry-specific levels of labour securities and these basic features of industries.

The economic reforms package in the labour market offers a strong plea for labour flexibility, recommending an end to labour market regulations as well as trade union pressures on wages and other terms of employment.

The validity of the strong plea for labour flexibility as above warrants a labour security status which, however, is far from what we found in our

Table 5.3 Labour security across industries

	Growth rates	Income security	Employment security	Job security	Skill reproduction security	Work security	Representation security	Financial security	Family support	CLSI
Wearing apparel (18)	16.55	0.27	0.51	0.38	0.44	0.44	0.28	0.48	0.25	0.38
Furniture (36)	13.17	0.22	0.40	0.52	0.58	0.26	0.02	0.40	0.50	0.36
Rubber and plastic (25)	12.02	0.27	0.50	0.38	0.42	0.56	0.23	0.21	0.54	0.39
Chemical (24)	9.11	0.53	0.49	0.69	0.47	0.83	0.31	0.35	0.44	0.51
Non-metallic mineral (26)	8.96	0.65	0.50	0.90	0.54	0.80	0.38	0.33	0.58	0.58
Motor vehicle (34)	8.9	0.69	0.53	0.60	0.58	0.77	0.25	0.42	0.63	0.56
Leather (19)	8.04	0.54	0.55	0.57	0.54	0.62	0.07	0.42	0.52	0.48
Other transport (35)	7.84	0.58	0.55	0.75	0.70	0.85	0.40	0.38	0.53	0.59
Textiles (17)	7.61	0.30	0.43	0.61	0.45	0.41	0.20	0.41	0.47	0.41
Fabricated metal (28)	7.12	0.39	0.46	0.79	0.41	0.78	0.35	0.42	0.40	0.50
Machinery (29)	6.85	0.33	0.45	0.70	0.52	0.50	0.09	0.24	0.49	0.41
Food and beverages (15)	6.17	0.66	0.58	0.75	0.38	0.68	0.45	0.41	0.52	0.55
Paper (21)	5.8	0.27	0.61	0.53	0.49	0.50	0.14	0.15	0.42	0.39
Basic metal (27)	5.54	0.54	0.52	0.46	0.42	0.72	0.23	0.32	0.39	0.45
Electrical machinery (31)	4.9	0.49	0.52	0.62	0.60	0.69	0.27	0.47	0.41	0.51
Printing and publishing (22)	2.52	0.46	0.48	0.34	0.53	0.60	0.17	0.35	0.34	0.41

Source: Authors' own calculations based on primary data collected through questionnaire-based field survey of 615 industrial workers in the organized manufacturing industries in some selected industrial areas of Delhi, Gujarat, Maharashtra, Uttar Pradesh and West Bengal during 2003–06.

Table 5.4 Some features of the industries in the sample

Industry name	AAGR of wage 1991–03	AAGR of employment 1991–03	AAGR of labour productivity	AAGR of capital–labour ratio
Furniture including jewellery (36)	20.05	31.23	29.05	33.28
Motor vehicle (34)	13.84	28.27	24.37	29.63
Printing and publishing (22)	19.68	14.99	30.21	32.20
Wearing apparel (18)	14.72	24.35	12.86	20.78
Chemical (24)	15.71	13.76	20.94	21.59
Food and beverages (15)	17.11	15.64	20.60	23.93
Paper (21)	17.36	17.20	20.54	27.25
Fabricated metal (28)	14.24	13.17	17.21	19.47
Other transport (35)	15.35	19.93	26.53	30.45
Machinery (29)	15.47	10.76	19.45	20.10
Rubber and plastic (25)	12.71	17.93	15.83	22.15
Non-metallic mineral (26)	21.94	15.33	28.36	41.52
Basic metal (27)	17.59	10.76	19.45	20.10
Electrical machinery (31)	13.42	14.18	17.05	21.65
Textiles (17)	10.79	13.89	16.40	21.67
Leather (19)	10.54	8.79	10.55	9.50

Source: Authors' own calculations based on primary data collected through questionnaire-based field survey of 615 industrial workers in the organized manufacturing industries in some selected industrial areas of Delhi, Gujarat, Maharashtra, Uttar Pradesh and West Bengal during 2003–06.

survey of industrial labour. Our findings, as mentioned in Chapter 3, confirm wide ranges of differentiation among labourers, say between labour employed on a permanent basis and the other 50 per cent or more of workers in our sample of 615 workers who are on a casual basis. As pointed out earlier, the CLSI of casual workers in our sample is only 0.36 as compared to 0.56 for permanent workers. It is a matter of concern for the new industrial economy of India with policies of growth-oriented flexible labour markets which has initiated wide ranging casualization of the workforce (see Table 5.5). As for the components of the CLSI, the income security of the casual worker is only 0.19 as compared to 0.70 of permanent workers. Similar discrepancies exist in the employment security between the casual workers (0.44) as compared to those for the permanent workers (0.57), in job security of casuals (0.55) as compared the permanent workers (0.60), skill reproduction security of casual workers (0.47) compared to the permanent workers (0.53), work security of casual workers at an abysmally low level (0.15) in comparison with that of permanent workers (0.34), financial security of casual workers (0.28)

Table 5.5 The composite and other security index for permanent and casual workers

	Income security	Employment security	Job security	Skill reproduction security	Work security
Casual (N = 344)	0.19	0.44	0.55	0.47	0.42
Permanent (N = 271)	0.70	0.57	0.60	0.53	0.53
Total (N = 615)	0.41	0.49	0.57	0.49	

	Voice representation security	Financial security	Family support index	CLSI
Casual (N = 344)	0.15	0.28	0.42	0.36
Permanent (N = 271)	0.34	0.47	0.51	0.56
Total (N = 615)	0.23	0.37	0.46	0.45

Source: Authors' own calculations based on primary data collected through questionnaire-based field survey of 615 industrial workers in the organized manufacturing industries in some selected industrial areas of Delhi, Gujarat, Maharashtra, Uttar Pradesh and West Bengal during 2003–06.

as compared to permanent workers (0.47), and family support security of casual workers (0.42) when compared to permanent workers (0.51).

Casualization, as pointed out earlier in Chapter 3, has been more common with young workers who are new entrants.[15] Thus age remains a major factor here which works against the young, entry level workers who face much lower levels of security. Exit-point workers, mostly permanent and also aged, as compared to the new entrants, enjoy some degree of social benefits during their working life which the new workers do not get.[16] Also, entry-point workers enjoy negligible voice representation—a point worth a mention here for policy articulation of the trade unions.

Conclusion

Aspects relating to the emerging patterns of the labour market in India, as will be pointed out in Chapter 6, may have important bearings for social cohesion in the years to come. The following aspects demand attention as our final observations on the field survey results:

We observe that with firms facing stiff competition in the product market, labour flexibility is demanded and implemented by the enterprises in their bid to cut costs. Dwindling labour security needs be viewed as a consequence of such cost cutting endeavour of the manufacturing enterprises which cuts across size classes of the industry. The voice of the enterprises is well represented in the push to do away with 'rigid' labour norms which are well encapsulated in the Second National Labour Commission's Report (National Commission on Labour 2002) and the Industrial Disputes Act.

Labour security needs be understood in the class focused distribution of surplus labour in the Marxist tradition. From this angle the payment which a worker receives may comprise *(a)* the necessary labour and *(b)* subsumed payments for providing conditions of existence to the enterprise. Growing casualization in the labour market is tantamount to reduced payments, even for necessary labour (as reflected in terms of the low level of minimum wage fixed by the state). This is related to *(a)* the existence of intermediaries/labour contractors and *(b)* payments below the minimum wage levels.

Labour market flexibility in terms of the lengthening of working hours and in dispensing with social benefits are both rationalized in the cost cutting attempts of enterprises in the face of growing competition. Those can be interpreted in terms of the distribution of surplus value, with the stake of labour at the lower end of the scale. A drop in labour market security clearly signifies a growing exploitation of labour.[17] In some instances, it even pertains to super-exploitation as we have found in the course of our field study among the manufacturing workers, especially at the Falta Special Economic Zone (SEZ) and in the *bidi* (tobacco processing) industry at Murshidabad in West Bengal (see Chapter 4 for details).

As for wage rates, these tend to vary widely across different regions. Even the minimum wages vary from area to area and from industry to industry. And a high output growth rate in particular industries does necessarily guarantee payment of minimum wages. For contractual workers, wage bargains cannot be made directly with the management. Here the labour contractors play a decisive role in deciding not only the wage levels but also the recruitment and retention of workers. This fact is often not paid the attention it deserves in most studies related to current labour status in India. As for the non-regular workers who are migrants, they often are forced to offer their labour at wages which are even below the prevailing rate of minimum wages. They are naturally not entitled to any social benefit from their employers and also lack of family support because their families happen to be far away. In-migration swells the ranks of reserve army of labour, which is an inevitable outcome of the accumulation process in industry under capitalism (Marx 1990: 631).[18]

As for the firms we came across, most of those increasingly use casual/contractual workers and thus less of regular permanent workers. An explanation, once again, may be offered in terms of the cost cutting devices of the manufacturing enterprises. Thus with a casual workforce, expenditure on the part of the employers as are needed for providing security to the workers is also proportionately less. We observe that contractual employment is on the rapid rise in organized manufacturing in the current phase of globalization—a process, which can be dubbed as 'informalization of formal space', which leads to a greater degree of insecurity for the workforce in the country. Thus the workforce now includes an increasing number of contractual workers who work for more than eight hours a day with hardly any overtime benefits and other social benefits as are usually given to the permanent workers. Dwindling labour security in the country is influenced by the rising uncertainty in a globalized economy, and intensified by subsidies and other advantages as are provided to capital at the cost of labour. Growing insecurity among workers, particularly among those who are at the entry points, makes the ILO declaration of decent work and decent life for all working men and women remain a far cry. The increasing worries about their insecure future coupled with widening inequality in the distribution of income and wealth may catapult a crisis in the country—a crisis of widespread social tension and turmoil in the days ahead.

As for trade unions, their bargaining strength has declined over the time. Labour unions are fast losing their strongholds in the face of growing casualization and the replacement of the so-called 'standard' work by the 'non-standard' work in these 'new economies'. Barring West Bengal, we did not come across a single state where a strong presence of trade unions among workers was visible. Further, the strategies of the trade unions at different tiers of their operation (from local to national) seemed to vary and the perception of the problem as well.[19] (See Chapter 6 for an elaboration of these arguments.)

Finally, we reiterate that labour market is a human social institution, a fact which is missing from the official perceptions relating to the current phase of globalization. This is evident with the emphasis which is placed on market-driven labour market reforms as the panacea to all problems in the economy. These observations indicate the rather unsustainable level of existence for a large part of working population in India. Thus insecurity of labour, as indicated by the facts relating to the organized manufacturing sector in our study, at best, provides only a partial picture.

The reality, especially when covering the status of labour deployed in unorganized manufacturing, and in agriculture, would turn out to be even more grim.

The deteriorating status of labour, despite the modest revival of the economy, has raised concerns within and outside the official circles which resulted in limited responses. A limited measure like 100 days of guaranteed employment programme in rural areas (National Rural Employment Guarantee Scheme) is one such gesture. Labour protests, increasingly difficult and hard to stage today, are treated by employers as dispensable costs of labour in terms of the new *mantra* of labour flexibility. However, both the state as well as the civil society are aware of the hazards of a unidirectional path to complete liberalization. This stalls the moves on part of capital to further enhance its share of output at cost of labour. The phase of unrelenting exploitation of labour thus has its own limits in history and a 'process of counter-globalization' at the level of local groups and civil society, as predicted by Polyani, does continue. With the process remaining undefined, especially in terms of the depth and intensity of the repressive phases, it becomes imperative for the concerned parties including the state, the non-governmental civil society, labour and capital to realize the limits of repression in non-authoritarian societies.

Appendix—Methodology of Construction of Security Indicators

INCOME SECURITY

1. Above minimum wage (1); otherwise (0)
2. Regular income (1); otherwise (0)
3. Wage revision in recent past (1); otherwise (0)
4. PF (1); otherwise (0)
5. ESI (1); otherwise (0)
6. Gratuity (1); otherwise (0)

EMPLOYMENT SECURITY

1. Long-term contract (1); otherwise (0)
2. No fear of losing job (1); otherwise (0)
3. No increased fear of losing job (1); otherwise (0)
4. Chances for alternative employment (1); otherwise (0)

JOB SECURITY

1. Good relationship with supervisor (1); otherwise (0)
2. Chances of promotion (1); otherwise (0)

SKILL REPRODUCTION SECURITY

1. Mean education and above (1); otherwise (0)
2. Access to special training (1); otherwise (0)
3. Special training (1); otherwise (0)
4. Opportunity to obtain training (1); otherwise (0)

WORK SECURITY

1. ESI (1); otherwise (0)
2. Worker works for normal working hour of eight hours (1); otherwise (0)

VOICE REPRESENTATION SECURITY

1. Union membership (1); otherwise (0)
2. Positive attitude towards union (1); otherwise (0)
3. Collective bargaining through union has increased (1); otherwise (0)

FINANCIAL SECURITY

1. Savings (1); otherwise (0)
2. Bank account (1); otherwise (0)
3. Asset holding (1); otherwise (0)

FAMILY SUPPORT SECURITY

1. More than one earning member (1); otherwise (0)
2. More than two dependent members (0); otherwise (1)

Notes

1. Manufacturing industries provide 12 per cent of total employment in India. The organized sector provides as little as 14 per cent of total employment in the manufacturing industry as a whole. Thus the organized manufacturing industry provides only 1.6 per cent of total employment in the country (Government of India, Annual Survey of Industries, Central Statistical Organisation).
2. After independence a Minimum Wages Act, 1948 was enacted by the Government of India empowering the state to fix minimum wages for employees working in specified employments. Payment of overtime in scheduled employments is also governed by this Act.
3. Employment security has different meanings according to the employment laws of each country. A worker in continental Europe enjoys a statutory employment contract. In the US, however, it refers to more to a worker's sense of having stability of maintaining a job resulting from the possession of special skills or seniority, though there are safeguards provided in many collective agreements against unanticipated technical changes.
4. In case of parameters quantitative in nature a threshold value is fixed either institutionally or on the basis of sample mean value of the parameter. In the case of qualitative (subjective) parameters the threshold is determined according to whether the particular parameter holds or not—assigning value 1 for 'yes' and value 0 for 'no'.

5. CLSI of Mumbai may be worse than is indicated here because of heavy weightage of electronics and gems and jewellery units located in the Santa Cruz SEZ in our study where workers are comparatively better off than their counterparts elsewhere in the city.

6. In Delhi, East Delhi and Mayapuri recorded the same level of CLSI whereas Okhla industrial area recorded a much higher level of CLSI. One reason for this may be the differences in nature of industries in which interviewed workers work. Within Uttar Pradesh, Ghaziabad recorded a lower CLSI than NOIDA and NOIDA SEZ. Within West Bengal, the Falta SEZ recorded the lowest CLSI, which is much below CLSIs recorded in the other areas of the same state. The highest CLSI is enjoyed by the industrial workers in the Hooghly area, which is an old industrial belt where large industries like automobiles, textile mills, and engineering are concentrated. CLSIs for Kalyani and Kolkata follow that of Hooghly. Howrah industrial area ranks just above the Falta SEZ at the bottom. Howrah is also an industrial area where mainly iron foundry, chemical and light engineering industries are located.

7. We define a fundamental class process as that confined to the performance and appropriation of surplus labour as in Marx and subsumed class process as distribution and receipt of surplus labour.

8. We have classified the interviewed workers into six different education categories—illiterate, literate, basic education (up to eighth standard), secondary, higher secondary (+2 or school leaving) and graduates and above. Very few workers in our sample have graduate and post-graduate degrees.

9. We define skill here as knowledge or apprenticeship which is specialized in nature and without which the present production cannot take place. This means unskilled workers are engaged in those types of works which can be done without any specialized knowledge and, which only supplements the jobs done by skilled workers in the factory space.

10. This passive attitude towards trade union activities is reflected in terms of the large number of negative ('no') responses when asked whether the worker finds the trade union interventions satisfactory. Also a large number replied in the negative when asked if the bargaining capability of unions has increased in recent past.

11. Union members possess higher CLSI than the non-union members. Unionized workers have significantly higher levels of job and social security than the non-unionized workers.

12. This is because, at individual level, a worker may have very high expenditure liability (often, this is influenced by socio-cultural background, say, looking after one's ailing and old parents and old people in the family) despite earning a high income. This would then adversely affect his/her savings potential. Or, sometimes it may be the case that the worker concerned spends exorbitantly on commodities (which are socially undesirable) like liquor, etc., which increases his monthly expenditure. In fact, in such cases he may be spending more than his income and get into a debt trap. This, in most cases, depends on the socio-cultural ambience in which the individual workers work and live.

13. We categorize the workers broadly into general, OBC and SC/ST, and minority. Our hypothesis is that in the Indian social stratification context, general category workers are better placed than the other categories.

14. We could make a list of 16 industry categories as per ASI 2-digit level codes. Note that the workers in the other transport industry (with ASI code 35) have highest CLSI and those in the furniture industries (with ASI code 36) have the lowest. Motor vehicle

industry workers (with ASI code 34) enjoy highest income security and the lowest by the furniture (code 36). Paper (code 21) industry workers enjoy highest employment security and lowest by furniture (code 36). In the non-metallic mineral industries (code 26) workers enjoy highest job security. The job security index in our calculation is lowest for the printing and publishing industry category (code 22). The skill reproduction security is highest for other transport (code 35) and lowest for food and beverages (code 15). The work security is highest for other transport (code 35) and lowest for furniture (code 36). The voice representation security is highest for food and beverages (code 15) and lowest for furniture (code 36). The financial security is observed to be highest among the workers in wearing apparel (code 18) and lowest for paper (code 21). Finally, family support index is highest in motor vehicle (code 34) and lowest in printing and publishing (code 22).

15. Individual workers aged up to 25 years are taken as entry point workers. They start job searching at the age of 15–16 years in the conditions prevailing in the Indian countryside and they generally remain in that state almost for next 10 years or so. Workers above 50 years of age, whose working life comes to an end within the next 5–10 years, are considered as exit point workers.

16. We categorize them into eight different age groups. Age-wise distribution of CLSI brings forth one interesting observation. As one moves up in the age ladder, CLSI increases more or less, with one negligible exception. Workers who are below 25 years of age enjoy lowest CLSI, which is true about their income security also. In fact, most of the young workers in these age-groups we could interview are casual in nature while most of the aged workers with more than 45 years of age are in present job for quite a long period of time and are permanent—the main reason behind high income security among the 51+ age group.

17. This refers to rise in s/v with s rising and v falling. Falling v indicates fall in costs pertaining to security provisions. Here s refers to 'surplus value' and v variable capital as in Marx, and s/v as rate of exploitation. There are multiplicity of class processes which may be exploitative and non-exploitative (Chakrabarti and Cullenberg 2003).

18. 'Thus it is capitalist accumulation itself that constantly produces, and produces in direct ratio of its own energy and extent, a relatively abundant population of labourers, that is, a population of greater extent than suffices for the average needs of the self-expansion of capital, and therefore a surplus population' (Marx 1990: 631).

19. For example, we find some local trade union leaders in one of our surveyed areas are actually playing the role of labour contractors for the sake of the working class cause. On the one hand, they are pragmatic in rationing daily jobs to a group of labourers and distributing equally the aggregate earnings of the day among the workers and taking care of social benefits of the labourers by forming a co-operative. On the other hand, they remain very passive to the very idea of fighting to change the situation. Rather, they seem to be content with what they are doing. The militancy in the activities of the central leaders of the same union is completely missing at the local level in this case. Similarly, in Murshidabad, trade unions are present and yet not present. Missing in their perceptions the difference in the class processes of *bidi*-manufacturing enterprises with those in the factory-based manufacturing.

Labour Market Policies in India 6

Labour policy reform remains a major agenda in India's second phase of economic reforms which is currently underway. This is backed by the neo-liberal prescription for deregulation which claims that the rigid labour market rules and regulations obfuscate the cutting edge of competitive efficiency for business firms, both in the domestic economy as well as in overseas markets in this age of globalization. The growth-centric agenda of free market reforms warrants flexibility in all markets including those in the labour market. Following the supply-side doctrines of the 1980s and 1990s, these theories negate the possibility of under-employment equilibrium in the labour market. Unemployment is thus viewed as the consequence of labour market rigidity, and particularly of wage rigidity. Thus it is maintained that the removal of all sorts of rigidities in the labour market would automatically ensure full employment in the labour market.

During the post-war years of the 1950s and 1960s, aptly described as the golden age of capitalism, advanced industrialized countries in the West embraced the Keynesian policy imperatives of fiscal expansion towards full-employment along with the Fordist pattern of expansion which ensured stability in the labour market. The 1980s, however, witnessed a reversal of such policies which came along with the upsurge of supply side economics of the Thatcher–Reagan variety. The micro foundation of macroeconomics which provided the basis for these policies advocated, among others, wage flexibility as the device to ensure cost-cutting technology and the clearing of labour markets. The different versions of the mainstream economic doctrines which included New Classical economics (relying on rational expectations), the supply-side theories, and the New Keynesian varieties—all held the rigid labour market as solely responsible for unemployment or the non-clearance of the labour market (see Mankiw 2004; Farmer 2002). Unemployment is viewed as frictional and/or structural in both New Classical and New Keynesian theories. Thus the policy prescriptions as follow to justify what is observed as the natural rate of unemployment (NRU) rely on giving up sticky wage policies and rigid labour rules and regulations in the economy as remedial measures. Models as shown here look at unemployment both at a micro as well as at the macro-level, from a supply side perspective, thus ignoring altogether the demand aspects as well as the social institutions which govern the labour market.

In their micro-theoretic approach to the functioning of the labour market, the neo-classical doctrines are dominated by the search theoretic models, as mentioned in Chapter 1. The issues cover, among others, the options (apparently) exercised by labourers between work and leisure, especially in turning down job offers; the lengths of employment and unemployment spells for individual workers; the coexistence of unemployed workers and unfilled vacancies; factors influencing aggregate unemployment and vacancy rates; wage disparities among groups of homogeneous workers; the relation between wages and turnover of labour and finally factors which affect the most efficient rate of labour turnover (see Rogerson et al. 2005).[1]

It does not require much introspection to identify the strong impact of a supply-side approach in these doctrines including the search model. The basic presumption underlying these constructions is that of an individual worker, viewed as a rational economic agent, and in his/her utility maximizing behaviour, who may remain unemployed by choice. Needless to say it hardly encompasses the concrete reality in terms of what labour experiences, particularly in developing countries, where options of availing unemployment benefits or other forms of social security are almost non-existent. To remain unemployed by choice may remain an option for only a handful of persons who can afford such luxuries; but employment, which means livelihood, cannot be an option which can be dispensed with by the majority, in developing as well as in developed countries.

An essential ingredient to these notions relates to what is known as the Washington consensus, which is responsible for pushing different national economies on to the path of free markets and economic liberalization and for its strong advocacy of labour market flexibility. Wage rigidity as well as the laws to protect labour, as mentioned earlier, have been held as factors responsible for the low employment growth as well as inefficiency in production.

Since the inception of economic reforms in 1991 labour market reforms have been on the agenda of the official reform initiatives, the implementation of which is still considered as incomplete. Labour flexibility in the day-to-day handling, recruiting and/or discharging of labour at the factory level, however, has started even without much change in the official labour laws. The changed scenario in the labour market, which has emerged is characterized by rampant contractualization, casualization, with erosions in labour security and voice representation, some details of which have been provided in the earlier chapters of this book.

Several commissions, dealing with labour reforms (including the National Commission of Labour 2002) were appointed by the government in recent years.[2] In addition, the Planning Commission constituted a task force under the chairmanship of M.S. Ahluwalia—the report of which came out in July 2001. The major thrust of all these official reports has been to do away with existing labour legislations and to permit flexible hiring policies. These removed most of the labour security measures, even for the organized sector where labour and other employees are often perceived as a *privileged* set among other workers, especially as compared to those in the unorganized sector.

It is important to assess the impact of these policy recommendations in terms of the status of labour in the organized sector. As we indicate in the rest of this chapter, the entire perspective of these labour market reforms as recommended by these official committees, are essentially from the perspective of capital, thus leaving behind the earlier experiments of state-led industrialization and development as was experimented earlier in the newly independent India.

We provide, in this chapter, an understanding of the policy imperative of these official reports in relation to the role of trade unions for organized factory workers in the country. The chapter is organized as follows. The first section goes through the principal recommendations of the National Commission on Labour Report (2002). The next section dwells on the role of trade unions in the broader context of industrial relations and economic development. The third section makes an attempt to draw some policy conclusions from the discussions in the earlier two sections while commenting on the Unorganized Workers Security Bill (2005). The last section sums up the major findings of the chapter.

Report of the National Commission on Labour (2002)— Reviewing the Official Position in India on Organized Labour

The National Commission on Labour (NCL) submitted its report in September 2002. Earlier there was one National Commission on Rural Labour in 1991. The last commission's policy goal was to change the labour laws. As a state appointed commission, its recommendations can be deemed as that of the ruling Indian state. As a background to an under-standing of the recommendations of the NCL, we recall that in a market economy the state brings its chosen set of processes which has an important bearing on the legally binding set of rules and regulations concerning the enterprises, including their running and closure. The labour laws, a subset of such legal systems, consist of processes which concern the working day, working conditions, right to strike, etc., relating to labour employed in the enterprise. Putting it in a slightly different way, *the labour laws, a state acknowledged intervention, is an acceptance of what can be termed as labour rights, a legal guarantee which refers to the various facilities the workers enjoy in a specific socio-historical setting.* However, one must also bear in mind that labour laws are outcomes of political decisions taken in a certain political and economic environment.

Implementation of any law is necessarily subject to how it is interpreted. We may question here the perspective taken by the NCL in formulating its recommendations regarding the changes in the prevailing labour laws. As mentioned earlier, we observe that labour as viewed by the NCL is grounded on the logic of global capital which provides an anchor to com-petitive capitalism. This, in effect, explicates the place and role of labour from the perspective of policy-making. The NCL is thus in a position which is quite paradoxical with its recommendations for labour-related legal changes which are from the perspective of capital.

There could be so many other ways to view labour laws. Thus one can consider labour as the point of reference by placing it at the centre of analysis. From such an angle, labour laws would address the NCL recom-mendations quite differently from what the official interpretation of NCL stands for. We offer in the rest of this section an analysis of the NCL report from a perspective which views labour in terms of the surplus approach as in the Marxist literature.

Our analysis is important since the NCL report remains an important document in providing the much needed ideological underpinnings for the state in dealing with labour which, if fully implemented, will change altogether the status of labour as also the judicial structure in favour of capital.

Organized vis-à-vis unorganized workers

At a basic level, the NCL draws a line between workers in the 'organized sector' and those in the 'unorganized sector'. Following the literature on dual economies in mainstream literature, the 'organized sector' is con-ceived as the site of the 'normal' economy and the 'unorganized sector' as the pathological, the *lacking other* of the 'normal' economy. Given this binary, the NCL report addresses two issues which include the 'labour reform' targeting the organized sector and a set of tentatively framed recommendations relating to social security for the unorganized sector, which include the women workforce and children.

We want to stress at this point that there seems to be one unifying theme to the seemingly disparate policy goals in the NCL. Thus, as pointed out earlier in this book, a major aspect of the ongoing process of globalization is to protract the system of competitive capitalism which requires linkages among the capitalist enterprises at a global level. For this to happen the global capitalist enterprises as also the non-capitalist enterprises in the unorganized sector need to pass through institutions facilitating such changes (for example, via the outsourcing process). The connecting processes for the global capitalist enterprises can be described as *circuits* of global capital which spins a space even wider than what is specified by the physical reach of all above combined. This process of creating and expanding of the circuits of global capital has allowed competitive capitalism to become a global phenomenon. And the NCL seems to precisely endorse this route of capitalist expansion by having the unorganized workers in its fold.

From our perspective, the NCL telescopes in its report the neo-classical position on distribution between wages and profits as 'fairness and just', as in the much celebrated marginal productivity principle of neo-classical doctrine. We mentioned this in Chapter 1. The principle signals the absence and indeed disavowal of an exploitation of labour by capital. The NCL thus wants to produce a 'work culture' that seeks to reproduce the wage–productivity nexus in case of the workers thereby expelling the spectre of exploitation from the social realm.

While the emphasis on the wage–productivity nexus is self-evident,[3] the report asserts that while the management is already committed to productivity, the workers are presumed to be not so.[4] One of the explicitly mentioned policy goals which underlies the NCL recommendations on labour laws is to produce what it says is a 'systematic arrangement' that will guarantee the social reproduction of this wage–productivity nexus, which in turn must form the founding basis of the relation between the workers/trade unions and employers. The social reproduction of the wage–productivity nexus is, however, assumed to depend upon a harmonious and stable relation between the two contending parties which include labour.[5]

A host of measures are sought by the NCL as part of this 'systematic arrangement'. Thus the labour laws, as suggested by the NCL, need to be reconsidered in terms of the process that globalization has opened up.[6] According to the NCL, competitive capitalism under globalization demands two things from the labourers: *(a)* acceptance of wholesale cost-cutting as a matter of right of employers which, by default, constitutes the right to shed labour (either by keeping the enterprises open or by closing the enterprise itself) and *(b)* acceptance of the wage–productivity principle that would guarantee the maximum intensity of labour usage. Both these conditions are deemed necessary for a capitalist enterprise to survive in the face of global competition and, in the process, to keep on 'pumping out' the maximum possible amount of surplus value by employing the workers.

Here, we can discern a definitive pattern in the policy prescriptions of the NCL. It concerns the social sanction of cost-cutting and wage–productivity nexus as a matter of right for the employers. This can only be guaranteed in a harmonious social scenario where the workers accept this right, a guarantee that NCL seeks to produce. For the NCL the existing labour laws in India along with the current conceptions of 'worker' and 'workers' rights' contravene the logic of (global) capital, posing serious barriers to the rights sought by the employers. Consequently, the NCL attempts to change within the organized sector the conception of the worker by invoking the aspect of 'work culture' and by seeking to institutionalize a change in the workers' 'mindset' regarding who they are and what is rightfully theirs. Such a social reproduction of the wage–productivity nexus is, however, assumed to depend upon harmonious and stable relations between the two contending parties which include labour.[7]

In sharp contrast, the wage–productivity nexus is downplayed in the NCL report as far as the unorganized sector is concerned. Thus the usual cost-cutting race observed between enterprises is also not what is seen as taking place within the unorganized sector which has enough leeway to reduce costs. What comes to the fore in the NCL report regarding the unorganized sector is the aspect of social security which, it says quite vaguely, is to be guaranteed by the employer and the state or some combination of both. In this sense, we aver that the recommendations of the NCL can be seen as reforming the labour laws in the organized sector and offering social security in the unorganized sector. These are not apparently different goals but instead could be seen as diverse components of a unifying logic. The recent legislations in the Parliament relating to the insurance facilities for the unorganized workers are a step in that direction.

A host of measures are sought by the NCL as part of this 'systematic arrangement.' Thus the labour laws, as suggested by the NCL, need to be reconsidered in terms of the process that globalization has opened up.[8] In terms of the NCL, competitive capitalism under globalization demands two things from the labourers:

1. Acceptance of wholesale cost-cutting as a matter of right of employers which, by default, constitutes the right to shed labour (either by keeping the enterprise open or by closing the enterprise itself).
2. Acceptance of the wage-productivity principle that would guarantee the maximum intensity of labour usage.

Both these conditions are deemed necessary for a capitalist enterprise to survive in the face of global competition and, in the process, to keep on 'pumping out' the maximum possible amount of surplus value from the workers.

A host of 'reforms' have been initiated in the name of New Economic Policy in India that would make this linkage feasible. These include efforts to restructure the unorganized sector and to articulate these enterprises within the broader circuits of global capital. As part of that policy the numerous subsidy protections for unorganized sector from government—some of which dates back to decades ago—are taken away or sharply reduced. Just as there is an international reserve army of labour from where enterprises in the organized sector can now pick and choose, there is similarly an effort to identify and create a reserve army of enterprises in the unorganized sector that can be possibly accessed by these organized sector enterprises, for outsourcing or for providing other services.

We can surmise that the emphasis of the NCL centres on the existing labour rights in the organized sector whose dismantling and even possible truncation is important because: (a) it allows the enterprises to directly compete against one another and (b) it allows the enterprises unlimited access to the unorganized sector thereby enabling these enterprises to remain competitive. Both these aspects, of course, help to secure and facilitate the process of extracting, appropriating and distributing the maximum amount of surplus value by 'productive' employers.

Redefining the worker

The NCL sets out to practically redefine the meaning of worker. NCL's goal is to redefine the worker and of 'working class' on two indicators: (a) income and (b) status fixed in terms of the type of work.[9]

As for income-based categories, it is clearly an attempt to redraw the meaning of worker while ignoring the relevance of property income. The focus of the report remains singularly trained on the wages which the segmented 'productive labourers' and 'unproductive labourers' respectively receive and then dividing the existing 'workers' into 'workers' and 'non-workers' on the basis of a wage income, the amount of which is decided in an ad hoc manner. The NCL, however, makes no such differences in the category of the term 'employers' concerning whether a corporate appropriates Rs 1 billion per year or another appropriates only Rs 1 million. Instead, all who employ labour in any form are clubbed under the term 'employer'.

To understand why NCL seeks to categorize workers in terms of level of wage income, it needs to be mentioned that competitive capitalism demands, among other things, assured protection from socially created barriers such as the received 'labour rights' and trade unions (whose existence is ensured by the prevalent labour laws). The NCL report meets this demand of competitive capitalism by excluding a major chunk of the workforce from the definition of the 'worker' by the criteria of income and status and in this way literally exclude them from any access to labour rights. Those who get above the specified sum designated as wage income (for example, white-collar workers) are not supposed to have the right to form labour unions, a practice widely followed in the industrial sector.

The second aspect used to differentiate the 'worker' is their 'status', as fixed in terms of the type of assigned job. It might very well happen that an individual is simultaneously occupying two positions within an enterprise, say as a productive labourer who takes part in the process of producing surplus value and as an unproductive labourer involved in the process of supervision, two distinctly different processes. The NCL categories as above do not work in such cases.

Work culture and voice representation

One more aspect that is given special importance by the NCL is 'work culture'.[10]

In a theme that recurs quite routinely throughout the NCL report, a worker must remain attentive to both the rights and responsibilities as suits the new work culture. 'Work culture' here demands that workers should stand ready to work for any duration, in whatever form required and with the greatest possible intensity (productivity). These constitute the responsibility on part of the workers, which comes with the rights handed over to them. Thus the 'rights' of the workers to have access to 'fair' wage and 'minimum social security' must be countervailed by a return in terms of maximum possible productivity they can deliver to the employers (or, more generally, any appropriator of surplus).

The 'rights', however, are fixed by the NCL in abstract terms. For example, the 'rights' of the workers can include ruling out any form of legal recourse to closure, retrenchment and lay-off for which no prior permission is required by the employer. The 'rights' also include those of employers when workers are being subjected to the 'act of misconduct' by refusing to undergo training and take up job assigned by the employers following any restructuring of the enterprise or even otherwise. Labour actions such as 'go slow' and 'work to rule' would also come under the 'act of misconduct' (NCL 6.41, p. 80). Misconduct are seen as social evils by NCL and the 'strong arm of the state' is recommended to ensure that severe penalties on the workers and their organizations are imposed.

The NCL recommends a ban on the right to strike by workers in establishments dealing with essential services like water supply, medical services, sanitation, electricity and transport (NCL 6.48, pp. 80–81). Denied rights could be taken instead as the social responsibility of the 'workers'. The only acknowledged 'right' in such cases is the 'right' to get ones dues (in wages or benefits), the delivery of which is seen as the responsibility of the employers.

The NCL recognises, in general, the right to strike of workers. But here too, 'rights' is defined as collective bargaining between the trade unions and employers to sort out the disputes relating to wages, with arbitrators at Labour Relations Commission and the Lok Adalats having a great degree of significance (NCL 6.90–6.97, pp. 87–90). However, it is not spelt out as to how, say, in case of the Lok Adalats, the 'justness' as expected would be guaranteed. To stop the workers/unions from attempting to take legal recourse through any other institutions, it is recommended that 'jurisdiction of civil courts be banned in respect of all matters for which provision is contained in the relevant labour laws' (NCL 6.99, pp. 90–91).

So, what remains of the workers' right to strike? As the NCL holds it,

Strike could be called only by the recognised negotiating agent and that too only after it had conducted a strike ballot amongst all the workers, of whom at least 51 per cent support the strike. Correspondingly, an employer will not be allowed to declare a lock out except with the approval of the highest level of management except in cases of actual or grave apprehension of physical threat to the management or to the establishment. The appropriate government will have the authority to prohibit a strike or lock-out by a general or special order and refer for adjudication the issue leading to the strike/lock-out. The general provisions like giving of notice of not less than 14 days, not declaring a strike or lock-out over a dispute which is in conciliation or adjudication and so on will be incorporated in the law. In this context we also recommend that an illegal strike or illegal lock-out should attract similar penalties. A worker who goes on illegal strike should lose three days wages for every day of illegal strike, and the management must pay the worker wages equivalent to three days wages per day of the duration of an illegal lock-out. The union which leads an illegal strike must be derecognised and debarred from applying for registration or recognition for a period of two or three years. (NCL 6.101, p. 91)

The above contains an important point of discrepancy between the closure (strike) by workers and closures (the lockouts) on part of the employers. The workers are required to approve the strike by satisfying the objective condition of 51 per cent approval that can be verified in a positive sense. The employers, on the other hand, are required to get the 'approval of the management' or hold a perceived apprehension of threat to the management or the enterprise per se. The latter is a very subjective condition which is non-verifiable in a positive sense. While the probability that the 'management' may run into conflict with the employers is always there, one can safely conjecture that with the senior level of management directly appointed by the employers, the two would remain in close relationship with one another. As for confronting labour, the employers and top management have rarely been found to be differing. Besides the term 'approval' by management is open to interpretation. If the 'approval of highest management' makes for the legal sanction of lockouts, it is further reinforced by the employers' 'perception' regarding the 'threat' coming from workers. This 'perception threat' is totally subjective and cannot be verified as and when invoked. Consequently, we can say that the NCL gives the employers a virtual free hand in declaring lockouts as and when deemed a fit case by the employers, without giving the same kind of right to the workers to declare strikes. As a contrast, even if the 51 per cent objective condition for strike is met by workers, the 'appropriate government' is given extraordinary authority to ban any strike violating which the workers will be subjected to a host of penalties and the unions leading the strike face derecognition. Overall, what we observe in the NCL is that the rights of workers and their responsibilities, and that of the employers' rights and responsibilities, remain heavily biased in favour of the latter.

Working hours

We now comment on the NCL's approach to hours of the average working day for a labourer. Previously, the idea of eight hours work (whether implemented or not) was considered as a socially acceptable workload that a worker could take in a day. It was understood that the workers will work for eight hours, sleep for eight hours and spend the rest of the eight hours pursuing their other interests. The concept of eight hours 'working day' as a right of the worker was won in the industrialized countries through hard struggles. While this right was more confirmed in the West, it had different degrees of success in the rest of the world. However, despite the regional and sectoral differences in terms of its applicability, it has wide acceptance as a desirable goal from the perspective of the worker functioning in any site of the economy.

Currently, the social acceptability of this norm is under attack in India, in terms of both the neo-liberal project of labour reforms and the recommendations by the NCL. It may be mentioned that the NCL points out that under competitive capitalism enterprises cannot afford the concept of a 'working day' as has been hitherto understood. As such the NCL has kept the working hours outside its self-proclaimed goal of ensuring the minimum level of protection and welfare for workers in all sections of the economy—organized as well as unorganized.[11]

From the perspective of labour, the links of productivity with both technology and working hours has a major bearing on the rate of exploitation and 'profit' of the employers. An increase in the length of the working day enables an increase in surplus labour time even as socially necessary labour time remains the same. In contrast, technical progress can reduce the necessary labour time by allowing the socially necessary subsistence basket of commodities to be produced with even less amount of necessary labour time. This means that even as the working time remains the same, with necessary labour time falling more surplus labour time is available to be appropriated. This achieves a higher level of labour productivity relative to real wages and, consequently, a larger amount of surplus labour is available to be extracted for the same working time. An increase in the rate of exploitation through productivity increase is considered to be even more dynamic than the first one which is based on an increased rate of exploitation due to longer working hours.

With the experiences of exploitative labour relations in the 18th and 19th century and with different social movements against those experiences, rules and regulations were enacted that, among other things, fixed the maximum working hours for workers, particularly in Europe and North America. In case of India, especially after independence in 1947, and not least because of strong trade union and social movements, the received concept of an eight hour 'working day' retained a degree of social acceptability despite its non-implementation in many areas; including the so-called unorganized sector. The idea of 'working day' is important because it is often taken as a marker for what is considered a 'humane' day of labour. With this social acceptability of a 'working day', and the limits it places to the competitiveness of the capitalist enterprises, the NCL felt the need to address the issue in its recommendations which called for a practical dissolution of the concept altogether. Indeed, the logic of competitive capitalism that globalization has let loose is in some ways already producing this dissolution which, now, the NCL wants to be accepted both socially and legally. Even for developed countries, technological change along with increasing working hours is offering hitherto unforeseen opportunities for capitalist appropriation of surplus value and its distribution.

It can be observed that the existing labour regulations in India (pertaining to working hours, working conditions, security of jobs and pay, etc.) are coming under severe attacks with different state governments competing to facilitate the entry of global capital and its circuits in their respective domain. The latter entails higher productivity with a combination of increased working hours and technical progress. From this angle, the recommendations of the NCL on the working hours are not surprising at all. We would like to emphasize that the issue here is not whether the workers would want to work more (they may very well like to do so). Instead one has to ask whether there is still a need for *the concept of a working day from the point of view of the workers. A need as above, if forsaken, would amount to accepting that, in the process of being employed, the workers are required to place their labour power at the disposal of the employers in a timeless space so that the latter can pump out the surplus value from the workers at will.*

Casualization and labour contractors

While the presence of labour contractors in the process of casualization is acknowledged by the NCL (NCL 6.109, p. 93), the role of the labour contractors is generally kept outside the purview of labour laws. This is particularly disturbing since, evidently, this group is currently acquiring an institutional form in terms of occupying the position of an intermediary between labourers and employers. The importance of a labour contractor is particularly evident in the process of casualization that needs to be acknowledged, accounted for and dealt with. The NCL has pointed out repeatedly that one important element of the current phase of global-ization is the casualization of labour.[12] However, the growing process of casualization is gaining its own momentum and creating powerful players who are the labour contractors. The latter provide the conditions of ex-istence to the enterprises through their control of the supply and terms of employment of casual labourers, against which they receive a payment. With this role in the process of casualization, the labour contractors emerge as critical components of that process.

With intense competition, which is affected through cost-cutting meas-ures that globalization has brought about, *enterprises have formed important linkages with these labour contractors.* These linkages are motivated by the fact that the presence of labour contractors reduces the cost of searching to find casual labourers which helps the employers to circumvent the legal barriers pertaining to labour use; thus enabling a reduction in those forms of surplus distributions (like medical benefits, cheap canteens, pension, pro-vident funds, etc.) which had to be otherwise provided to the permanent workers in addition to the wage rate. The spectre of casualization also contains all upward movements in the wage rate including those of the permanent workers (who are threatened with replacements by the casual workers). Finally, the casualization process debilitates the power of the trade unions, thereby enabling other actors such as the board of directors and top management to acquire a decisive hold over the decision-making process within the enterprise. The presence of labour contractors is thus of critical importance in enabling enterprises to exercise a control over labour and, through that, a control over the cost-cutting procedure. In so far as dismantling the labour rights within an enterprise helps un-bundle the permanent workforce into a casual workforce, the enterprise in the organized sector mimics the 'work-conducive' environment within the un-organized sector. The role of labour contractors in producing this 'informal' environment within the enterprises in the organized sector is thus vital. Ironically, while the workers in the 'unorganized sector' per se possess different kinds of rights and securities which are guaranteed as part of the social norms and customs, this new force of casualized labourers in the organized sector are left with little rights and securities.

In countries like India, we not only come across labour contractors in traditional industries such as jute and construction, where the practice had existed for a long time, but also in the more 'sophisticated' industries such as engineering, finance and IT where the so-called placement and 'head-hunting' agencies are often found to be participating in the process of contracting casual/contractual labour.

The process of casualization can also have a significant impact on the wage rate of the labourers. One possibility is that the enterprise would have to provide a payment to the labour contractors for the service they provide through the supply of casual workers. This means that if an increasing amount of surplus value is extracted by intensifying the use of casual labourers, then even after paying for the labour contractors, the distributed surplus to the enterprise will not decline. There is another possibility that instead of the labourers, the enterprises hand over the wages directly to the labour contractors who then distribute the wage amount to the casual workers employed by the enterprise. In this case, while the enterprise pays the minimum wage, the workers may not be receiving it since the labour contractors would deduct part of that. Thus the workers could be subjected to what we may call super exploitation. Not only is their surplus value (labour) appropriated by the employers, the labourers are not even receiving the value of labour power equivalent to the socially necessary amount of basket of goods and services they require to reproduce their labour power, which is the minimum wage.[13] Possibilities as above are hardly given any consideration in the NCL and no effort is made to institutionalize the laws which would prevent such deplorable cases of super exploitation. However, given that the NCL report is in complicity with the logic of competitive capitalism, all these are hardly surprising.

Trade Unions in the Changing Circumstances

There remain a few aspects to the changing perception of trade unionism in general. Thus, 'It is by now a commonplace argument that the trade union movement in general and the Indian trade union movement in particular are, at best, under strain and, at worst, in a state of crisis' (Hariss-White 2003; Thomas 1995; Tulpule 1996). While globalization of late has aggravated the situation, some have claimed that the so-called crisis of trade unionism can be traced to the 1970s with the decline in its memberships (Thomas 1995). For the trade unions, the excluded or demoted sites, say, within the unorganized sector, cannot be independent of its activities in the organized sector.

Let us now look at some of the empirical facts regarding Indian labour force and trade unions. Tables 6.1 and 6.2 give the picture of employment in terms of different types of employment in urban India as per the National Sample Survey Organization (NSSO) findings. We draw attention

Table 6.1   Employment and unemployment in India per 1,000 male populations

NSSO Round	Self-employed	Regular employees	Casual workers	Unemployed	Not in labour force
50th	319	326	123	32	199
55th	312	314	125	35	213
60th	232	218	81	25	443

Source: NSSO 50th, 55th and 60th round.

Table 6.2   Employment and unemployment in India per 1,000 female populations

NSSO Round	Self-employed	Regular employees	Casual workers	Unemployed	Not in labour force
50th	99	65	58	15	762
55th	89	66	42	12	791
60th	44	53	24	12	867

Source: NSSO 50th, 55th and 60th round.

to the steady declines in regular employment between the 50th (July 1993–June 1994) and 55th Round (July 1999–June 2000); and the 55th Round (July 1999–June 2000) and 60th Round (January–June 2004). All the rounds indicate considerable proportion of self-employed for both male and female. Any labour policy reform, naturally needs to take these facts into account.

Let us now turn to the trade unions. Table 6.3 indicates the declining trade union density over the years since 1989. As per various issues of official reports which include the *Indian Labour Year Book,* and as cited in the literature, there is a steady decline in membership from 8.19 million in 1986 to 5.61 million in 1996 (Sengupta 2003). Note that in India most of the union members are organized sector workers. So, the decline in union memberships points to an erosion in trade union penetration among these categories while the other categories of workers in the unorganized sector including self-employed remain mostly non-unionized. In fact, organizing unorganized and self-employed workers is the greatest challenge that the trade unions are facing today. There is a need on the part of the trade unions to understand the fragmented space of labour, created by capital, where the earlier notion homogeneous classes of proletariat and bourgeois capitalists is not tenable. The requirements of voice representation on the part of a self-employed or on the part of an un-organized worker differ from those of the organized workers. Even within

Table 6.3 Trade union density in India, 1974–93 (in percentage)

Year	Union density
1974	16.55
1975	16.64
1976	16.82
1977	16.98
1978	17.16
1979	17.60
1980	18.17
1981	18.00
1982	18.32
1983	18.54
1984	18.81
1985	19.09
1986	19.36
1987	19.60
1988	19.79
1989	19.57
1990	19.40
1991	19.22
1992	19.07
1993	18.91

Source: Sengupta (2003).

the space of organized workforce labour flexibility has triggered a process of continuous fragmentation of workers in terms of regular and contractual, permanent and casual, standard and non-standard whatever may be the different nomenclature. Hence, trade unions need to have an innovative approach and appropriate strategies to make all these fragmented voices be represented properly.

As noted in the preceding section, the recommendations of the National Commission on Labour Report, if implemented, will go a long way in further thwarting the voice representation space of the organized as well as the unorganized workers. Trade unionism is perceived as inimical to economic growth as it threatens the very logic of competitive capitalism to usher in efficiency and competitive edge for the enterprises by relying on cost-cutting devices which primarily include labour costs. The steady erosion in the base of trade unions in industry continues unabated with casualization and contractualization, outsourcing of factory-based jobs to households and family labour, and labour-recruiting (intermediating) agencies operating between the enterprise and the self-employed workers outside factories. Further, the closure of many manufacturing factories in the last two decades, like the closure of many textile mills in the western

India, jute mills in West Bengal, etc., have reduced the strength of the trade unions in these industries, where they used to have large strongholds. New space for industries is being created in Special Economic Zones (SEZs), IT sector, etc., where trade union rights are officially denied.

It thus remains as a challenge now for the trade unions to reshape their activities with innovative ideas about penetration among the workers in the New Economy. They have to understand the empirical reality on the ground relating to the working class in the new environment of work. For this they need a proper theory of labour—a theory which would enable and sharpen their understandings of the disaggregated, fragmented space which is currently endangered by the global circuits of capital. Such theories can provide them the necessary insights for devising strategies to defend the diverse interests of the fragmented labour in this era of globalization.

Following Banuri and Amadeo (1991), one can identify four different categories of models of labour market institutions—decentralized, pluralist, polarized and social corporatist. While in the decentralized models bargaining takes place at the plant-level (of which East Asian economies are examples), in a polarized model it takes place at the industry level (as in the Latin American economies). The social corporatist framework garners institutional resources of the state to foster co-operative behaviour (as happens in the Scandinavian countries). India is an example of the pluralist model where features of both decentralized and polarized models are present. The bargaining structure here is varied, ranging from plant-level to industry-level negotiation and then to state intervention. Multiplicity of labour laws has rendered the labour negotiation process quite cumbersome over the years—a point aptly identified in NCL but with a biased interpretation from the perspective of capital.

With the advent of free-market-based economic policies the days of Keynesian state-led demand management is now passé. However, one major Keynesian proposition pertaining to effective demand is yet to lose its presence, if not in corporate strategy, at least in vestiges of official pronouncements on the need for 'inclusive growth'. The above seems to dwell on the fact that the worker is not just a factor of production as is viewed in mainstream neo-classical theory, but also a consumer whose marginal propensity to consume is much higher than what it is for other classes of economic agents. From this angle, protection of labour rights and labour security not only protects the very interests of labour but may go a long way in reviving effective aggregate demand with their spending. It remains to be seen how far such wisdom can travel in today's corporatist global industrial culture!

Labour Reform—What is to be Done?

We mention here that the basic criteria for labour reform should be transparency and accountability. As it has been aptly put,

> Transparency is required to ensure the free flow and the consequent sharing of all relevant information, and accountability is required so as to ensure that elected officials, public agencies, and Government employees, in sum, all those whose salaries are paid for by the average citizen, are held responsible for their actions (inertia). (Bhattacharjea 2006)

Viewed in this light there is a need to reform Indian labour rules to save time and resources from the clutches of multiple legal clauses as are embedded in the various overlapping laws (Kumar 2003; Jetli 2004).[14]

As for the NCL, it also has asked for a comprehensive review of labour laws.[15] For this purpose NCL has identified the Industrial Disputes Act (1948) or the IDA in short, the Trade Unions Act (1926), and the Contract Labour (Abolition and Regulation) Act (1970). As felt by NCL, 'the most important change needed is to abolish the requirement of prior permission of government for retrenchment, lay-offs or closure by deleting Chapter VB from the Industrial Disputes Act, as it would help to restore the position prevailing prior to 1976' (italics added). Also, as warranted by NCL, the Contract Labour Act 'needs to be suitably amended to allow all peripheral activities to be freely outsourced from specialized firms, even if it means employees of the specialized firms provide the services on the premises of the outsourcing units' (NCL 2002). Suggested changes as above which are offered by the NCL, as pointed out earlier in this chapter, are geared to ensure flexibility in the labour rules so that competitive capitalism gets the *de jure* sanction in terms of cost-cutting—the brunt of which is obviously on labour.

One can cite here the urge publicly expressed by the Government of India for labour reforms very recently:

> Various studies indicate that Indian labour laws are highly protective of labour, and labour markets are relatively inflexible. These laws apply only to the organized sector. Consequently, these laws have restricted labour mobility, have led to capital-intensive methods in the organized sector and adversely affected the sector's long-run demand for labour. Labour being a subject in the concurrent list, State-level labour regulations are also an important determinant of industrial performance. Evidence suggests that States, which have enacted more pro-worker regulations, have lost out on industrial production in general. (Government of India 2006: 209)

There also are quite a few studies which seek to indicate that pro-worker legislation impaired industrial performance (see Besley and Burgess 2004; Fallon and Lucas 1993). These tend to have a strong impact in shaping the official position on labour in countries like India. As pointed out in one of the critiques:

> This entire literature places excessive weight on *de jure* changes in the IDA, which is just one out of scores of labour laws, and whose *de facto* implementation has been vitiated by administrative slackness. Reading labour market conditions from the IDA are like reading traffic conditions from the Delhi Motor Vehicles Act. (Bhattacharjea 2006)

Contesting the mainstream position, three recent surveys of the literature can be mentioned here all of which have provided evidence to the contrary (Anant et al. 2006; Sharma 2006; Shyam Sundar 2005). They dispute the claim that Chapter VB of Industrial Dispute Act and existing Contract Labour Act are hindering industrial performance and, thereby, growth. In fact, these studies point at the fact that the industrial performance had in no way been affected adversely by the labour regulations, particularly by the amendment in 1976 (Chapter VB); and nor had these affected employment and productivity. Instead it is the growing trend of casualization and outsourcing which indicate a *de facto* regime of labour flexibility.

A successful run of the political economy of labour under globalization warrants a thorough review of labour policy in India which is capable of initiating a reversal of the ongoing trends in the direction of labour market flexibility and the scratching of protective labour legislation. There needs to be new labour legislations as are conducive to the well-being for the major sections of the working population, in the interest of equity, stability and long term economic growth. Finally there has to be a transparent and accountable system with strict and swift enforcement mechanism of affirmative actions in order to make possible a humane face for Indian labour in this second largest democracy of the world. We need to address the question as to economic growth for whom? Unless the ultimate benefits do not percolate to the direct producers—the performers of surplus labour—and labour continues to remain the risk-bearing factor for the current cycles of growth, which bears the burden of adjustments to accommodate and expand the global circuits of capital, we can never have growth as an inclusive one. The current pattern of high growth in India is clearly opposed to such possibilities. These changes warrant the co-ordinated and strong political will of the state on one hand and an innovative penetration of the labour organizations among the workforce on the other.

Notes

1. This chapter provides a broad survey of all the relevant search theoretic models of labour market which were constructed during 1980s and 1990s to address the questions mentioned in the text.
2. The National Commission on Labour brought out its report in 2002 and the National Commission on Rural Labour put forth its report in 1991. Besides, there is a report of the Steering Committee on Labour and Employment for the 10th Five Year Plan (2002–07) under the chairmanship of S.P. Gupta.
3. Thus the NCL claims, 'Competitiveness and low costs of production have to be achieved through increased productivity, improved quality, uniqueness, and so on. The workers/ unions will also have to accept the crucial role that productivity and productivity norms play in ensuring the competitiveness necessary for the survival of the industry' (NCL 2.123, pp. 29–30). '...the commitment of the workforce to quality and productivity must be high...' (NCL 1.20, p. 21). 'The crucial link between productivity and industrial efficiency cannot be denied. The level of wages depends on the economic efficiency of an undertaking or industry. Workers have to be as interested in productivity as the management is' (NCL 1.21, p. 21).
4. 'In the evidence tendered before the Commission, many witnesses pointed out that many workers in private and public undertakings work only 4 or 5 hours a day. This is not only true of Government or administrative offices, but true of factory workers as well' (NCL 5.10, p. 68). Also see NCL 5.10, 5.11, 5.12 for further evidence in NCL on worker's lack of responsibility towards the norm of productivity.
5. Thus, '...in a regime of competition, this means that every nation has to acquire and retain sufficient competitiveness to be able to survive and prosper in world markets. This competitiveness cannot be acquired without harmonious relations or at least peaceful relations in industry. The first requisite for the employers and employees today, therefore, is to develop a mindset that looks upon each other as partners, to develop a work culture that new technology and the context of globalization demand' (NCL 5.3, p. 67).
6. 'Because of global competition most of the companies want to reduce costs and be competitive' (NCL 4.276, p. 60). '...in the new circumstances of global competition, it may not be possible for some enterprises to continue and meet the economic consequences of competition....They should therefore have the option to close down' (NCL 6.87, pp. 86). '...organisations must have the flexibility to adjust the number of this workforce based on economic efficiency...' (NCL 6.109, p. 92).
7. Thus, '...in a regime of competition, this means that every nation has to acquire and retain sufficient competitiveness to be able to survive and prosper in world markets. This competitiveness cannot be acquired without harmonious relations or at least peaceful relations in industry. The first requisite for the employers and employees today, therefore, is to develop a mindset that looks upon each other as partners, to develop a work culture that new technology and the context of globalisation demand' (NCL 5.3, p. 67).

8. Thus, 'because of global competition most of the companies want to reduce costs and be competitive' (NCL 4.276, p. 60).

'...in the new circumstances of global competition, it may not be possible for some enterprises to continue and meet the economic consequences of competition.... They should, therefore, have the option to close down' (NCL 6.87, p. 86).

'....organisations must have the flexibility to adust the number of this workforce based on economic efficiency...' (NCL 6.109, p. 92).

9. Thus,

'...the Commission considered the question whether there should be any salary limit above which the protection of the labour laws will not be available or there should not be any such limit for coverage of workers under the labour laws' (NCL 6.18, p. 76).

'Relatively better off section of employees categorized as workmen like Airlines Pilots etc., do not merely carry out instructions from superior authority but are also required and empowered to take various kinds of on the spot decisions in various situations and particularly in exigencies. Their functions, therefore, cannot merely be categorized as those of ordinary workmen. We, therefore, recommend that Government may lay down a list of such highly paid jobs who are presently deemed as workmen category as being outside the purview of the laws relating to workmen and included in the proposed law for the protection of non workmen. Another alternative is that the Government fix a cut-off limit of remuneration which is substantially high enough, in the present context, such as Rs 25, 000 per month beyond which employees will not be treated as ordinary "workmen"' (NCL 6.19, p. 76).

'It would be logical to keep all the supervisory personnel, irrespective of their wage/salary, outside the rank of worker and keep them out of the purview of the labour laws meant for workers. All such supervisory category of employees should be clubbed along with the category of persons who discharge managerial and administrative functions. The Commission would also recommend that such a modified definition of worker could be adopted in all the labour laws. We expect managements to take care of the interests of supervisory staff as they will now be part of the managerial fraternity' (NCL 6.20, p. 76).

10. Thus,

'...in a regime of competition, this means that every nation has to acquire and retain sufficient competitiveness to be able to survive and prosper in world markets. This competitiveness cannot be acquired without harmonious relations or at least peaceful relations in industry. The first requisite for the employers and employees today, there-fore, is to develop a mindset that looks upon each other as partners, to develop a work culture that new technology and the context of globalization demand' (NCL 5.3, p. 67).

'Most of the witnesses before the Commission, talked of the imperative need to evolve a new work culture in our country' (NCL 5.7, p. 68).

'It has to be conceded that the workers have a stake in the viability and growth of the undertaking, and an attendant responsibility as well as right. Wages have to be looked upon as incomes that are earned through hard work, not merely monetary payment but also a balance of responsibilities and rights' (NCL 5.8, p. 68).

'The individual worker's attitude to work has to include, (i) pride in maximizing his own productivity to repay his debt to society and (ii) pride in his commitment to excellence, as reflected in the quality of his work' (NCL 5.9, p. 68).

'The work environment also plays a role in promoting good work culture. A vibrant work environment will result in greater output' (NCL 5.20, p. 69).

11. '...we have the maximum number of holidays.... We recommend that: the Central Government and all State Governments should have a uniform policy on holidays.... Saturday should be a working day, and the movement of quality circles should be encouraged. This will enable workers to take interest in the work they perform and contribute to the improvement in the overall work culture in the organization.... The attitude to hours of work should not be rigid. The total number of hours per day should not be more than nine, and hours of work per week should not be more than 48. But within these limits there may be flexibility, and compensation for overtime' (NCL 5.24, 5.29, 5.32, pp. 69–70).

12. Thus,
    'There is a trend in growth of casual labour in the total workforce during all these years. The proportion of self-employed has come down from 58.9 per cent in 1977–78 to 52.9 per cent in 1999–2000. But the number of casual workers has gone up substantially from 27.2 per cent to 33.2 per cent' (NCL 4.274[d], p. 59).

    'Because of global competition most of the companies want to reduce costs and be competitive...' (NCL 4.278, p. 60).

    'Most of those who demand the right to hire and fire also want to bring about a fundamental change in the nature or perception of employment. They want all employment to be on the basis of contracts for stipulated periods.... If transforming the basis of all employment is a social necessity because it has become an economic necessity for industrial or commercial enterprises, then, it is equally necessary to create social acceptability for the change, and the social institutions that can take care of the consequences' (NCL 5.34, p. 70).

13. Of course, there are controversies whether minimum wages, as they are generally set in different industries and in different locations from time to time, do really constitute the values of bare minimum socially necessary basket of commodities. Moreover, minimum wages are not revised frequently, as they should be, keeping in pace with inflation and changes that are occurring in the socio-economic ambience almost day-by-day in this age of globalization, liberalization and privatization.

14. There is multiplicity of laws affecting industrial labour like Industrial Disputes Act, Trade Union Act, Contract Labour (Abolition and Regulation Act), and Minimum Wages Act, etc.

15. 'A comprehensive review of all these laws is definitely needed. They need to be simplified and brought in line with contemporary economic realities, including especially current international practice....' (NCL 2002).

Conclusion 7

We offer in this chapter a concluding note to our analysis and observations in the present study on the unfreedom and waged labour in India's organized manufacturing industry.

The two major observations as have emerged from our analysis include the jobless nature of the growth process in these industries and the precarious level of living even for those having jobs in this sector. Thus employment growth has been consistently slow, near zero or even negative in most of these industries, including those with high growth rates. Industries in this sector have also been experiencing fluctuating growth rates, largely with rising uncertainty in the product markets as were prominent with the steady opening up of markets after 1991. The *second* important aspect of our findings relates to the level of living of workers, as can be judged on the basis of information available from our field surveys in selected pockets of manufacturing (including a few sites located within the export-oriented Special Economic Zones [SEZs]). All these narrate a dismal story. Workers seem to be facing hardships even in terms of their survival strategy, with low levels of subsistence and miserable dimensions of security.

As we have mentioned earlier, we have conducted this analysis both on the basis of data sets as are available from the published official sources and from what we gathered in our field surveys. We have looked at the published official statistics relating to the post-reform years between 1991 and 2003. We also have looked, for comparability, at the data set relating to the pre-reform years preceding 1991. To decipher the performance pattern of individual industries groups we have looked at disaggregated industry statistics at the 3-digit level. Using the appropriate deflators we were able to arrive at a data set of these industries at constant prices, both for the pre- and post-reform years. This disaggregated data set, as mentioned earlier, has been constructed for the first time in the literature. It has provided valuable insights to us in arriving at some meaningful and relevant results in our study.

As mentioned earlier, our findings confirm a pattern of 'jobless growth', not only in the stagnant industries like man-made fibre, tobacco manufacture, publishing, etc. (which, incidentally, are found to be relatively labour intensive) but also in the high growth and relatively capital intensive industries. (The latter include manufacture of aircraft and spacecraft, motor vehicles, electronic valves and tubes, electric motors, generators and transformers and jewellery, etc., with individual growth rates well above 20 per cent.) Employment growth has consistently been at a much slower rate relative to output growth rate, both in the high growth and in low growth industries, and during the reform years which started in 1991.

The output growth scenario, high, moderate, low or even negative shares the common feature of a volatile performance. Instability of output has been common, especially during the more recent years which also mark the advances of economic reforms in the country. Employment fluctuated with similar fluctuations in output, both in the high and low growth sectors. Thus labour has been turned into a 'risk-bearing' factor of production in this age of liberalized output and flexible labour markets. It appears that workers do not get more jobs in industries which are passing though a boom while jobs are equally scarce in industries experiencing a downturn in production.

These aspects, as observed in the available statistics, make us contest the validity of the standard mainstream arguments in support of economic reforms. We have questioned, in particular, the proclaimed benefits of economic reforms and liberalization in terms of their contribution to 'efficient growth' as has been claimed in the neo-liberal doctrines. We point at the low employment growth as has resulted during the reform period and argue that such outcomes are not at all consistent to what in neo-classical economics is claimed as a part of the of the so-called 'efficient growth' package. We chose to look into the links between the openness of the economy (signified by the pace of trade and capital flows) and growth, the causal link between which provides a major plank in the construction of these doctrines and policies. Using micro-level data for 400 major firms (which are listed on the country's stock exchanges), we observe that net exports and foreign equity holdings had failed to register any impact, whatsoever, on sales and/or net value added of these firms in the year 2004. We also arrived at the argument that these major firms in the industrial sector did not seem to experience any fillip from what can be identified as a greater degree of openness as have taken place in recent years. We could not, however, due to data inadequacy, substantiate a similar argument as with macro-data, in terms of employment at the firm level.

We also checked, with macro-level data, the pattern of wage and profit shares of output in these industries. As could be expected in terms of the relative growth rates of employment which were lower than those of output, the wage share of output showed a distinct drop during the period. Probing further into the causal factors as might be responsible for the relatively lower employment growth, we identified the rising capital-output ratio as a major labour-displacing factor. Paradoxically, while a rise in this ratio, as can be expected, contributed to a rise in labour productivity, the impact on employment growth had been adverse. Underlying this process are two forces which include, first, the absence of a growth inducing impact (a rise in scale of production) on output and second, the on-going cost-cutting exercise which the owner–managers of industrial enterprises have embraced today, by displacing labour with capital.

Official statistics can also be used to provide information on the status of workers in the manufacturing industry, according to whether they are employed directly or are recruited via contractors. We notice the dominance of the second type, a consequence largely of the new norm of labour flexibility which is advocated and adopted in the new economy under globalization.

Our study would have remained incomplete if we stopped at this point and concluded on the basis of the aggregative statistics. To substantiate our critique of the mainstream theory and policy prescriptions relating to the labour market, we probed into the findings from a field survey which was conducted by our research team during 2003–05.The survey provides a set of revealing facts which relate to the quality of jobs and life in general for the workers we interviewed. The majority of workers in our sample seem to have a precarious state of living as well as conditions of work, as can be judged in terms of what we constructed as the composite and individual levels of labour security. We have computed indices of securities as above by following the method used in an earlier study by another scholar. Levels of labour security seem to be low on most counts, which include income, jobs, employment, skill, social support, job-tenure, etc. Permanence of jobs and migration status seem to be the two major factors which push down the overall (composite) level of security for these industrial workers. Export orientation of the units as in the three SEZ areas or even in the otherwise prosperous diamond industry of Surat does not help to pull up the composite labour security index; and more so with the majority of workers in these units having work contracts with a casualized status. Thus the results of our survey complement and corroborate the aggregative analysis based on secondary data sources, with information relating to multiple aspects of the working population in the units we had surveyed.

Our survey results, to repeat, highlight the prime significance of casualization and migration as factors behind the poor conditions of existence undermining the security of these industrial workers. The two aspects remain interrelated, with migration often a consequence of the temporary nature of jobs in the industrial units. In the labour market, casualization (or labour flexibility) has spawned one or more additional layers of agents (or intermediaries) who are far removed from the production process. These include the labour contractors who have come to stay in the labour market as major conduits between employers and the supply of workers. These people volunteer the responsibility of mobilizing the migrant workforce, their recruitments and even wage payments. Often the share appropriated by these men is disproportionately high as compared to what the worker finally gets. This works as a marriage of convenience for employers and even for the exploited workers who are left with no other option other than to accept what the contractor would offer. No amount of state or labour union intervention is visible to mend the situation by tilting the balance in favour of the working population.

Absence of an effective social protection of labour which includes legislation and trade union or community level interventions, as observed, is not an accident. Since the beginning of the liberalization drive in 1991, there has been a very conscious effort on the part of the Indian state (backed earlier by local and later, by foreign capital), to disarm labour. This was done by dismantling, as much as possible, the erstwhile legislations to protect labour. There has been an open consent and encouragement at official level to casualize the workforce which removes the union leadership at the back stage. These are the arrangements which suit the employers and are recommended by the state to achieve competitive efficiency in the age of globalized markets. The impact, as discussed in our study, is neither growth-efficient, nor sustainable, especially as one considers the demeaning of the major part of the country's population to levels around bare subsistence.

Issues of employment and the labour status concerns, as viewed by us, do not remain confined to equity and fairness as such. Instead these involve the wider aspects of sustainability in the development process over time. Thus the prevailing arrangement between the owners of capital and the Indian state on the question of labour use may turn out as non-viable over not too distant a future. We hope that the present study will be of use to sensitize and change the mindset of corporate capital as well as the policy makers in India.

Bibliography

Adam, P. and P. Caniziani. 1998. 'Partial De-regulation: Fixed-term Contracts in Italy and Spain', Discussion Paper No. 386, Centre for Economic Performance, London.

Agarwala, Ramgopal, Nagesh Kumar and Michelle Riboud (eds). 2004. *Reforms, Labour Markets, and Social Security in India*. New Delhi: Oxford University Press.

Ahluwalia, I.J. 1992. *Productivity and Growth in Indian Manufacturing*. New Delhi: Oxford University Press.

Alchain, A. and H. Demsetz. 1972. 'Production, Information Costs, and Economic Organization', *American Economic Review*, 62: 777–95.

Anant, T.C.A., R. Hasan, P. Mohapatra and R. Nagaraj. 2006. 'Labor Markets in India: Issues and Perspectives', in J. Felipe and R. Hasan (eds), *Labor Markets in Asia: Issues and Perspectives*. Basingstoke: Palgrave Macmillan.

Anderson, L. and B. Trentin. 1996. *Trabajo, derechos y sindicato en el mundo*. Caracas: Nueva Sociedad.

Bagchi, Amiya Kumar. 2002. *Capital and Labour Re-defined: India and the Third World*. New Delhi: Tulika Books.

Balakrishnan, Pulapre. 2004. 'Measuring Productivity in the Manufacturing Sector', *Economic and Political Weekly*, April: 3–10.

Baldoz, Rick, Charles Koeber and Philip Kraft (eds). 2001. *The Critical Study of Work: Labour, Technology and Global Production*. Philadelphia: Temple University Press.

Banuri, T. and E.J. Amadeo. 1991. 'Worlds within the Third World: Labour Market Institutions in Asia and Latin America', in T. Banuri (ed.), *Economic Liberalization: No Panacea*, pp. 171–230. New Delhi: Oxford University Press.

Basu, Indrani. Unpublished. 'Formal Informal Linkage: A Case Study of the Closure of the Dunlop Tyre Factory', unpublished M. Phil dissertation, Department of Economics, University of Kalyani, 2004.

Besley, Timothy and Robin Burgess. 2004. 'Can Regulation Hinder Economic Performance? Evidence from India', *Quarterly Journal of Economics*, 119(February): 91–134.

Bhattacharjea, Aditya. 2006. 'Labour Market Regulation and Industrial Performance in India—A Critical Review of the Empirical Evidence', *The Indian Journal of Labour Economics*, June.

Bhattacharjee, Debasish. 1996. 'Economic Liberalization, Democracy and Industrial Relations: India in a Comparative Perspective', *The Indian Journal of Labour Economics*, 39(4): 1011–022.

Blanchflower, David G. and Andrew J. Oswald. 1995. *The Wage Curve*. Cambridge, MA: MIT Press.

Boyer, R. 1987. 'Labour Flexibilities: Many Forms, Uncertain Effects', *Labour and Society*, 12: 107–29.

Braverman, Harry. 1974. *Labour and Monopoly Capital: The Deregulation of Work in the Twentieth Century*. New York: Monthly Review Press.

Bremen, Jan. 1996. *Footloose Labour: Working in India's Informal Economy*. Cambridge, UK: Cambridge University Press.

Brenner, C. 2002. *Work in the New Economy—Flexible Labour Markets in Silicon Valley*. Oxford: Blackwell Publishing.

Buchanan, D.H. 1934. *The Development of Capitalist Enterprise in India*. New York and London: Macmillan.

Callenberg, A. 1990. 'Commitment and Flexibility: Changing Employment Relations in Industrial Societies', paper presented at the workshop on 'The Nature of Consensus at the Place of Production', Siena, 14–15 June.

Card, David. 1995. 'The Wage Curve: A Review', *Journal of Economic Literature*, 33(June): 285–99.

Chakrabarti, Anjan and Steven Cullenberg. 2003. *Transition and Development in India*. New York and London: Routledge.

Chaudhuri, Sudip. 2002. 'Economic Reform and Industrial Structure in India', *Economic and Political Weekly*, 12 January: pp. 155–62.

Debroy, Bibek. 2005. 'Issues in Labour Law Reform', in Bibek Debroy and P.D. Kaushik (eds), *Reforming the Labour Market*, pp. 37–76. New Delhi: Academic Foundation.

Deshpande, Lalit K., Alak N. Sharma, Anup K. Karan and Sandip Sarkar. 2004. *Liberalisation and Labour: Labour Flexibility in Indian Manufacturing*. New Delhi: Institute of Human Development.

Dutt, Rudder. 2003. *Lockouts in India*. New Delhi: Manohar.

EIRR. 1985. 'European Industrial Relations Conference', *European Industrial Relations Review*, 138(July): 24–27.

Esping-Anderson, Gosta. 1990. *The Three Worlds of Welfare—Capitalism*. Prineton: Prineton University Press.

Fallon, Peter and Robert E.B. Lucas. 1986. 'An Overview of the Labour Market in India', Discussion Paper, Report No. DRD153, Development Research Department, World Bank, Washington, DC (mimeo).

———. 1993. 'Job Security Regulations and the Dynamic Demand for Labor in India and Zimbabwe', *Journal of Development Economics*, 40: 241–75.

Farmer, Roger E.A. 2002. *Macroeconomics* (Second edition). London: Thomson South-Western.

Felstead, A. and N. Jewson (eds). 1999. *Global Trends in Flexible Labour*. London: Macmillan.

Ghosh, Ajit K. 2001 *Globalisation, Growth and Poverty: Building an Inclusive World Economy*. Washington, DC: World Bank.

————. 2003a. *Globalisation, Growth and Poverty: Building an Inclusive World Economy*. London: Oxford University Press.

————. 2003b. 'Trade Liberalisation and Manufacturing Employment', International Labour Organization (ILO) Employment Paper, 2000/3.

————. 2005a. *Jobs and Incomes in a Globalising World*. New Delhi. BookWell.

————. 2005b. 'High Wage–Low Productivity Organised Manufacturing and the Employment Challenge in India', *The Indian Journal of Labour Economics*, 48: 231–42.

Government of India. 1991. Census of India, 1991.

————. 1991. *Report of the National Commission on Rural Labour (1991)*.

————. 2001. Census of India, 2001.

————. 2002. *Report of the National Commission on Labour*. Government of India.

————. 2006. *Economic Survey 2005–06*. Ministry of Finance, Government of India.

————. 2007. *Economic Survey 2006–07*. Ministry of Finance, Government of India.

————. *Report of the Steering Committee on Labour and Employment for the 10th Five Year Plan (2002–2007)* under the chairmanship of S.P. Gupta.

————. *Annual Survey of Industries* (various issues). Central Statistical Organization.

————. *Indian Labour Year Book* (various issues), Government of India.

Haltwanger, John. 1987. 'The Natural Rate of Unemployment', in John Eatwell, Murry Milgate and Peter Newman (eds), *The New Palgrave*, pp. 610–12. New York: Stockton Press.

Hariss-White, B. 2003. *India Working: Essays on Society and Economy*. Cambridge, UK: Cambridge University Press.

Hasan, R., Devashish Moitra and K.V. Ramaswami. 2003. 'Trade Reforms, Labor Regulations and Labor Demand Elasticities: Empirical Evidence from India', NBER Working Paper 9879.

Jetli, N.K. 2004. *India: Economic Reforms and Labour Policy*. New Delhi: New Century Publications.

Johnsson, E. 1978. 'Labour as Risk-bearer', *Cambridge Journal of Economics*,

Kumar, Arun. 2003. *Industrial Law* (Volume 1 and 2). New Delhi: Atlantic Publishers and Distributors.

Lilien, David M. 1982. 'Sectoral Shifts and Cyclical Unemployment', *Journal of Political Economy*, 90(August): 777–93.

Lucas, Robert E.B. 1986. 'An Overview of the Labour Market in India', Discussion Paper, Report No. DRD153, Development Research Department, World Bank, Washington, DC (mimeo).

Lucas, Robert E. and Leonard Rapping. 1969. 'Real Wages, Employment, and Inflation', *Journal of Political Economy*, 77(September/October): 721–54.

Mankiw, N. Gregory. 2004. *Macroeconomics* (Fifth edition). New York: Worth Publishers. Originally published in 2003 with reprint edition in 2004.

Marx, Karl. *Capital: A Critical Analysis of Capitalist Production Volume I*. Moscow: Progressive Publishers.

————. 1990 (Reprinted in 1997). *Capital—A Critique of Political Econnomy* (Vol 1). Penguin Books.

Mazumdar, D. and S. Sarkar. 2004. 'Reforms and Employment Elasticity in Organised Manufacturing', *Economic and Political Weekly*, 39(28).

Mortensen, Dale T. 1986. 'Job Search and Labour Market Analysis', in Orley C. Ashenfelter and Richard Layard (eds), *Handbook of Labour Economics* (Volume 2), pp. 849–919. Amsterdam: North-Holland.

Munck, Ronaldo. 2003. *Globalization and Labour—The New Great Transformation*. Delhi: Madhyam Books (Originally published by Zed Books, London, 2002).

Nagaraj, R. 2004. 'Fall in Manufacturing Employment: A Brief Note', *Economic and Political Weekly*, 39: 3387–90.

————. 2006. 'Employment and Wages in Manufacturing Industries: Trends, Hypotheses and Evidence', in R. Nagraj (ed.), *India's Economic Growth and Reforms*. New Delhi: Academic Foundation.

National Commission on Labour. 2003. 'Report of the National Commission on Labour (2002)', *Economicaindia*, INFO-SERVICE, Academic Foundation, New Delhi.

NSSO. *Employment and Unemployment Report* (50th, 55th and 60th Round), National Sample Survey Organization, Government of India.

Panchmukhi, V.R. 2000. 'Trade, Technology and Employment: A Profile of Systemic Dilemmas and Paradoxes', *The Indian Journal of Labour Economics*, 43(1).

Panchmukhi, V.R., Nagesh Kumar and Ram Upendra Das. 2004. 'Economic Reforms and Implications for Labour Markets', in Ramgopal Agarwala, Nagesh Kumar and Michelle Riboud (eds), *Reforms, Labour Markets, and Social Security in India*. New Delhi: Oxford University Press.

Panchmukhi V.R. and Ram Upendra Das. 1999. *Economic Reforms, Regional Integration and Labour Markets in the SAARC Region*, International Labour Organization-South Asia Advisory Team (ILO-SAAT), New Delhi.

Papola, T.S. 1992. 'Labour Institutions and Economic Development: The Case of Indian Industrialisation', in T.S. Papola and G.S. Rogers (eds), *Institutions and Economic Development in India*, International Institute for Labour Studies (IILS) Research Series No. 97, International Labour Organization (ILO), Geneva.

Papola, T.S. and G.S. Rogers (eds). 1992. *Institutions and Economic Development in India*, International Institute for Labour Studies (IILS) Research Series No. 97, International Labour Organization (ILO), Geneva.

Planning Commission Reports on Labour and Employment. 2002. *Economicaindia*, INFO-SERVICE, Academic Foundation, New Delhi.

Polyani, Karl. 1944. *The Great Transformation: The Political and Economic Origin of our Time*. Boston: Beacon Press.

Polyani Levitt, Kari. 2005. 'Karl Polyali as a Developmental Economist', in K.S. Jomo (ed.), *Pioneers of Development Economists*, pp. 165–80. London and New York: Zed Books.

Regini, M. 1997. 'Social Institutions and Production Structure—The Italian Variety of Capitalism in the 1980s', in C. Crouch and W. Streeck (eds), *Political Economy and Modern Capitalism: Mapping and Divergence*, pp. 102–16. London: Sage Publications.

———. 2000. 'The Dilemmas of Labour Market Regulation', in Gosta Esping-Andersen and Marino Regini (eds), *Why Deregulate Labour Markets?* London: Oxford University Press.

Rogerson, Richard, Robert Shimer and Randall Wright. 2005. 'Search Theoretic Models of the Labor Market: A Survey', *Journal of Economic Literature*, XLIII(December): 959–88.

Rosen, Sherwin. 1985. 'Implicit Contracts: A Survey', *Journal of Economic Literature* 23(September): 1144–75.

Roy, T. 2002. 'Social Costs of Reforms: A Study of Job Loss with Special Reference to Declining Industries in 1990–98', in Shuji Uchikawa (ed.), *Economic Reforms and Industrial Structure in India*. New Delhi: Manohar.

Sen, Sunanda. 2007. *Globalisation and Development*. New Delhi: National Book Trust.

Sen, Sunanda and Byasdeb Dasgupta. 2006a. 'Labour in India's Manufacturing Sector', *Indian Journal of Labour Economics*, January–March, 49(1): 79–101.

———. 2006b. *Political Economy of Labour under Globalization—A Study of Labour in India's Manufacturing Industry*. IDPAD–ICSSR report, September 2006.

———. 2007. 'SEZs: Modern Enclaves to Reward Capital by Exploiting Labour and Displacing Livilihood in the Agrarian Economy', *Mainstream*, 4 May 2007.

Sen, Sunanda and Soumya Kanti Ghosh. 2005. 'Basel Norms, Indian Banking Sector and Impact on Credit on SMEs and the Poor', *Economic and Political Weekly*, 40(12).

Sengupta, Anil K. 2003. 'Decline of Trade Union Power in India', *The Indian Journal of Labour Economics*, 46(4): 685–701.

Shapiro, Carl and Joseph E. Stiglitz. 1984. 'Equilibrium Unemployment as a Worker Device', *American Economic Review*, 74(June): 433–44.

Sharma, Alakh N. 2004. 'Employment Generation Policy and Social Safety Nets in India', in Ramgopal Agarwala, Nagesh Kumar and Michelle Riboud (eds), *Reforms, Labour Markets, and Social Security in India*. New Delhi: Oxford University Press.

———. 2006. 'Flexibility, Employment and Labour Market Reforms in India', *Economic and Political Weekly*, 41: 2078–86.

Shyam Sundar, K.R. 2005. 'Labour Flexibility Debate in India: A Comprehensive Review and Some Suggestions', *Economic and Political Weekly*, 28 May–4 June: 2274–85

Soskice, D. 1990. 'Reinterpreting Corporatism and Explaining Unemployment: Coordinated and Non-Coordinated Market Economies', in R. Brunetta and

C. Dell'Aringa (eds), *Markets, Institutions and Corporations: Labour Relations and Economic Performance*, pp. 170–211. London: Macmillan.

Stigler, George J. 1961. 'The Economics of Information', *Journal of Political Economy*, 69(June): 213–25.

————. 1962. 'Information in the Labour Market', *Journal of Political Economy*, 70(October): 94–104.

Standing, Guy. 1999. *Global Labour Flexibility—Seeking Distributive Justice*. pp 51–53. London: Macmillan Press Ltd.

————. 2002. *Beyond New Paternalism—Basic Security as Equality*. New York: Verso.

————. 2004, *Economic Security for a Better World*. Geneva: International Labour Organization (ILO).

State Development Report of Government of West Bengal. 2008.

Streeck, W. 1991. 'On the Institutional Conditions of Diversified Quality Production', in E. Matzner and W. Streeck (eds), *Beyond Keynesianism*, pp. 21–61. Aldershot: Edward Elgar.

Thomas, H. 1995. 'The Erosion of Trade Unions', in Henk Thomas (ed.), *Globalization and Third World Trade Unions: The Challenge of Rapid Economic Change*. New Delhi: Madhyam Books.

Tulpule, B. 1996. 'Segmented Labour and Fragmented Trade Unions', in T.V. Sathamurth (ed.), *Class Formation and Political Transformation in Post-colonial India*. New Delhi: Oxford University Press.

Uchikawa, S. (ed.). 2002. *Economic Reforms and Industrial Structure in India*. New Delhi: Manohar.

Wood, A. 1994. *North–South Trade Employment and Inequality: Changing Fortunes in a Skill-Driven World*. Oxford: Clarendon Press.

www.Indiastat.com online data during 2004–06 (downloaded the data on 15 April 2004). http://commerce.nic.in (downloaded on 20 April 2004).

Index

About the Authors

Sunanda Sen is currently a Visiting Professor at Jamia Milia Islamia as well as at Institute of Industrial Studies, both in New Delhi. She has retired from the Jawaharlal Nehru University. Her publications include several books including *Global Finance at Risk* (2004) and *Globalisation and Development* (2007) and articles in reputed journals and edited volumes.

Byasdeb Dasgupta is Reader at the Department of Economics at University of Kalyani, West Bengal. He has published articles in journals and in edited volumes on issues such as external debt problems of developing countries, international trade in the context of India and labour.